COMMENTARIES ON LIVING
SECOND SERIES

Born near Madras, Jiddu Krishnamurti (1895–1986) was fourteen when he was taken under the guardianship of Mrs Annie Besant, socialist, reformer and President of the International Theosophical Society at Adyar, near Madras. She and her colleague, C. W. Leadbeater, believed that Krishnamurti was the vehicle for the Messiah whose coming the Theosophists had predicted. The Order of the Star in the East, an organisation dedicated to preparing mankind for the coming of the World Teacher, was formed in 1911 with Krishnamurti at its head. In the same year he was brought to England to be privately educated and trained for his coming role. In 1929, however, he dissolved the order and relinquished the money and property which had accumulated in his name. He declared that truth cannot be found through any sect or religion but only by freeing oneself from all forms of conditioning. "You can form other organisations and expect someone else," he said. "With that I am not concerned, nor with creating new cages . . . My only concern is to set men absolutely, unconditionally free."

Long recognised as one of the world's foremost spiritual teachers, Krishnamurti dedicated his life to speaking throughout the world. Staying nowhere for more than a few months at a time, he did not consider himself as belonging to any race or country. Over the years, his annual gatherings in India, at Ojai, California, at Saanen in Switzerland and at Brockwood Park in Hampshire attracted thousands of people of different nationality, occupation and outlook.

Krishnamurti's  m, made a considerable by Gollancz in 1954 a s. *Commentaries on Li* n 1959) was his fourth n overleaf.

COMMENTARIES
ON LIVING:

Second Series

from the notebooks of
J. KRISHNAMURTI

edited by
D. Rajagopal

LONDON
VICTOR GOLLANCZ LTD
1986

First published in Great Britain 1959
by Victor Gollancz Ltd,
14 Henrietta Street, London WC2E 8QJ

Reprinted 5 times

First published in Gollancz Paperbacks 1986

British Library Cataloguing in Publication Data
Krishnamurti, J.
    Commentaries on living: second series:
    from the notebooks of J. Krishnamurti.
    1. Ethics
    I. Title   II. Rajagopal, D.
    170   BJ1012

ISBN 0-575-03949-3

Printed in Great Britain by
St Edmundsbury Press Ltd, Bury St Edmunds, Suffolk

CONTENTS

COMMENTARIES ON LIVING
Second Series

CREATIVE HAPPINESS

THERE IS A city by the magnificent river; wide and long steps lead down to the water's edge, and the world seems to live on those steps. From early morning till well after dark, they are always crowded and noisy; almost level with the water are little projecting steps on which people sit and are lost in their hopes and longings, in their gods and chants. The temple bells are ringing, the muezzin is calling; someone is singing, and a huge crowd has gathered, listening in appreciative silence.

Beyond all this, round the bend and higher up the river, there is a pile of buildings. With their avenues of trees and wide roads, they stretch several miles inland; and along the river, through a narrow and dirty lane, one enters into this scattered field of learning. So many students from all over the country are there, eager, active and noisy. The teachers are pompous, intriguing for better positions and salaries. No one seems to be greatly concerned with what happens to the students after they leave. The teachers impart certain knowledge and techniques which the clever ones quickly absorb; and when they graduate, that is that. The teachers have assured jobs, they have families and security; but when the students leave, they have to face the turmoil and the insecurity of life. There are such buildings, such teachers and students all over the land. Some students achieve fame and position in the world; others breed, struggle and die. The State wants competent technicians, administrators to guide and to rule; and there is always the army, the church, and business. All the world over, it is the same.

It is to learn a technique and to have a job, a profession, that we go through this process of having the upper mind stuffed with facts and knowledge, is it not? Obviously, in the modern world, a good technician has a better chance of earning a livelihood; but then what? Is one who is a technician better able to face the complex problem of living than one who is not? A profession is only a part of life; but there are also those parts which are hidden, subtle and mysterious. To emphasize the one and to deny or neglect the rest must inevitably lead to very lop-sided and disintegrating activity. This is precisely what is taking place in the world to-day, with ever-mounting conflict, confusion and misery. Of course there are a few exceptions, the creative, the happy, those who are in touch with something that is not man-made, who are not dependent on the things of the mind.

You and I have intrinsically the capacity to be happy, to be creative, to be in touch with something that is beyond the clutches of time. Creative happiness is not a gift reserved for the few; and why is it that the vast majority do not know that happiness? Why do some seem to keep in touch with the profound in spite of circumstances and accidents, while others are destroyed by them? Why are some resilient, pliable, while others remain unyielding and are destroyed? In spite of knowledge, some keep the door open to that which no person and no book can offer, while others are smothered by technique and authority. Why? It is fairly clear that the mind wants to be caught and made certain in some kind of activity, disregarding wider and deeper issues, for it is then on safer ground; so its education, its exercises, its activities are encouraged and sustained on that level, and excuses are found for not going beyond it.

Before they are contaminated by so-called education, many children are in touch with the unknown; they show this in so many ways. But environment soon begins to close around them, and after a certain age they lose that light, that beauty which is not found in any book or school. Why? Do not say that life is too much for them, that they have to face hard realities, that it is their karma, that it is their fathers' sin; this is all nonsense. Creative happiness is for all and not for the few alone. You may express it in one way and I in another, but it is for all. Creative happiness has no value on the market; it is not a commodity to be sold to the highest bidder, but it is the one thing that can be for all.

Is creative happiness realizable? That is, can the mind keep in touch with that which is the source of all happiness? Can this openness be sustained in spite of knowledge and technique, in spite of education and the crowding in of life? It can be, but only when the educator is educated to this reality, only when he who teaches is himself in touch with the source of creative happiness. So our problem is not the pupil, the child, but the teacher and the parent. Education is a vicious circle only when we do not see the importance, the essential necessity above all else, of this supreme happiness. After all, to be open to the source of all happiness is the highest religion; but to realize this happiness, you must give right attention to it, as you do to business. The teacher's profession is not a mere routine job, but the expression of beauty and joy, which cannot be measured in terms of achievement and success.

The light of reality and its bliss are destroyed when the mind, which is the seat of self, assumes control. Self-knowledge is the beginning of wisdom; without self-knowledge, learning leads to ignorance, strife and sorrow.

CONDITIONING

HE WAS VERY concerned with helping humanity, with doing good works, and was active in various social-welfare organizations. He said he had literally never taken a long holiday, and that since his graduation from college he had worked constantly for the betterment of man. Of course he wasn't taking any money for the work he was doing. His work had always been very important to him, and he was greatly attached to what he did. He had become a first-class social worker, and he loved it. But he had heard something in one of the talks about the various kinds of escape which condition the mind, and he wanted to talk things over.

"Do you think being a social worker is conditioning? Does it only bring about further conflict?"

Let us find out what we mean by conditioning. When are we

aware that we are conditioned? Are we ever aware of it? Are you aware that you are conditioned, or are you only aware of conflict, of struggle at various levels of your being? Surely, we are aware, not of our conditioning, but only of conflict, of pain and pleasure.

"What do you mean by conflict?"

Every kind of conflict: the conflict between nations, between various social groups, between individuals, and the conflict within oneself. Is not conflict inevitable as long as there is no integration between the actor and his action, between challenge and response? Conflict is our problem, is it not? Not any one particular conflict, but all conflict: the struggle between ideas, beliefs, ideologies, between the opposites. If there were no conflict there would be no problems.

"Are you suggesting that we should all seek a life of isolation, of contemplation?"

Contemplation is arduous, it is one of the most difficult things to understand. Isolation, though each one is consciously or unconsciously seeking it in his own way, does not solve our problems; on the contrary, it increases them. We are trying to understand what are the factors of conditioning which bring further conflict. We are only aware of conflict, of pain and pleasure, and we are not aware of our conditioning. What makes for conditioning?

"Social or environmental influences: the society in which we were born, the culture in which we have been raised, economic and political pressures, and so on."

That is so; but is that all? These influences are our own product, are they not? Society is the outcome of man's relationship with man, which is fairly obvious. This relationship is one of use, of need, of comfort, of gratification, and it creates influences, values that bind us. The binding is our conditioning. By our own thoughts and actions we are bound; but we are not aware that we are bound, we are only aware of the conflict of pleasure and pain. We never seem to go beyond this; and if we do, it is only into further conflict. We are not aware of our conditioning, and until we are, we can only produce further conflict and confusion.

"How is one to be aware of one's conditioning?"

It is possible only by understanding another process, the process of attachment. If we can understand why we are attached, then perhaps we can be aware of our conditioning.

"Isn't that rather a long way round to come to a direct question?"

Is it? Just try to be aware of your conditioning. You can only know it indirectly, in relation to something else. You cannot be aware of your conditioning as an abstraction, for then it is merely verbal, without much significance. We are only aware of conflict. Conflict exists when there is no integration between challenge and response. This conflict is the result of our conditioning. Conditioning is attachment: attachment to work, to tradition, to property, to people, to ideas, and so on. If there were no attachment, would there be conditioning? Of course not. So why are we attached? I am attached to my country because through identification with it I become somebody. I identify myself with my work, and the work becomes important. I am my family, my property; I am attached to them. The object of attachment offers me the means of escape from my own emptiness. Attachment is escape, and it is escape that strengthens conditioning. If I am attached to you, it is because you have become the means of escape from myself; therefore you are very important to me and I must possess you, hold on to you. You become the conditioning factor, and escape is the conditioning. If we can be aware of our escapes, we can then perceive the factors, the influences that make for conditioning.

"Am I escaping from myself through social work?"

Are you attached to it, bound to it? Would you feel lost, empty, bored, if you did not do social work?

"I am sure I would."

Attachment to your work is your escape. There are escapes at all the levels of our being. You escape through work, another through drink, another through religious ceremonies, another through knowledge, another through God, and still another is addicted to amusement. All escapes are the same, there is no superior or inferior escape. God and drink are on the same level as long as they are escapes from what we are. When we are aware of our escapes, only then can we know of our conditioning.

"What shall I do if I cease to escape through social work? Can I do anything without escaping? Is not all my action a form of escape from what I am?"

Is this question merely verbal, or does it reflect an actuality, a fact which you are experiencing? If you did not escape, what would happen? Have you ever tried it?

"What you are saying is so negative, if I may say so. You don't offer any substitute for work."

Is not all substitution another form of escape? When one particular form of activity is not satisfactory or brings further conflict, we turn to another. To replace one activity by another without understanding escape is rather futile, is it not? It is these escapes and our attachment to them that make for conditioning. Conditioning brings problems, conflict. It is conditioning that prevents our understanding of the challenge; being conditioned, our response must inevitably create conflict.

"How can one be free from conditioning?"

Only by understanding, being aware of our escapes. Our attachment to a person, to work, to an ideology, is the conditioning factor; this is the thing we have to understand, and not seek a better or more intelligent escape. All escapes are unintelligent, as they inevitably bring about conflict. To cultivate detachment is another form of escape, of isolation; it is attachment to an abstraction, to an ideal called detachment. The ideal is fictitious, ego-made, and becoming the ideal is an escape from what *is*. There is the understanding of what *is*, an adequate action towards what *is*, only when the mind is no longer seeking any escape. The very thinking about what *is* is an escape from what *is*. Thinking about the problem is escape from the problem; for thinking *is* the problem, and the only problem. The mind, unwilling to be what it is, fearful of what it is, seeks these various escapes; and the way of escape is thought. As long as there is

6

thinking, there must be escapes, attachments, which only strengthen conditioning.

Freedom from conditioning comes with the freedom from thinking. When the mind is utterly still, only then is there freedom for the real to be.

THE FEAR OF INNER SOLITUDE

HOW NECESSARY IT is to die each day, to die each minute to everything, to the many yesterdays and to the moment that has just gone by! Without death there is no renewing, without death there is no creation. The burden of the past gives birth to its own continuity, and the worry of yesterday gives new life to the worry of to-day. Yesterday perpetuates to-day, and to-morrow is still yesterday. There is no release from this continuity except in death. In dying there is joy. This new morning, fresh and clear, is free from the light and darkness of yesterday; the song of that bird is heard for the first time, and the noise of those children is not that of yesterday. We carry the memory of yesterday, and it darkens our being. As long as the mind is the mechanical machine of memory, it knows no rest, no quietude, no silence; it is ever wearing itself out. That which is still can be reborn, but a thing that is in constant activity wears out and is useless. The well-spring is in ending, and death is as near as life.

She said she had studied for a number of years with one of the famous psychologists and had been analysed by him, which had taken considerable time. Though she had been brought up as a Christian and had also studied Hindu philosophy and its teachers, she had never joined any particular group or associated herself with any system of thought. As always, she was still dissatisfied, and had even put aside the psycho-analysis; and now she was engaged in some kind of welfare work. She had been married and had known all the misfortunes of family life as well as its joys.

7

She had taken refuge in various ways: in social prestige, in work, in money, and in the warm delight of this country by the blue sea. Sorrows had multiplied, which she could bear; but she had never been able to go beyond a certain depth, and it was not very deep.

Almost everything is shallow and soon comes to an end, only to begin again with a further shallowness. The inexhaustible is not to be discovered through any activity of the mind.

"I have gone from one activity to another, from one misfortune to another, always being driven and always pursuing. Now that I have reached the end of one urge, and before I follow another which will carry me on for a number of years, I have acted on a stronger impulse, and here I am. I have had a good life, gay and rich. I have been interested in many things and have studied certain subjects fairly deeply; but somehow, after all these years, I am still on the fringe of things, I don't seem able to penetrate beyond a certain point; I want to go deeper, but I cannot. I am told I am good at what I have been doing, and it is that very goodness that binds me. My conditioning is of the beneficent kind: doing good to others, helping the needy, consideration, generosity, and so on; but it is binding, like any other conditioning. My problem is to be free, not only of this conditioning, but of all conditioning, and to go beyond. This has become an imperative necessity, not only from hearing the talks, but also from my own observation and experience. I have for the time being put aside my welfare work, and whether or not I shall continue with it will be decided later."

Why have you not previously asked yourself the reason for all these activities?

"It has never before occurred to me to ask myself why I am in social work. I have always wanted to help, to do good, and it wasn't just empty sentimentality. I have found that the people with whom I live are not real, but only masks; it is those who need help that are real. Living with the masked is dull and stupid, but with the others there is struggle, pain."

Why do you engage in welfare or in any other kind of work?

8

"I suppose it is just to carry on. One must live and act, and my conditioning has been to act as decently as possible. I have never questioned why I do these things, and now I must find out. But before we go any further, let me say that I am a solitary person; though I see many people, I am alone and I like it. There is something exhilarating in being alone."

To be alone, in the highest sense, is essential; but the aloneness of withdrawal gives a sense of power, of strength, of invulnerability. Such aloneness is isolation, it is an escape, a refuge. But isn't it important to find out why you have never asked yourself the reason for all your supposedly good activities? Shouldn't you inquire into that?

"Yes, let us do so. I think it is the fear of inner solitude that has made me do all these things."

Why do you use the word 'fear' with regard to inner solitude? Outwardly you don't mind being alone, but from inner solitude you turn away. Why? Fear is not an abstraction, it exists only in relationship to something. Fear does not exist by itself; it exists as a word, but it is felt only in contact with something else. What is it that you are afraid of?

"Of this inner solitude."

There is fear of inner solitude only in relation to something else. You cannot be afraid of inner solitude, because you have never looked at it; you are measuring it now with what you already know. You know your worth, if one may put it that way, as a social worker, as a mother, as a capable and efficient person, and so on; you know the worth of your outer solitude. So it is in relation to all this that you measure or approach inner solitude; you know what has been, but you don't know what *is*. The known looking at the unknown brings about fear; it is this activity that causes fear.

"Yes, that is perfectly true. I am comparing the inner solitude with the things I know through experience. It is these experiences that are causing fear of something I have really not experienced at all."

So your fear is really not of the inner solitude, but the past is

9

afraid of something it does not know, has not experienced. The past wants to absorb the new, make of it an experience. But can the past, which is you, experience the new, the unknown? The known can experience only that which is of itself, it can never experience the new, the unknown. By giving the unknown a name, by calling it inner solitude, you have only recognized it verbally, and the word is taking the place of experiencing; for the word is the screen of fear. The term 'inner solitude' is covering the fact, the what *is*, and the very word is creating fear.

"But somehow I don't seem to be able to look at it."

Let us first understand why we are not capable of looking at the fact, and what is preventing our being passively watchful of it. Don't attempt to look at it now, but please listen quietly to what is being said.

The known, past experience, is trying to absorb what it calls the inner solitude; but it cannot experience it, for it does not know what it is; it knows the term, but not what is behind the term. The unknown cannot be experienced. You may think or speculate about the unknown, or be afraid of it; but thought cannot comprehend it, for thought is the outcome of the known, of experience. As thought cannot know the unknown, it is afraid of it. There will be fear as long as thought desires to experience, to understand the unknown.

"Then what . . . ?"

Please listen. If you listen rightly, the truth of all this will be seen; and then truth will be the only action. Whatever thought does with regard to inner solitude is an escape, an avoidance of what *is*. In avoiding what *is*, thought creates its own conditioning which prevents the experiencing of the new, the unknown. Fear is the only response of thought to the unknown; thought may call it by different terms, but still it is fear. Just see that thought cannot operate upon the unknown, upon what *is* behind the term 'inner solitude'. Only then does what *is* unfold itself, and it is inexhaustible.

Now, if one may suggest, leave it alone; you have heard, and let that work as it will. To be still after tilling and sowing is to give birth to creation.

THE PROCESS OF HATE

SHE WAS A teacher, or rather had been one. She was affectionate and kindly, and this had almost become a routine. She said she had taught for over twenty-five years and had been happy in it; and although towards the end she had wanted to get away from the whole thing, she had stuck to it. Recently she had begun to realize what was deeply buried in her nature. She had suddenly discovered it during one of the discussions, and it had really surprised and shocked her. It was there, and it wasn't a mere self-accusation; and as she looked back through the years she could now see that it had always been there. She really hated. It was not hatred of anyone in particular, but a feeling of general hate, a suppressed antagonism towards everyone and everything. When she first discovered it, she thought it was something very superficial which she could easily throw off; but as the days went by she found that it wasn't just a mild affair, but a deep-rooted hatred which had been going on all her life. What shocked her was that she had always thought she was affectionate and kind.

Love is a strange thing; as long as thought is woven through it, it is not love. When you think of someone you love, that person becomes the symbol of pleasant sensations, memories, images; but that is not love. Thought is sensation, and sensation is not love. The very process of thinking is the denial of love. Love is the flame without the smoke of thought, of jealousy, of antagonism, of usage, which are things of the mind. As long as the heart is burdened with the things of the mind, there must be hate; for the mind is the seat of hate, of antagonism, of opposition, of conflict. Thought is reaction, and reaction is always, in one way or another, the source of enmity. Thought is opposition, hate; thought is always in competition, always seeking an end, success; its fulfilment is pleasure and its frustration is hate. Conflict is thought caught in the opposites; and the synthesis of the opposites is still hate, antagonism.

"You see, I always thought I loved the children, and even when they grew up they used to come to me for comfort when they were in trouble. I took it for granted that I loved them, especially those who were my favourites away from the classroom; but now I see there has always been an undercurrent of hate, of deep-rooted antagonism. What am I to do with this discovery? You have no idea how appalled I am by it, and though you say we must not condemn, this discovery has been very salutary."

Have you also discovered the process of hate? To see the cause, to know why you hate, is comparatively easy; but are you aware of the ways of hate? Do you observe it as you would a strange new animal?

"It is all so new to me, and I have never watched the process of hate."

Let us do so now and see what happens; let us be passively watchful of hate as it unrolls itself. Don't be shocked, don't condemn or find excuses; just passively watch it. Hate is a form of frustration, is it not? Fulfilment and frustration always go together.

What are you interested in, not professionally, but deep down?

"I always wanted to paint."

Why haven't you?

"My father used to insist that I should not do anything that didn't bring in money. He was a very aggressive man, and money was to him the end of all things; he never did a thing if there was no money in it, or if it didn't bring more prestige, more power. 'More' was his god, and we were all his children. Though I liked him, I was opposed to him in so many ways. This idea of the importance of money was deeply embedded in me; and I liked teaching, probably because it offered me an opportunity to be the boss. On my holidays I used to paint, but it was most unsatisfactory; I wanted to give my life to it, and I actually gave only a couple of months a year. Finally I stopped painting, but it was burning inwardly. I see now how it was breeding antagonism."

Were you ever married? Have you children of your own?

"I fell in love with a married man, and we lived together secretly. I was furiously jealous of his wife and children, and I was scared to have babies, though I longed for them. All the natural things, the everyday companionship and so on, were denied me, and jealousy was a consuming fury. He had to move to another town, and my jealousy never abated. It was an unbearable thing. To forget it all, I took to teaching more intensely. But now I see I am still jealous, not of him, for he is dead, but of happy people, of married people, of the successful, of almost anyone. What we could have been together was denied to us!"

Jealousy is hate, is it not? If one loves, there is no room for anything else. But we do not love; the smoke chokes our life, and the flame dies.

"I can see now that in school, with my married sisters, and in almost all my relationships, there was war going on, only it was covered up. I was becoming the ideal teacher; to become the ideal teacher was my goal, and I was being recognized as such."

The stronger the ideal, the deeper the suppression, the deeper the conflict and antagonism.

"Yes, I see all that now; and strangely, as I watch, I don't mind being what I actually am."

You don't mind it because there is a kind of brutal recognition, is there not? This very recognition brings a certain pleasure; it gives vitality, a sense of confidence in knowing yourself, the power of knowledge. As jealousy, though painful, gave a pleasurable sensation, so now the knowledge of your past gives you a sense of mastery which is also pleasurable. You have now found a new term for jealousy, for frustration, for being left: it is hate and the knowledge of it. There is pride in knowing, which is another form of antagonism. We move from one substitution to another; but essentially, all substitutions are the same, though verbally they may appear to be dissimilar. So you are caught in the net of your own thought, are you not?

"Yes, but what else can one do?"

Don't ask, but watch the process of your own thinking. How cunning and deceptive it is! It promises release, but only produces another crisis, another antagonism. Just be passively watchful of this and let the truth of it be.

"Will there be freedom from jealousy, from hate, from this constant, suppressed battle?"

When you are hoping for something, positively or negatively, you are projecting your own desire; you will succeed in your desire, but that is only another substitution, and so the battle is on again. This desire to gain or to avoid is still within the field of opposition, is it not? See the false as the false, then the truth is. You don't have to look for it. What you seek you will find, but it will not be truth. It is like a suspicious man finding what he suspects, which is comparatively easy and stupid. Just be passively aware of this total thought-process, and also of the desire to be free of it.

"All this has been an extraordinary discovery for me, and I am beginning to see the truth of what you are saying. I hope it won't take more years to go beyond this conflict. There I am hoping again! I shall silently watch and see what happens."

PROGRESS AND REVOLUTION

THEY WERE CHANTING in the temple. It was a clean temple of carved stone, massive and indestructible. There were over thirty priests, naked to the waist; their pronunciation of the Sanskrit was precise and distinct, and they knew the meaning of the chant. The depth and sound of the words made those walls and pillars almost tremble, and instinctively the group that was there became silent. The creation, the beginning of the world was being chanted, and how man was brought forth. The people had closed their eyes, and the chant was producing a pleasant disturbance: nostalgic remembrances of their childhood, thoughts of the progress they had made since those youthful days, the strange effect of Sanskrit words, delight in hearing the chant again. Some were repeating the chant to themselves, and their lips were moving. The atmosphere was getting charged with strong emotions, but the priests went on with the chant and the gods remained silent.

How we hug to ourselves the idea of progress. We like to think we shall achieve a better state, become more merciful, peaceful and virtuous. We love to cling to this illusion, and few are deeply aware that this becoming is a pretence, a satisfying myth. We love to think that someday we shall be better, but in the meantime we carry on. Progress is such a comforting word, so reassuring, a word with which we hypnotize ourselves. The thing which *is* cannot become something different; greed can never become non-greed, any more than violence can become non-violence. You can make pig-iron into a marvellous, complicated machine, but progress is illusion when applied to self-becoming. The idea of the 'me' becoming something glorious is the simple deception of the craving to be great. We worship the success of the State, of the ideology, of the self, and deceive ourselves with the comforting illusion of progress. Thought may progress, become something more, go towards a more perfect end, or make itself silent; but as long as thought is a movement of acquisitiveness or renunciation, it is always a mere reaction. Reaction ever produces conflict, and progress in conflict is further confusion, further antagonism.

He said he was a revolutionary, ready to kill or be killed for his cause, for his ideology. He was prepared to kill for the sake of a better world. To destroy the present social order would of course produce more chaos, but this confusion could be used to build a classless society. What did it matter if you destroyed some or many in the process of building a perfect social order? What mattered was not the present man, but the future man; the new world that they were going to build would have no inequality, there would be work for all, and there would be happiness.

How can you be so sure of the future? What makes you so certain of it? The religious people promise heaven, and you promise a better world in the future; you have your book and your priests, as they have theirs, so there is really not much difference between you. But what makes you so sure that you are clear-sighted about the future?

"Logically, if we follow a certain course the end is certain. Moreover, there is a great deal of historical evidence to support our position."

We all translate the past according to our particular conditioning and interpret it to suit our prejudices. You are as uncertain of
to-morrow as the rest of us, and thank heaven it is so! But to
sacrifice the present for an illusory future is obviously most
illogical.

"Do you believe in change, or are you a tool of the capitalist
bourgeoisie?"

Change is modified continuity, which you may call revolution;
but fundamental revolution is quite a different process, it has
nothing to do with logic or historical evidence. There is fundamental revolution only in understanding the total process of
action, not at any particular level, whether economic or ideological, but action as an integrated whole. Such action is not
reaction. You only know reaction, the reaction of antithesis, and
the further reaction which you call synthesis. Integration is not an
intellectual synthesis, a verbal conclusion based on historical study.
Integration can come into being only with the understanding of
reaction. The mind is a series of reactions; and revolution based
on reactions, on ideas, is no revolution at all, but only a modified
continuity of what has been. You may call it revolution, but
actually it is not.

"What to you is revolution?"

Change based on an idea is not revolution; for idea is the response of memory, which is again a reaction. Fundamental revolution is possible only when ideas are not important and so have
ceased. A revolution born of antagonism ceases to be what it says
it is; it is only opposition, and opposition can never be creative.

"The kind of revolution you are talking about is purely an
abstraction, it has no reality in the modern world. You are a vague
idealist, utterly impractical."

, On the contrary, the idealist is the man with an idea, and it is
he who is not revolutionary. Ideas divide, and separation is disintegration, it is not revolution at all. The man with an ideology
is concerned with ideas, words, and not with direct action; he
avoids direct action. An ideology is a hindrance to direct action.

"Don't you think there can be equality through revolution?"

Revolution based on an idea, however logical and in accordance with historical evidence, cannot bring about equality. The very function of idea is to separate people. Belief, religious or political, sets man against man. So-called religions have divided people, and still do. Organized belief, which is called religion, is, like any other ideology, a thing of the mind and therefore separative. You with your ideology are doing the same, are you not? You also are forming a nucleus or group around an idea; you want to include everyone in your group, just as the believer does. You want to save the world in your way, as he in his. You murder and liquidate each other, all for a better world. Neither of you is interested in a better world, but in shaping the world according to your idea. How can idea make for equality?

"Within the fold of the idea we are all equal, though we may have different functions. We are first what the idea represents, and afterwards we are individual functionaries. In function we have gradations, but not as representatives of the ideology."

This is precisely what every other organized belief has proclaimed. In the eyes of God we are all equal, but in capacity there is variation; life is one, but social divisions are inevitable. By substituting one ideology for another you have not changed the fundamental fact that one group or individual treats another as inferior. Actually, there is inequality at all the levels of existence. One has capacity, and another has not; one leads, and another follows; one is dull, and another is sensitive, alert, adaptable; one paints or writes, and another digs; one is a scientist, and another a sweeper. Inequality is a fact, and no revolution can do away with it. What so-called revolution does is to substitute one group for another, and the new group then assumes power, political and economic; it becomes the new upper class which proceeds to strengthen itself by privileges, and so on; it knows all the tricks of the other class, which has been thrown down. It has not abolished inequality, has it?

"Eventually it will. When the whole world is of our way of thinking, then there will be ideological equality."

Which is not equality at all, but merely an idea, a theory, the dream of another world, like that of the religious believer. How very near you are to each other! Ideas divide, they are separative, opposing, breeding conflict. An idea can never bring about equality, even in its own world. If we all believed the same thing, at the same time, at the same level, there would be equality of a sort; but that is an impossibility, a mere speculation which can only lead to illusion.

"Are you scouting all equality? Are you being cynical and condemning all efforts to bring about equal opportunity for all?"

I am not being cynical, but am merely stating the obvious facts; nor am I against equal opportunity. Surely, it is possible to go beyond and perhaps discover an effective approach to this problem of inequality, only when we understand the actual, the what *is*. To approach what *is* with an idea, a conclusion, a dream, is not to understand what *is*. Prejudiced observation is no observation at all. The fact is, there is inequality at all the levels of consciousness, of life; and do what we may, we cannot alter that fact.

Now, is it possible to approach the fact of inequality without creating further antagonism, further division? Revolution has used man as a means to an end. The end was important, but not man. Religions have maintained, at least verbally, that man is important; but they too have used man for the building up of belief, of dogma. The utilizing of man for a purpose must of necessity breed the sense of the superior and the inferior, the one who is near and the one who is far, the one who knows and the one who does not know. This separation is psychological inequality, and it is the factor of disintegration in society. At present we know relationship only as utility; society uses the individual, just as individuals use each other, in order to benefit in various ways. This using of another is the fundamental cause of the psychological division of man against man.

We cease to use one another only when idea is not the motivating factor in relationship. With idea comes exploitation, and exploitation breeds antagonism.

"Then what is the factor that comes into being when idea ceases?"

It is love, the only factor that can bring about a fundamental revolution. Love is the only true revolution. But love is not an idea; it *is* when thought is not. Love is not a tool of propaganda;

it is not something to be cultivated and shouted about from the house tops. Only when the flag, the belief, the leader, the idea as planned action, drop away, can there be love; and love is the only creative and constant revolution.

"But love won't run machinery, will it?"

BOREDOM

It HAD STOPPED raining; the roads were clean, and the dust had been washed from the trees. The earth was refreshed, and the frogs were loud in the pond; they were big, and their throats were swollen with pleasure. The grass was sparkling with tiny drops of water, and there was peace in the land after the heavy downpour. The cattle were soaking wet, but during the rain they never took shelter, and now they were contentedly grazing. Some boys were playing in the little stream that the rain had made by the roadside; they were naked, and it was good to see their shining bodies and their bright eyes. They were having the time of their life, and how happy they were! Nothing else mattered, and they smiled out of joy as one said something to them, though they didn't understand a word. The sun was coming out and the shadows were deep.

How necessary it is for the mind to purge itself of all thought, to be constantly empty, not *made* empty, but simply empty; to die to all thought, to all of yesterday's memories, and to the coming hour! It is simple to die, and it is hard to continue; for continuity is effort to be or not to be. Effort is desire, and desire can die only when the mind ceases to acquire. How simple it is just to live! But it is not stagnation. There is great happiness in not wanting, in not being something, in not going somewhere. When the mind purges itself of all thought, only then is there the silence of creation. The mind is not tranquil as long as it is travelling in order to arrive. For the mind, to arrive is to succeed, and success is ever the same, whether at the beginning or at the end. There is no purgation of the mind if it is weaving the pattern of its own becoming.

She said she had always been active in one way or another, either with her children, or in social affairs, or in sports; but behind this activity there was always boredom, pressing and constant. She was bored with the routine of life, with pleasure, pain, flattery, and everything else. Boredom was like a cloud that had hung over her life for as long as she could remember. She had tried to escape from it, but every new interest soon became a further boredom, a deadly weariness. She had read a great deal, and had had the usual turmoils of family life, but through it all there was this weary boredom. It had nothing to do with her health, for she was very well.

Why do you think you get bored? Is it the outcome of some frustration, of some fundamental desire which has been thwarted?

"Not especially. There have been some superficial obstructions, but they have never bothered me; or when they have, I have met them fairly intelligently and have never been stumped by them. I don't think my trouble is frustration, for I have always been able to get what I want. I haven't cried for the moon, and have been sensible in my demands; but there has nevertheless been this sense of boredom with everything, with my family and with my work."

What do you mean by boredom? Do you mean dissatisfaction? Is it that nothing has given you complete satisfaction?

"It isn't quite that. I am as dissatisfied as any normal person, but I have been able to reconcile myself to the inevitable dissatisfactions."

What are you interested in? Is there any deep interest in your life?

"Not especially. If I had a deep interest I would never be bored. I am naturally an enthusiastic person, I assure you, and if I had an interest I wouldn't easily let it go. I have had many intermittent interests, but they have all led in the end to this cloud of boredom."

What do you mean by interest? Why is there this change from

interest to boredom? What does interest mean? You are interested in that which pleases you, gratifies you, are you not? Is not interest a process of acquisitiveness? You would not be interested in anything if you did not get something out of it, would you? There is sustained interest as long as you are acquiring; acquisition is interest, is it not? You have tried to gain satisfaction from everything you have come in contact with; and when you have thoroughly used it, naturally you get bored with it. Every acquisition is a form of boredom, weariness. We want a change of toys; as soon as we lose interest in one, we turn to another, and there is always a new toy to turn to. We turn to something in order to acquire; there is acquisition in pleasure, in knowledge, in fame, in power, in efficiency, in having a family, and so on. When there is nothing further to acquire in one religion, in one saviour, we lose interest and turn to another. Some go to sleep in an organization and never wake up, and those who do wake up put themselves to sleep again by joining another. This acquisitive movement is called expansion of thought, progress.

"Is interest always acquisition?"

Actually, are you interested in anything which doesn't give you something, whether it be a play, a game, a conversation, a book, or a person? If a painting doesn't give you something, you pass it by; if a person doesn't stimulate or disturb you in some way, if there is no pleasure or pain in a particular relationship, you lose interest, you get bored. Haven't you noticed this?

"Yes, but I have never before looked at it in this way."

You wouldn't have come here if you didn't want something. You want to be free of boredom. As I cannot give you that freedom, you will get bored again; but if we can together understand the process of acquisition, of interest, of boredom, then perhaps there will be freedom. Freedom cannot be acquired. If you acquire it, you will soon be bored with it. Does not acquisition dull the mind? Acquisition, positive or negative, is a burden. As soon as you acquire, you lose interest. In trying to possess, you are alert, interested; but possession is boredom. You may want to possess more, but the pursuit of more is only a movement towards boredom. You try various forms of acquisition, and as long as there is the effort to acquire, there is interest; but there is always an end to acquisition, and so there is always boredom. Isn't this what has been happening?

"I suppose it is, but I haven't grasped the full significance of it."

That will come presently.

Possessions make the mind weary. Acquisition, whether of knowledge, of property, of virtue, makes for insensitivity. The nature of the mind is to acquire, to absorb, is it not? Or rather, the pattern it has created for itself is one of gathering in; and in that very activity the mind is preparing its own weariness, boredom. Interest, curiosity, is the beginning of acquisition, which soon becomes boredom; and the urge to be free from boredom is another form of possession. So the mind goes from boredom to interest to boredom again, till it is utterly weary; and these successive waves of interest and weariness are regarded as existence.

"But how is one to be free from acquiring without further acquisition?"

Only by allowing the truth of the whole process of acquisition to be experienced, and not by trying to be non-acquisitive, detached. To be non-acquisitive is another form of acquisition which soon becomes wearisome. The difficulty, if one may use that word, lies, not in the verbal understanding of what has been said, but in experiencing the false as the false. To see the truth in the false is the beginning of wisdom. The difficulty is for the mind to be still; for the mind is always worried, it is always after something, acquiring or denying, searching and finding. The mind is never still, it is in continuous movement. The past, overshadowing the present, makes its own future. It is a movement in time, and there is hardly ever an interval between thoughts. One thought follows another without a pause; the mind is ever making itself sharp and so wearing itself out. If a pencil is being sharpened all the time, soon there will be nothing left of it; similarly, the mind uses itself constantly and is exhausted. The mind is always afraid of coming to an end. But, living is ending from day to day; it is the dying to all acquisition, to memories, to experiences, to the past. How can there be living if there is experience? Experience is knowledge, memory; and is memory the state of experiencing? In the state of experiencing, is there memory as the experiencer? The purgation of the mind is living, is creation. Beauty is in experiencing, not in experience; for experience is ever of the past, and the past is not the experiencing, it is not the living. The purgation of the mind is tranquillity of heart.

DISCIPLINE

WE HAD DRIVEN through heavy traffic, and presently we turned off the main road into a sheltered lane. Leaving the car, we followed a path that wove through palm groves and along a field of green, ripening rice. How lovely was that long, curving rice-field, bordered by the tall palms! It was a cool evening, and a breeze was stirring among the trees with their heavy foliage. Unexpectedly, round a bend, there was a lake. It was long, narrow and deep, and on both sides of it the palms stood so close together as to be almost impenetrable. The breeze was playing with the water, and there was murmuring along the shore. Some boys were bathing, naked, unashamed and free. Their bodies were glistening and beautiful, well-formed, slender and supple. They would swim out into the middle of the lake, then come back and start again. The path led on past a village, and on the way back the full moon made deep shadows; the boys had gone, the moonlight was upon the waters, and the palms were like white columns in the shadowy dark.

He had come from some distance, and was eager to find out how to subdue the mind. He said that he had deliberately withdrawn from the world and was living very simply with some relatives, devoting his time to the overcoming of the mind. He had practised a certain discipline for a number of years, but his mind was still not under control; it was always ready to wander off, like an animal on a leash. He had starved himself, but that did not help; he had experimented with his diet, and that had helped a little, but there was never any peace. His mind was forever

23

throwing up images, conjuring up past scenes, sensations and incidents; or it would think of how it would be quiet to-morrow. But to-morrow never came, and the whole process became quite nightmarish. On very rare occasions the mind was quiet, but the quietness soon became a memory, a thing of the past.

What is overcome must be conquered again and again. Suppression is a form of overcoming, as are substitution and sublimation. To desire to conquer is to give birth to further conflict. Why do you want to conquer, to calm the mind?

"I have always been interested in religious matters; I have studied various religions, and they all say that to know God the mind must be still. Ever since I can remember I have always wanted to find God, the pervading beauty of the world, the beauty of the rice-field and the dirty village. I had a very promising career, had been abroad and all that kind of thing; but one morning I just walked out to find that stillness. I heard what you said about it the other day, and so I have come."

To find God, you try to subdue the mind. But is calmness of mind a way to God? Is calmness the coin which will open the gates of heaven? You want to buy your way to God, to truth, or what name you will. Can you buy the eternal through virtue, through renunciation, through mortification? We think that if we do certain things, practise virtue, pursue chastity, withdraw from the world, we shall be able to measure the measureless; so it's just a bargain, isn't it? Your 'virtue' is a means to an end.

"But discipline is necessary to curb the mind, otherwise there is no peace. I have just not disciplined it sufficiently; it's my fault, not the fault of the discipline."

Discipline is a means to an end. But the end is the unknown. Truth is the unknown, it cannot be known; if it is known, it is not truth. If you can measure the immeasurable, then it is not. Our measurement is the word, and the word is not the real. Discipline is the means; but the means and the end are not two dissimilar things, are they? Surely, the end and the means are one; the means is the end, the only end; there is no goal apart from the means. Violence as a means to peace is only the perpetuation of violence. The means is all that matters, and not the end; the end is determined by the means; the end is not separate, away from the means.

"I will listen and try to understand what you are saying. When I don't, I will ask."

You use discipline, control, as a means to gain tranquillity, do you not? Discipline implies conformity to a pattern; you control in order to be this or that. Is not discipline, in its very nature, violence? It may give you pleasure to discipline yourself, but is not that very pleasure a form of resistance which only breeds further conflict? Is not the practice of discipline the cultivation of defence? And what is defended is always attacked. Does not discipline imply the suppression of what *is* in order to achieve a desired end? Suppression, substitution and sublimation only increase effort and bring about further conflict. You may succeed in suppressing a disease, but it will continue to appear in different forms until it is eradicated. Discipline is the suppression, the overcoming of what *is*. Discipline is a form of violence; so, through a 'wrong' means we hope to gain the 'right' end. Through resistance, how can there be the free, the true? Freedom is at the beginning, not at the end; the goal is the first step, the means is the end. The first step must be free, and not the last. Discipline implies compulsion, subtle or brutal, outward or self-imposed; and where there is compulsion, there is fear. Fear, compulsion, is used as a means to an end, the end being love. Can there be love through fear? Love is when there is no fear at any level.

"But without some kind of compulsion, some kind of conformity, how can the mind function at all?"

The very activity of the mind is a barrier to its own understanding. Have you never noticed that there is understanding only when the mind, as thought, is not functioning? Understanding comes with the ending of the thought-process, in the interval between two thoughts. You say the mind must be still, and yet you desire it to function. If we can be simple in watchfulness, we shall understand; but our approach is so complex that it prevents understanding. Surely, we are not concerned with discipline, control, suppression, resistance, but with the process and the ending of thought itself. What do we mean when we say that the mind wanders? Simply that thought is everlastingly enticed from one attraction to another, from one association to another, and is in constant agitation. Is it possible for thought to come to an end?

"That is exactly my problem. I want to end thought. I can see now the futility of discipline; I really see the falseness, the stupidity of it, and I won't pursue that line any more. But how can I end thought?"

Again, listen without prejudice, without interposing any conclusions, either your own or those of another; listen to understand and not merely to refute or accept. You ask how you can put an end to thought. Now, are you, the thinker, an entity separate from your thoughts? Are you entirely dissimilar from your thoughts? Are you not your own thoughts? Thought may place the thinker at a very high level and give a name to him, separate him from itself; yet the thinker is still within the process of thought, is he not? There is only thought, and thought creates the thinker; thought gives form to the thinker as a permanent, separate entity. Thought sees itself to be impermanent, in constant flux, so it breeds the thinker as a permanent entity apart and dissimilar from itself. Then the thinker operates on thought; the thinker says, "I must put an end to thought". But there is only the process of thinking, there is no thinker apart from thought. The experiencing of this truth is vital, it is not a mere repetition of phrases. There are only thoughts, and not a thinker who thinks thoughts.

"But how did thought arise originally?"

Through perception, contact, sensation, desire and identification; 'I want', 'I don't want', and so on. That is fairly simple, is it not? Our problem is, how can thought end? Any form of compulsion, conscious or unconscious, is utterly futile, for it implies a controller, one who disciplines; and such an entity, as we see, is non-existent. Discipline is a process of condemnation, comparison, or justification; and when it is clearly seen that there is no separate entity as the thinker, the one who disciplines, then there are only thoughts, the process of thinking. Thinking is the response of memory, of experience, of the past. This again must be perceived, not on the verbal level, but there must be an experiencing of it. Then only is there passive watchfulness in which the thinker is not, an awareness in which thought is entirely absent. The mind, the totality of experience, the self-consciousness which is ever in the past, is quiet only when it is not projecting itself; and this projection is the desire to become.

The mind is empty only when thought is not. Thought cannot come to an end save through passive watchfulness of every thought. In this awareness there is no watcher and no censor; without the censor, there is only experiencing. In experiencing there is neither the experiencer nor the experienced. The experienced is the thought, which gives birth to the thinker. Only when the mind is experiencing is there stillness, the silence which is not made up, put together; and only in that tranquillity can the real come into being. Reality is not of time and is not measurable.

Conflict—Freedom—Relationship

"The conflict between thesis and antithesis is inevitable and necessary; it brings about synthesis, from which again there is a thesis with its corresponding antithesis, and so on. There is no end to conflict, and it is only through conflict that there can ever be any growth, any advance."

Does conflict bring about a comprehension of our problems? Does it lead to growth, advancement? It may bring about secondary improvements, but is not conflict in its very nature a factor of disintegration? Why do you insist that conflict is essential?

"We all know there is conflict at every level of our existence, so why deny or be blind to it?"

One is not blind to the constant strife within and without; but if I may ask, why do you insist that it is essential?

"Conflict cannot be denied, it is part of the human structure, and we use it as a means to an end, the end being the right environment for the individual. We work towards that goal and use every means to bring it about. Ambition, conflict, is the way of man, and it can be used either against him or for him. Through conflict we move to greater things."

What do you mean by conflict? Conflict between what?

"Between what has been and what will be."

The 'what will be' is the further response of what has been and is. By conflict we mean the struggle between two opposing ideas. But is opposition in any form conducive to understanding? When is there understanding of any problem?

"There is class conflict, national conflict, and ideological conflict. Conflict is opposition, resistance due to ignorance of certain fundamental historical facts. Through opposition there is growth, there is progress, and this whole process is life."

We know there is conflict at all the different levels of life, and it would be foolish to deny it. But is this conflict essential? We have so far assumed that it is, or have justified it with cunning reason. In nature, the significance of conflict may be quite different; among the animals, conflict as we know it may not exist at all. But to us, conflict has become a factor of enormous importance. Why has it become so significant in our lives? Competition, ambition, the effort to be or not to be, the will to achieve, and so on—all this is part of conflict. Why do we accept conflict as being essential to existence? This does not imply, on the other hand, that we should accept indolence. But why do we tolerate conflict within and without? Is conflict essential to understanding, to the resolution of a problem? Should we not investigate rather than assert or deny? Should we not attempt to find the truth of the matter rather than hold to our conclusions and opinions?

"How can there be progress from one form of society to another without conflict? The 'haves' will never voluntarily give up their wealth, they must be forced, and this conflict will bring about a new social order, a new way of life. This cannot be done pacifically. We may not want to be violent, but we have to face facts."

You assume that you know what the new society should be, and that the other fellow does not; you alone have this extraordinary knowledge, and you are willing to liquidate those who stand in your way. By this method, which you think is essential, you only bring about opposition and hate. What you know is merely another form of prejudice, a different kind of conditioning. Your historical studies, or those of your leaders, are interpreted according to a particular background which determines your response; and this response you call the new approach, the new ideology. All response of thought is conditioned, and to bring about a revolution based on thought or idea is to perpetuate a modified form of what was. You are essentially reformers, and not real revolutionaries. Reformation and revolution based on idea are retrogressive factors in society.

You said, did you not, that the conflict between thesis and antithesis is essential, and that this conflict of opposites produces a synthesis?

"Conflict between the present society and its opposite, through the pressure of historical events and so on, will eventually bring about a new social order."

Is the opposite different or dissimilar from what *is?* How does the opposite come into being? Is it not a modified projection of what *is?* Has not the antithesis the elements of its own thesis? The one is not wholly different or dissimilar from the other, and the synthesis is still a modified thesis. Though periodically coated a different colour, though modified, reformed, reshaped according to circumstances and pressures, the thesis is always the thesis. The conflict between the opposites is utterly wasteful and stupid. Intellectually or verbally you can prove or disprove anything, but that cannot alter certain obvious facts. The present society is based on individual acquisitiveness; and its opposite, with the resulting synthesis, is what you call the new society. In your new society, individual acquisitiveness is opposed by State acquisitiveness, the State being the rulers; the State is now all-important, and not the individual. From this antithesis you say there will eventually be a synthesis in which all individuals are important. This future is imaginary, an ideal; it is the projection of thought, and thought is always the response of memory, of conditioning. It is really a vicious circle with no way out. This conflict, this struggling within the cage of thought, is what you call progress.

"Do you say, then, that we must stay as we are, with all the exploitation and corruption of the present society?"

Not at all. But your revolution is no revolution, it is only a change of power from one group to another, the substitution of one class for another. Your revolution is merely a different structure built of the same material and within the same underlying pattern. There *is* a radical revolution which is not a conflict, which is not based on thought with its ego-made projections, ideals, dogmas, Utopias; but as long as we think in terms of changing this into that, of becoming more or becoming less, of achieving an end, there cannot be this fundamental revolution.

"Such a revolution is an impossibility. Are you seriously proposing it?"

It is the only revolution, the only fundamental transformation.

"How do you propose to bring it about?"

By seeing the false as the false; by seeing the truth in the false. Obviously, there must be a fundamental revolution in man's relationship to man; we all know that things cannot go on as they are without increasing sorrow and disaster. But all reformers, like the so-called revolutionaries, have an end in view, a goal to be achieved, and both use man as a means to their own ends. The use of man for a purpose is the real issue, and not the attainment of a particular end. You cannot separate the end from the means, for they are a single, inseparable process. The means is the end; there can be no classless society through the means of class conflict. The results of using wrong means for a so-called right end are fairly obvious. There can be no peace through war, or through being prepared for war. All opposites are self-projected; the ideal is a reaction from what *is*, and the conflict to achieve the ideal is a vain and illusory struggle within the cage of thought. Through this conflict there is no release, no freedom for man. Without freedom, there can be no happiness; and freedom is not an ideal. Freedom is the only means to freedom.

As long as man is psychologically or physically used, whether in the name of God or of the State, there will be a society based on violence. Using man for a purpose is a trick employed by the politician and the priest, and it denies relationship.

"What do you mean by that?"

When we use each other for our mutual gratification, can there be any relationship between us? When you use another for your comfort, as you use a piece of furniture, are you related to that person? Are you related to the furniture? You may call it yours, and that is all; but you have no relationship with it. Similarly, when you use another for your psychological or physical advantage, you generally call that person yours, you possess him or her; and is possession relationship? The State uses the individual and calls him its citizen; but it has no relationship with the individual, it merely uses him as a tool. A tool is a dead thing, and there can be no relationship with that which is dead. When we use man for a purpose, however noble, we want him as an instrument, a dead thing. We cannot use a living thing, so our demand is for dead things; our society is based on the use of dead things. The use of another makes that person the dead instrument of our gratification. Relationship can exist only between the living, and usage is a process of isolation. It is this isolating process that breeds conflict, antagonism between man and man.

"Why do you lay so much emphasis on relationship?"

Existence is relationship; to be is to be related. Relationship is society. The structure of our present society, being based on mutual use, brings about violence, destruction and misery; and if the so-called revolutionary State does not fundamentally alter this usage, it can only produce, perhaps at a different level, still further conflict, confusion and antagonism. As long as we psychologically need and use each other, there can be no relationship. Relationship is communion; and how can there be communion if there is exploitation? Exploitation implies fear, and fear inevitably leads to all kinds of illusions and misery. Conflict exists only in exploitation and not in relationship. Conflict, opposition, enmity, exists between us when there is the use of another as a means of pleasure, of achievement. This conflict obviously cannot be resolved by using it as a means to a self-projected goal; and all ideals, all Utopias are self-projected. To see this is essential, for then we shall experience the truth that conflict in any form destroys relationship, understanding. There is understanding only when the mind is quiet; and the mind is not quiet when it is held in any ideology, dogma or belief, or when it is bound to the pattern of its own experience, memories. The mind is not quiet when it is acquiring or becoming. All acquisition is conflict; all becoming is a process of isolation. The mind is not quiet when it is disciplined, controlled and checked; such a mind is a dead mind, it is isolating itself through various forms of resistance, and so it inevitably creates misery for itself and for others.

The mind is quiet only when it is not caught in thought, which is the net of its own activity. When the mind is still, not made still, a true factor, love, comes into being.

EFFORT

IT BEGAN TO rain gently enough, but suddenly it was as though the heavens had opened and there was a deluge. In the street the water was almost knee-deep, and it was well over the pavement. There was not a flutter among the leaves, and they too were silent in their surprise. A car passed by and then stalled, water having gotten into its essential parts. People were wading across the street, soaked to the skin, but they were enjoying this downpour. The garden beds were being washed out and the lawn was covered with several inches of brown water. A dark blue bird with fawn-coloured wings was trying to take shelter among the thick leaves, but it got wetter and wetter and shook itself so often. The downpour lasted for some time, and then stopped as suddenly as it had begun. All things were washed clean.

How simple it is to be innocent! Without innocence, it is impossible to be happy. The pleasure of sensations is not the happiness of innocence. Innocence is freedom from the burden of experience. It is the memory of experience that corrupts, and not the experiencing itself. Knowledge, the burden of the past, is corruption. The power to accumulate, the effort to become, destroys innocence; and without innocence, how can there be wisdom? The merely curious can never know wisdom; they will find, but what they find will not be truth. The suspicious can never know happiness, for suspicion is the anxiety of their own being,

and fear breeds corruption. Fearlessness is not courage but freedom from accumulation.

"I have spared no effort to get somewhere in the world, and
have become a very successful money-maker; my efforts in that
direction have produced the results I wanted. I have also tried
hard to make a happy affair of my family life, but you know how
it is. Family life is not the same as making money or running an
industry. One deals with human beings in business, but it is at a
different level. At home there is a great deal of friction with very
little to show for it, and one's efforts in this field only seem to
increase the mess. I am not complaining, for that is not my
nature, but the marriage system is all wrong. We marry to satisfy
our sexual urges, without really knowing anything about each
other; and though we live in the same house and occasionally
and deliberately produce a child, we are like strangers to each
other, and the tension that only married people know is always
there. I have done what I think is my duty, but it has not produced the best results, to put it mildly. We are both dominant
and aggressive people, and it is not easy. Our efforts to co-operate
have not brought about a deep companionship between us.
Though I am very interested in psychological matters, it has not
been of great help, and I want to go much more deeply into this
problem."

The sun had come out, the birds were calling, and the sky was
clear and blue after the storm.

What do you mean by effort?

"To strive after something. I have striven after money and
position, and I have won both. I have also striven to have a
happy family life, but this has not been very successful; so now I
am struggling after something deeper."

We struggle with an end in view; we strive after achievement;
we make a constant effort to become something, positively or
negatively. The struggle is always to be secure in some way, it is
always towards something or away from something. Effort is
really an endless battle to acquire, is it not?

"Is it wrong to acquire?"

33

We shall go into that presently; but what we call effort is this constant process of travelling and arriving, of acquiring in different directions. We get tired of one kind of acquisition, and turn to another; and when that is gathered, we again turn to something else. Effort is a process of gathering knowledge, experience, efficiency, virtue, possessions, power, and so on; it is an endless becoming, expanding, growing. Effort towards an end, whether worthy or unworthy, must always bring conflict; conflict is antagonism, opposition, resistance. Is that necessary?

"Necessary to what?"

Let us find out. Effort at the physical level may be necessary; the effort to build a bridge, to produce petroleum, coal, and so on, is or may be beneficial; but how the work is done, how things are produced and distributed, how profits are divided, is quite another matter. If at the physical level man is used for an end, for an ideal, whether by private interests or by the State, effort only produces more confusion and misery. Effort to acquire for the individual, for the State, or for a religious organization, is bound to breed opposition. Without understanding this striving after acquisition, effort at the physical level will inevitably have a disastrous effect on society.

Is effort at the psychological level—the effort to be, to achieve, to succeed—necessary or beneficial?

"If we made no such effort, would we not just rot, disintegrate?"

Would we? So far, what have we produced through effort at the psychological level?

"Not very much, I admit. Effort has been in the wrong direction. The direction matters, and rightly directed effort is of the greatest significance. It is because of the lack of right effort that we are in such a mess."

So you say there is right effort and wrong effort, is that it? Do not let us quibble over words, but how do you distinguish between right and wrong effort? According to what criterion do you judge? What is your standard? Is it tradition, or is it the future ideal, the 'ought to be'?

"My criterion is determined by what brings results. It is the result that is important, and without the enticement of a goal we would make no effort."

If the result is your measure, then surely you are not concerned with the means; or are you?

"I will use the means according to the end. If the end is happiness, then a happy means must be found."

Is not the happy means the happy end? The end is in the means, is it not? So there is only the means. The means itself is the end, the result.

"I have never before looked at it this way, but I see that it is so."

We are inquiring into what is the happy means. If effort produces conflict, opposition within and without, can effort ever lead to happiness? If the end is in the means, how can there be happiness through conflict and antagonism? If effort produces more problems, more conflict, it is obviously destructive and disintegrating. And why do we make effort? Do we not make effort to be more, to advance, to gain? Effort is for more in one direction, and for less in another. Effort implies acquisition for oneself or for a group, does it not?

"Yes, that is so. Acquiring for oneself is at another level the acquisitiveness of the State or the church."

Effort is acquisition, negative or positive. What is it, then, that we are acquiring? At one level we acquire the physical necessities, and at another we use these as a means of self-aggrandizement; or, being satisfied with a few physical necessities, we acquire power, position, fame. The rulers, the representatives of the State, may live outwardly simple lives and possess but few things, but they have acquired power and so they resist and dominate.

"Do you think all acquisition is baneful?"

Let us see. Security, which is having the essential physical needs, is one thing, and acquisitiveness is another. It is acquisitiveness in the name of race or country, in the name of God; or in the name of the individual, that is destroying the sensible and efficient organization of physical necessities for the well-being of man. We must all have adequate food, clothing and shelter, that is simple and clear. Now, what is it that we are seeking to acquire, apart from these things?

One acquires money as a means to power, to certain social and psychological gratifications, as a means to the freedom to do what one wants to do. One struggles to attain wealth and position in order to be powerful in various ways; and having succeeded in outer things, one now wants to be successful, as you say, with regard to inner things.

What do we mean by power? To be powerful is to dominate, to overcome, to suppress, to feel superior, to be efficient, and so on. Consciously or unconsciously the ascetic as well as the worldly person feels and strives for this power. Power is one of the completest expressions of the self, whether it be the power of knowledge, the power over oneself, worldly power, or the power of abstinence. The feeling of power, of domination, is extraordinarily gratifying. You may seek gratification through power, another through drink, another through worship, another through knowledge, and still another through trying to be virtuous. Each may have its own particular sociological and psychological effect, but all acquisition is gratification. Gratification at any level is sensation, is it not? We are making effort to acquire greater or more subtle varieties of sensation, which at one time we call experience, at another knowledge, at another love, at another the search for God or truth; and there is the sensation of being righteous, or of being the efficient agent of an ideology. Effort is to acquire gratification, which is sensation. You have found gratification at one level, and now you are seeking it at another; and when you have acquired it there, you will move to another level, and so keep going. This constant desire for gratification, for more and more subtle forms of sensation, is called progress, but it is ceaseless conflict. The search after ever wider gratification is without end, and so there is no end to conflict, antagonism, and hence no happiness.

"I see your point. You are saying that the search for gratification in any form is really the search for misery. Effort towards gratification is everlasting pain. But what is one to do? Give up seeking gratification and just stagnate?"

If one does not seek gratification, is stagnation inevitable? Is the state of non-anger necessarily a lifeless state? Surely, gratification at any level is sensation. Refinement of sensation is only the refinement of word. The word, the term, the symbol, the image, plays an extraordinarily important part in our lives, does it not? We may no longer seek the touch, the satisfaction of physical contact, but the word, the image becomes very significant. At one level we gather gratification through crude means, and at another through means that are more subtle and refined; but the gathering of words is for the same purpose as the gathering of things, is it not? Why do we gather?

"Oh, I suppose it is because we are so discontented, so utterly bored with ourselves, that we will do anything to get away from our own shallowness. That is really so—and it just strikes me that I am exactly in that position. This is rather extraordinary!"

Our acquisitions are a means of covering up our own emptiness; our minds are like hollow drums, beaten upon by every passing hand and making a lot of noise. This is our life, the conflict of never-satisfying escapes and mounting misery. It is strange how we are never alone, never strictly alone. We are always with something, with a problem, with a book, with a person; and when we are alone, our thoughts are with us. To be alone, naked, is essential. All escapes, all gatherings, all effort to be or not to be, must cease; and then only is there the aloneness that can receive the alone, the measureless.

"How is one to stop escaping?"

By seeing the truth that all escapes only lead to illusion and misery. The truth frees; you cannot do anything about it. Your very action to stop escaping is another escape. The highest state of inaction is the action of truth.

DEVOTION AND WORSHIP

A MOTHER WAS beating her child, and there were painful screams. The mother was very angry, and while she was beating she was talking to it violently. When presently we came back she was caressing the child, hugging as though she would squeeze the life out of it. She had tears in her eyes. The child was rather bewildered, but was smiling up at the mother.

Love is a strange thing, and how easily we lose the warm flame of it! The flame is lost, and the smoke remains. The smoke fills our hearts and minds, and our days are spent in tears and bitterness. The song is forgotten, and the words have lost their meaning; the perfume has gone, and our hands are empty. We never know how to keep the flame clear of smoke, and the smoke always smothers the flame. But love is not of the mind, it is not in the net of thought, it cannot be sought out, cultivated, cherished; it is there when the mind is silent and the heart is empty of the things of the mind.

The room overlooked the river, and the sun was upon its waters.

He was by no means foolish, but was full of emotion, an exuberant sentiment in which he must have taken delight, for it seemed to give him great pleasure. He was eager to talk; and when a green-golden bird was pointed out to him, he turned on his sentiment and gushed over it. Then he talked of the beauty of the river, and sang a song about it. He had a pleasant voice, but the room was too small. The green-golden bird was joined by another, and the two sat very close together, preening themselves.

"Is not devotion a way to God? Is not the sacrifice of devotion the purification of the heart? Is not devotion an essential part of our life?"

What do you mean by devotion?

"Love of the highest; the offering of a flower before the image, the symbol of God. Devotion is complete absorption, it is a love that excels the love of the flesh. I have sat for many hours at a time, completely lost in the love of God. In that state I am nothing and I know nothing. In that state all life is a unity, the sweeper and the king are one. It is a wondrous state. Surely you must know it."

Is devotion love? Is it something apart from our daily existence? Is it an act of sacrifice to be devoted to an object, to knowledge, to service, or to action? Is it self-sacrifice when you are lost in your devotion? When you have completely identified yourself with the object of your devotion, is that self-abnegation? Is it selflessness to lose yourself in a book, in a chant, in an idea? Is devotion the worship of an image, of a person, of a symbol? Has reality any symbol? Can a symbol ever represent truth? Is not the symbol static, and can a static thing ever represent that which is living? Is your picture you?

Let us see what we mean by devotion. You spend several hours a day in what you call the love, the contemplation of God. Is that devotion? The man who gives his life to social betterment is devoted to his work; and the general, whose job is to plan destruction, is also devoted to his work. Is that devotion? If I may say so, you spend your time being intoxicated by the image or idea of God, and others do the same thing in a different way. Is there a fundamental distinction between the two? Is it devotion that has an object?

"But this worship of God consumes my whole life. I am not aware of anything but God. He fills my heart."

And the man who worships his work, his leader, his ideology, is also consumed by that with which he is occupied. You fill your heart with the word 'God', and another with activity; and is that devotion? You are happy with your image, your symbol, and another with his books or music; and is that devotion? Is it devotion to lose oneself in something? A man is devoted to his wife for various gratifying reasons; and is gratification devotion? To identify oneself with one's country is very intoxicating; and is identification devotion?

"But giving myself over to God does nobody any harm. On the contrary, I both keep out of harm's way and do no harm to others."

That at least is something; but though you may not do any outward harm, is not illusion harmful at a deeper level both to you and to society?

"I am not interested in society. My needs are very few; I have controlled my passions and I spend my days in the shadow of God."

Is it not important to find out if that shadow has any substance behind it? To worship illusion is to cling to one's own gratification; to yield to appetite at any level is to be lustful.

"You are very disturbing, and I am not at all sure that I want to go on with this conversation. You see, I came to worship at the same altar as yourself; but I find that your worship is entirely different, and what you say is beyond me. But I would like to know what is the beauty of your worship. You have no pictures, no images, and no rituals, but you must worship. Of what nature is your worship?"

The worshipper is the worshipped. To worship another is to worship oneself; the image, the symbol, is a projection of oneself. After all, your idol, your book, your prayer, is the reflection of your background; it is your creation, though it be made by another. You choose according to your gratification; your choice is your prejudice. Your image is your intoxicant, and it is carved out of your own memory; you are worshipping yourself through the image created by your own thought. Your devotion is the love of yourself covered over by the chant of your mind. The picture is yourself, it is the reflection of your mind. Such devotion is a form of self-deception that only leads to sorrow and to isolation, which is death.

Is search devotion? To search after something is not to search; to seek truth is not to find it. We escape from ourselves through search, which is illusion; we try in every way to take flight from what we are. In ourselves we are so petty, so essentially nothing, and the worship of something greater than ourselves is as petty and stupid as we are. Identification with the great is still a projection of the small. The more is an extension of the less. The small in search of the large will find only what it is capable of finding. The escapes are many and various, but the mind in escape is still fearful, narrow and ignorant.

The understanding of escape is the freedom from what *is*. The what *is* can be understood only when the mind is no longer in search of an answer. The search for an answer is an escape from what *is*. This search is called by various names, one of which is devotion; but to understand what *is,* the mind must be silent.

"What do you mean by 'what *is*'?"

The what *is* is that which is from moment to moment. To understand the whole process of your worship, of your devotion to that which you call God, is the awareness of what *is*. But you do not desire to understand what *is;* for your escape from what *is,* which you call devotion, is a source of greater pleasure, and so illusion becomes of greater significance than reality. The understanding of what *is* does not depend upon thought, for thought itself is an escape. To think about the problem is not to understand it. It is only when the mind is silent that the truth of what *is* unfolds.

"I am content with what I have. I am happy with my God, with my chant and my devotion. Devotion to God is the song of my heart, and my happiness is in that song. Your song may be more clear and open, but when I sing my heart is full. What more can a man ask than to have a full heart? We are brothers in my song, and I am not disturbed by your song."

When the song is real there is neither you nor I, but only the silence of the eternal. The song is not the sound but the silence. Do not let the sound of your song fill your heart.

INTEREST

HE WAS A school principal with several college degrees. He had been very keenly interested in education, and had also worked hard for various kinds of social reform; but now, he said, though still quite young, he had lost the spring of life. He carried on with his duties almost mechanically, going through the daily routine with weary boredom; there was no longer any zest in what he did, and the drive which he had once felt was completely gone. He had been religiously inclined and had striven to bring about certain reforms in his religion, but that too had dried up.

41

He saw no value in any particular action.

Why?

"All action leads to confusion, creating more problems, more mischief. I have tried to act with thought and intelligence, but it invariably leads to some kind of mess; the several activities in which I have engaged have all made me feel depressed, anxious and weary, and they have led nowhere. Now I am afraid to act, and the fear of doing more harm than good has caused me to withdraw from all save the minimum of action."

What is the cause of this fear? Is it the fear of doing harm? Are you withdrawing from life because of the fear of bringing about more confusion? Are you afraid of the confusion that you might create, or of the confusion within yourself? If you were clear within yourself and from that clarity there were action, would you then be fearful of any outward confusion which your action might create? Are you afraid of the confusion within or without?

"I have not looked at it in this way before, and I must consider what you say."

Would you mind bringing about more problems if you were clear in yourself? We like to run away from our problems, by whatever means, and thereby we only increase them. To expose our problems may appear confusing, but the capacity to meet the problems depends on the clarity of approach. If you were clear, would your actions be confusing?

"I am not clear. I don't know what I want to do. I could join some ism of the left or of the right, but that would not bring about clarity of action. One may shut one's eyes to the absurdities of a particular ism and work for it, but the fact remains that there is essentially more harm than good in the action of all isms. If I were very clear within myself, I would meet the problems and try to clear them up. But I am not clear. I have lost all incentive for action."

Why have you lost incentive? Have you lost it in the over-expenditure of limited energy? Have you exhausted yourself in doing things that have no fundamental interest for you? Or is it that you have not yet found out what you are genuinely interested in?

"You see, after college I was very keen on social reform, and I ardently worked at it for some years; but I began to see the pettiness of it, so I dropped it and took up education. I really worked hard at education for a number of years, not caring for anything else; but that too I finally dropped because I was getting more and more confused. I was ambitious, not for myself, but for the work to succeed; but the people with whom I worked were always quarrelling, they were jealous and personally ambitious."

Ambition is an odd thing. You say you were not ambitious for yourself, but only for the work to succeed. Is there any difference between personal and so-called impersonal ambition? You would not consider it personal or petty to identify yourself with an ideology and work ambitiously for it; you would call that a worthy ambition, would you not? But is it? Surely, you have only substituted one term for another, 'impersonal' for 'personal'; but the drive, the motive is still the same. You want success for the work with which you are identified. For the term 'I' you have substituted the term 'work', 'system', 'country', 'God', but you are still important. Ambition is still at work, ruthless, jealous, fearful. Is it because the work was not successful that you dropped it? Would you have carried on if it had been?

"I don't think that was it. The work was fairly successful, as any work is if one gives time, energy and intelligence to it. I gave it up because it led nowhere; it brought about some temporary alleviation, but there was no fundamental and lasting change."

You had the drive when you were working, and what has happened to it? What has happened to the urge, the flame? Is that the problem?

"Yes, that is the problem. I had the flame once, but now it is gone."

Is it dormant, or is it burnt out through wrong usage so that only ashes are left? Perhaps you have not found your real interest. Do you feel frustrated? Are you married?

"No, I do not think I am frustrated, nor do I feel the need of a family or of the companionship of a particular person. Economically I am content with little. I have always been drawn to religion in the deep sense of the word, but I suppose I wanted to be 'successful' in that field too."

If you are not frustrated, why aren't you content just to live?

"I am not getting any younger, and I don't want to rot, to vegetate."

Let us put the problem differently. What are you interested in? Not what you *should* be interested in, but actually?

"I really don't know."

Aren't you interested in finding out?

"But how am I to find out?"

Do you think there is a method, a way to find out what you are interested in? It is really important to discover for yourself in what direction your interest lies. So far you have tried certain things, you have given your energy and intelligence to them, but they have not deeply satisfied you. Either you have burnt yourself out doing things that were not of fundamental interest to you, or your real interest is still dormant, waiting to be awakened. Now which is it?

"Again, I don't know. Can you help me to find out?"

Don't you want to know for yourself the truth of the matter? If you have burnt yourself out, the problem demands a certain approach; but if your fire is still dormant, then the awakening of it is important. Now which is it? Without my telling you which it is, don't you want to discover the truth of it for yourself? The truth of what *is* is its own action. If you are burnt out, then it is a matter of healing, recuperating, lying creatively fallow. This creative fallowness follows from the movement of cultivating and sowing; it is inaction for complete future action. Or it may be that your real interest has not yet been awakened. Please listen and find out. If the intention to find out is there, you will find out, not by constant inquiry, but by being clear and ardent in your intention. Then you will see that during the waking hours there is an alert watchfulness in which you are picking up every intimation of that latent interest, and that dreams also play a part. In other words, the intention sets going the mechanism of discovery.

"But how am I to know which interest is the real one? I have had several interests, and they have all petered out. How do I know that what I may discover to be my real interest won't also peter out?"

There is no guarantee, of course; but since you are aware of this petering out, there will be alert watchfulness to discover the real. If I may put it this way, you are not seeking your real interest; but being in a passively watchful state, the real interest will show itself. If you try to find out what your real interest is, you will choose one as against another, you will weigh, calculate, judge. This process only cultivates opposition; you spend your energies wondering if you have chosen rightly, and so on. But when there is passive awareness, and not a positive effort on your part to find, then into that awareness comes the movement of interest. Experiment with this and you will see.

"If I am not too hasty, I think I am beginning to sense my genuine interest. There is a vital quickening, a new *élan*."

EDUCATION AND INTEGRATION

IT WAS A beautiful evening. The sun was setting behind huge, black clouds, and against them stood a clump of tall, slender palms. The river had become golden, and the distant hills were aglow with the setting sun. There was thunder, but towards the mountains the sky was clear and blue. The cattle were coming back from pasture, and a little boy was driving them home. He couldn't have been more than ten or twelve, and though he had spent the whole day by himself, he was singing away and occasionally flicking the cattle that wandered off or were too slow. He smiled, and his dark face lit up. Stopping out of curiosity, and distantly eager, he began to ask questions. He was a village boy and would have no education; he would never be able to read and write, but he already knew what it was to be alone with himself. He did not know that he was alone; it probably never even occurred to him, nor was he depressed by it. He was just alone and contented. He was not contented with something, he was just contented. To be contented with something is to be discontented. To seek contentment through relationship is to be in fear. Contentment that depends on relationship is only gratification. Contentment is a state of non-dependency. Dependency always brings conflict and opposition. There must be freedom to be content. Freedom is and must always be at the beginning; it is not an end, a goal to be achieved. One can never be free in the future. Future freedom has no reality, it is only an idea. Reality is what *is;* and passive awareness of what *is* is contentment.

The professor said he had been teaching for many years, ever since he graduated from college, and had a large number of boys under him in one of the governmental institutions. He turned out students who could pass examinations, which was what the government and the parents wanted. Of course, there were exceptional boys who were given special opportunities, granted scholarships, and so on, but the vast majority were indifferent, dull, lazy, and somewhat mischievous. There were those who made something of themselves in whatever field they entered, but only very few had the creative flame. During all the years he had taught, the exceptional boys had been very rare; now and then there would be one who perhaps had the quality of genius, but it generally happened that he too was soon smothered by his environment. As a teacher he had visited many parts of the world to study this question of the exceptional boy, and everywhere it was the same. He was now withdrawing from the teaching profession, for after all these years he was rather saddened by the whole thing. However well boys were educated, on the whole they turned out to be a stupid lot. Some were clever or assertive and attained high positions, but behind the screen of their prestige and domination they were as petty and anxiety-ridden as the rest.

"The modern educational system is a failure, as it has produced two devastating wars and appalling misery. Learning to

46

read and write and acquiring various techniques, which is the cultivation of memory, is obviously not enough, for it has produced unspeakable sorrow. What do you consider to be the end-purpose of education?"

Is it not to bring about an integrated individual? If that is the 'purpose' of education, then we must be clear as to whether the individual exists for society, or whether society exists for the individual. If society needs and uses the individual for its own purposes, then it is not concerned with the cultivation of an integrated human being; what it wants is an efficient machine, a conforming and respectable citizen, and this requires only a very superficial integration. As long as the individual obeys and is willing to be thoroughly conditioned, society will find him useful and will spend time and money on him. But if society exists for the individual, then it must help in freeing him from its own conditioning influence. It must educate him to be an integrated human being.

"What do you mean by an integrated human being?"

To answer that question one must approach it negatively, obliquely; one cannot consider its positive aspect.

"I don't understand what you mean."

Positively to state what an integrated human being is, only creates a pattern, a mould, an example which we try to imitate; and is not the imitation of a pattern, an indication of disintegration? When we try to copy an example, can there be integration? Surely, imitation is a process of disintegration; and is this not what is happening in the world? We are all becoming very good gramophone records; we repeat what so-called religions have taught us, or what the latest political, economic, or religious leader has said. We adhere to ideologies and attend political mass-meetings; there is mass-enjoyment of sport, mass-worship, mass-hypnosis. Is this a sign of integration? Conformity is not integration, is it?

"This leads to the very fundamental question of discipline. Are you opposed to discipline?"

What do you mean by discipline?

"There are many forms of discipline: the discipline in a school, the discipline of citizenship, the party discipline, the social and religious disciplines, and self-imposed discipline. Discipline may be according to an inner or an outer authority."

Fundamentally, discipline implies some kind of conformity, does it not? It is conformity to an ideal, to an authority; it is the cultivation of resistance, which of necessity breeds opposition. Resistance is opposition. Discipline is a process of isolation, whether it is isolation with a particular group, or the isolation of individual resistance. Imitation is a form of resistance, is it not?

"Do you mean that discipline destroys integration? What would happen if you had no discipline in a school?"

Is it not important to understand the essential significance of discipline, and not jump to conclusions or take examples? We are trying to see what are the factors of disintegration, or what hinders integration. Is not discipline in the sense of conformity, resistance, opposition, conflict, one of the factors of disintegration? Why do we conform? Not only for physical security, but also for psychological comfort, safety. Consciously or unconsciously, the fear of being insecure makes for conformity both outwardly and inwardly. We must all have some kind of physical security; but it is the fear of being psychologically insecure that makes physical security impossible except for the few. Fear is the basis of all discipline: the fear of not being successful, of being punished, of not gaining, and so on. Discipline is imitation, suppression, resistance, and whether it is conscious or unconscious, it is the result of fear. Is not fear one of the factors of disintegration?

"With what would you replace discipline? Without discipline there would be even greater chaos than now. Is not some form of discipline necessary for action?"

Understanding the false as the false, seeing the true in the false, and seeing the true as the true, is the beginning of intelligence. It is not a question of replacement. You cannot replace fear with something else; if you do, fear is still there. You may successfully cover it up or run away from it, but fear remains. It is the elimination of fear, and not the finding of a substitute for it, that is important. Discipline in any form whatsoever can never

bring freedom from fear. Fear has to be observed, studied, understood. Fear is not an abstraction; it comes into being only in
relation to something, and it is this relationship that has to be
understood. To understand is not to resist or oppose. Is not discipline, then, in its wider and deeper sense, a factor of disintegration? Is not fear, with its consequent imitation and suppression, a
disintegrating force?

"But how is one to be free from fear? In a class of many students, unless there is some kind of discipline—or, if you prefer,
fear—how can there be order?"

By having very few students and the right kind of education.
This, of course, is not possible as long as the State is interested in
mass-produced citizens. The State prefers mass-education; the
rulers do not want the encouragement of discontent, for their
position would soon be untenable. The State controls education,
it steps in and conditions the human entity for its own purposes;
and the easiest way to do this is through fear, through discipline,
through punishment and reward. Freedom from fear is another
matter; fear has to be understood and not resisted, suppressed, or
sublimated.

The problem of disintegration is quite complex, like every
other human problem. Is not conflict another factor of disintegration?

"But conflict is essential, otherwise we would stagnate. Without striving there would be no progress, no advancement, no culture. Without effort, conflict, we would still be savages."

Perhaps we still are. Why do we always jump to conclusions or
oppose when something new is suggested? We are obviously
savages when we kill thousands for some cause or other, for our
country; killing another human being is the height of savagery.
But let us get on with what we were talking about. Is not conflict
a sign of disintegration?

"What do you mean by conflict?"

Conflict in every form: between husband and wife, between
two groups of people with conflicting ideas, between what *is* and
tradition, between what *is* and the ideal, the *should* be, the
future. Conflict is inner and outer strife. At present there is con-

49

flict at all the various levels of our existence, the conscious as well as the unconscious. Our life is a series of conflicts, a battleground —and for what? Do we understand through strife? Can I understand you if I am in conflict with you? To understand there must be a certain amount of peace. Creation can take place only in peace, in happiness, not when there is conflict, strife. Our constant struggle is between what *is* and what *should* be, between thesis and antithesis; we have accepted this conflict as inevitable, and the inevitable has become the norm, the true—though it may be false. Can what *is* be transformed by the conflict with its opposite? I am *this,* and by struggling to be *that,* which is the opposite, have I changed *this*? Is not the opposite, the antithesis, a modified projection of what *is*? Has not the opposite always the elements of its own opposite? Through comparison is there understanding of what *is*? Is not any conclusion about what *is* a hindrance to the understanding of what *is*? If you would understand something, must you not observe it, study it? Can you study it freely if you are prejudiced in favour of or against it? If you would understand your son must you not study him, neither identifying yourself with nor condemning him? Surely, if you are in conflict with your son, there is no understanding of him. So, is conflict essential to understanding?

"Is there not another kind of conflict, the conflict of learning how to do a thing, acquiring a technique? One may have an intuitive vision of something, but it has to be made manifest, and carrying it out is strife, it involves a great deal of trouble and pain."

A certain amount, it is true; but is not creation itself the means? The means is not separate from the end; the end is according to the means. The expression is according to creation; the style is according to what you have to say. If you have something to say, that very thing creates its own style. But if one is merely a technician, then there is no vital problem.

Is conflict in any field productive of understanding? Is there not a continuous chain of conflict in the effort, the will to be, to become, whether positive or negative? Does not the cause of conflict become the effect, which in its turn becomes the cause? There is no release from conflict until there is an understanding of what *is*. The what *is* can never be understood through the screen of idea; it must be approached afresh. As the what *is* is never static, the mind must not be bound to knowledge, to an ideology, to a belief, to a conclusion. In its very nature, conflict is separative, as all opposition is; and is not exclusion, separation, a factor of disintegration? Any form of power, whether individual or of the State, any effort to become more or to become less, is a process of disintegration. All ideas, beliefs, systems of thought, are separative, exclusive. Effort, conflict, cannot under any circumstances bring understanding, and so it is a degenerating factor in the individual as well as in society.

"What, then, is integration? I more or less understand what are the factors of disintegration, but that is only a negation. Through negation one cannot come to integration. I may know what is wrong, which does not mean that I know what is right."

Surely, when the false is seen as the false, the true *is*. When one is aware of the factors of degeneration, not merely verbally but deeply, then is there not integration? Is integration static, something to be gained and finished with? Integration cannot be arrived at; arrival is death. It is not a goal, an end, but a state of being; it is a living thing, and how can a living thing be a goal, a purpose? The desire to be integrated is not different from any other desire, and all desire is a cause of conflict. When there is no conflict, there is integration. Integration is a state of complete attention. There cannot be complete attention if there is effort, conflict, resistance, concentration. Concentration is a fixation; concentration is a process of separation, exclusion, and complete attention is not possible when there is exclusion. To exclude is to narrow down, and the narrow can never be aware of the complete. Complete, full attention is not possible when there is condemnation, justification, or identification, or when the mind is clouded by conclusions, speculations, theories. When we understand the hindrances, then only is there freedom. Freedom is an abstraction to the man in prison; but passive watchfulness uncovers the hindrances, and with freedom from these, integration comes into being.

CHASTITY

THE RICE WAS ripening, the green had a golden tinge, and the evening sun was upon it. There were long, narrow ditches filled with water, and the water caught the darkening light. The palm trees hung over the rice-fields all along their edge, and among the palms there were little houses, dark and secluded. The lane meandered lazily through the rice-fields and palm groves. It was a very musical lane. A boy was playing the flute, with the rice-field before him. He had a clean, healthy body, well-proportioned and delicate, and he wore only a clean white cloth around his loins; the setting sun had just caught his face, and his eyes were smiling. He was practising the scale, and when he got tired of that, he would play a song. He was really enjoying it, and his enjoyment was contagious. Though I sat down only a little distance away from him, he never stopped playing. The evening light, the green-golden sea of the field, the sun among the palms, and this boy playing his flute, seemed to give to the evening an enchantment that is rarely felt. Presently he stopped playing and came over and sat beside me; neither of us said a word, but he smiled and it seemed to fill the heavens. His mother called from some house hidden among the palms; he did not respond immediately, but at the third call he got up, smiled, and went away. Further along the path a girl was singing to some stringed instrument, and she had a fairly nice voice. Across the field someone picked up the song and sang with full-throated ease, and the girl stopped and listened till the male voice had finished it. It was getting dark now. The evening star was over the field, and the frogs began to call.

How we want to possess the cocoa-nut, the woman, and the heavens! We want to monopolize, and things seem to acquire greater value through possession. When we say, 'It is mine', the picture seems to become more beautiful, more worth-while; it seems to acquire greater delicacy, greater depth and fullness. There is a strange quality of violence in possession. The moment one says, 'It is mine', it becomes a thing to be cared for, defended, and in this very act there is a resistance which breeds violence. Violence is ever seeking success; violence is self-fulfilment. To succeed is always to fail. Arrival is death and travelling is eternal. To gain, to be victorious in this world, is to lose life. How eagerly we pursue an end! But the end is everlasting, and so is the conflict of its pursuit. Conflict is constant overcoming, and what is conquered has to be conquered again and again. The victor is ever in fear, and possession is his darkness. The defeated, craving victory, loses what is gained, and so he is as the victor. To have the bowl empty is to have life that is deathless.

They had been married for only a short time and were still without a child. They seemed so young, so distant from the market place, so timid. They wanted to talk things over quietly, without being rushed and without the feeling that they were keeping others waiting. They were a nice-looking couple, but there was strain in their eyes; their smiles were easy, but behind the smile was a certain anxiety. They were clean and fresh, but there was a whisper of inner struggle. Love is a strange thing, and how soon it withers, how soon the smoke smothers the flame! The flame is neither yours nor mine; it is just flame, clear and sufficient; it is neither personal nor impersonal; it is not of yesterday or to-morrow. It has healing warmth, and a perfume that is never constant. It cannot be possessed, monopolized, or kept in one's hand. If it is held, it burns and destroys, and smoke fills our being; and then there is no room for the flame.

He was saying that they had been married for two years, and were now living quietly not far from a biggish town. They had a small farm, twenty or thirty acres of rice and fruit, and some cattle. He was interested in improving the breed, and she in some local hospital work. Their days were full, but it was not the fullness of escape. They had never tried to run away from anything—except from their relations, who were very traditional and rather tiresome. They had married in spite of family opposition, and were living alone with very little help. Before they married they had talked things over and decided not to have children.

Why?

"We both realized what a frightful mess the world is in, and to produce more babies seemed a sort of crime. The children would almost inevitably become mere bureaucratic officials, or slaves to some kind of religious-economic system. Environment would make them stupid, or clever and cynical. Besides, we had not enough money to educate children properly."

What do you mean by properly?

"To educate children properly we would have to send them to school not only here but abroad. We would have to cultivate their intelligence, their sense of value and beauty, and help them to take life richly and happily so that they would have peace in themselves; and of course they would have to be taught some kind of technique which wouldn't destroy their souls. Besides all this, considering how stupid we ourselves were, we both felt that we should not pass on our own reactions and conditioning to our children. We didn't want to propagate modified examples of ourselves."

Do you mean to say you both thought all this out so logically and brutally before you got married? You drew up a good contract; but can it be fulfilled as easily as it was drawn up? Life is a little more complex than a verbal contract, is it not?

"That is what we are finding out. Neither of us has talked about all this to anyone else either before or since our marriage, and that has been one of our difficulties. We didn't know anybody with whom we could talk freely, for most older people take such arrogant pleasure in disapproving or patting us on the back. We heard one of your talks, and we both wanted to come and discuss our problem with you. Another thing is that, before our marriage, we vowed never to have any sexual relationship with each other."

Again, why?

"We are both very religiously inclined and we wanted to lead a spiritual life. Ever since I was a boy I have longed to be unworldly, to live the life of a *sannyasi*. I used to read a great many religious books, which only strengthened my desire. As a matter of fact, I wore the saffron robe for nearly a year."

And you too?

"I am not as clever or as learned as he is, but I have a strong religious background. My grandfather had a fairly good job, but he left his wife and children to become a *sannyasi*, and now my father wants to do the same; so far my mother has won out, but one day he too may disappear, and I have the same impulse to lead a religious life."

Then, if I may ask, why did you marry?

"We wanted each other's companionship," he replied; "we loved each other and had something in common. We had felt this ever since our very young days together, and we didn't see any reason for not getting officially married. We thought of not marrying and living together without sex, but this would have created unnecessary trouble. After our marriage everything was all right for about a year, but our longing for each other became almost intolerable. At last it was so unbearable that I used to go away; I couldn't do my work, I couldn't think of anything else, and I would have wild dreams. I became moody and irritable, though not a harsh word passed between us. We loved and could not hurt each other in word or act; but we were burning for each other like the mid-day sun, and we decided at last to come and talk it over with you. I literally cannot carry on with the vow that she and I have taken. You have no idea what it has been like."

And what about you?

"What woman doesn't want a child by the man she loves? I didn't know I was capable of such love, and I too have had days of torture and nights of agony. I became hysterical and would weep at the least thing, and during certain times of the month it became a nightmare. I was hoping something would happen, but even though we talked things over, it was no good. Then they started a hospital nearby and asked my help, and I was delighted to get away from it all. But it was still no good. To see him so close every day . . ." She was crying now, with her heart. "So we have come to talk it all over. What do you say?"

Is it a religious life to punish oneself? Is mortification of the body or of the mind a sign of understanding? Is self-torture a way to reality? Is chastity denial? Do you think you can go far through renunciation? Do you really think there can be peace through conflict? Does not the means matter infinitely more than the end? The end *may* be, but the means *is*. The actual, the what *is,* must be understood and not smothered by determinations, ideals and clever rationalizations. Sorrow is not the way of happiness. The thing called passion has to be understood and not suppressed or sublimated, and it is no good finding a substitute for it. Whatever you may do, any device that you invent, will only strengthen that which has not been loved and understood. To love what we call passion is to understand it. To love is to be in direct communion; and you cannot love something if you resent it, if you have ideas, conclusions about it. How can you love and understand passion if you have taken a vow against it? A vow is a form of resistance, and what you resist ultimately conquers you. Truth is not to be conquered; you cannot storm it; it will slip through your hands if you try to grasp it. Truth comes silently, without your knowing. What you know is not truth, it is only an idea, a symbol. The shadow is not the real.

Surely, our problem is to understand ourselves and not to destroy ourselves. To destroy is comparatively easy. You have a pattern of action which you hope will lead to truth. The pattern is always of your own making, it is according to your own conditioning, as the end also is. You make the pattern and then take a vow to carry it out. This is an ultimate escape from yourself. You are not that self-projected pattern and its process; you are what you actually are, the desire, the craving. If you really want to transcend and be free of craving, you have to understand it completely, neither condemning nor accepting it; but that is an art which comes only through watchfulness tempered with deep passivity.

"I have read some of your talks and can follow what you mean. But what actually are we to do?"

It is your life, your misery, your happiness, and dare another tell you what you should or should not do? Have not others already told you? Others are the past, the tradition, the conditioning of which you also are a part. You have listened to others, to yourself, and you are in this predicament; and do you still seek advice from others, which is from yourself? You will listen, but you will accept what is pleasing and reject what is painful, and both are binding. Your taking a vow against passion is the beginning of misery, just as the indulgence of it is; but what is important is to understand this whole process of the ideal, the taking of a vow, the discipline, the pain, all of which is a deep escape from inward poverty, from the ache of inward insufficiency, loneliness. This total process is yourself.

"But what about children?"

Again, there is no 'yes' or 'no'. The search for an answer through the mind leads nowhere. We use children as pawns in the game of our conceit, and we pile up misery; we use them as another means of escape from ourselves. When children are not used as a means, they have a significance which is not the significance that you, or society, or the State may give them. Chastity is not a thing of the mind; chastity is the very nature of love. Without love, do what you will, there can be no chastity. If there is love, your question will find the true answer.

They remained in that room, completely silent, for a long time. Word and gesture had come to an end.

THE FEAR OF DEATH

ON THE RED earth in front of the house there were quantities of trumpet-like flowers with golden hearts. They had large, mauve petals and a delicate scent. They would be swept away during the day, but in the darkness of night they covered the red earth. The creeper was strong, with serrated leaves which glistened in the morning sun. Some children carelessly trod on the flowers, and a man getting hurriedly into his car never even looked at them. A passer-by picked one, smelt it, and carried it away, to be dropped presently. A woman who must have been a servant came out of the house, picked a flower, and put it in her hair. How beautiful those flowers were, and how quickly they were withering in the sun!

"I have always been haunted by some kind of fear. As a child I was very timid, shy and sensitive, and now I am afraid of old age and death. I know we must all die, but no amount of rationalizing seems to calm this fear. I have joined the Psychical Research Society, attended a few séances, and read what the great teachers have said about death; but fear of it is still there. I even tried psycho-analysis, but that was no good either. This fear has become quite a problem to me; I wake up in the middle of the night with frightful dreams, and all of them are in one way or another concerned with death. I am strangely frightened of violence and death. The war was a continual nightmare to me, and now I am really very disturbed. It is not a neurosis, but I can see that it might become one. I have done everything that I possibly can to control this fear; I have tried to run away from it, but at the end of my escape I have not been able to shake it off. I have listened to a few rather stupid lectures on reincarnation, and have somewhat studied the Hindu and Buddhist literature concerning it. But all this has been very unsatisfactory, at least to me. I am not just superficially afraid of death, but there is a very deep fear of it."

How do you approach the future, the to-morrow, death? Are you trying to find the truth of the matter, or are you seeking reassurance, a gratifying assertion of continuity or annihilation? Do you want the truth, or a comforting answer?

"When you put it that way, I really do not know what I am afraid of; but the fear is both there and urgent."

What is your problem? Do you want to be free from fear, or are you seeking the truth regarding death?

"What do you mean by the truth regarding death?"

Death is an unavoidable fact; do what you will, it is irrevocable, final and true. But do you want to know the truth of what is beyond death?

"From everything I have studied and from the few materializations I have seen at séances, there is obviously some kind of continuity after death. Thought in some form continues, which you yourself have asserted. Just as the broadcasting of songs, words and pictures requires a receiver at the other end, so thought which continues after death needs an instrument through which it can express itself. The instrument may be a medium, or thought may incarnate itself in another manner. This is all fairly clear and can be experimented with and understood; but even though I have gone into this matter fairly deeply, there is still an unfathomable fear which I think is definitely connected with death."

Death is inevitable. Continuity can be ended, or it can be nourished and maintained. That which has continuity can never renew itself, it can never be the new, it can never understand the unknown. Continuity is duration, and that which is everlasting is not the timeless. Through time, duration, the timeless is not. There must be ending for the new to be. The new is not within the continuation of thought. Thought is continuous movement in time; this movement cannot enclose within itself a state of being which is not of time. Thought is founded on the past, its very being is of time. Time is not only chronological, but it is thought as a movement of the past through the present to the future; it is the movement of memory, of the word, the picture, the symbol, the record, the repetition. Thought, memory, is continuous through word and repetition. The ending of thought is the beginning of the new; the death of thought is life eternal. There must be constant ending for the new to be. That which is new is not continuous; the new can never be within the field of time. The new is only in death from moment to moment. There must be death every day for the unknown to be. The ending is the beginning, but fear prevents the ending.

"I know I have fear, and I don't know what is beyond it."

What do we mean by fear? What is fear? Fear is not an abstraction, it does not exist independently, in isolation. It comes into being only in relation to something. In the process of relationship, fear manifests itself; there is no fear apart from relationship. Now what is it that you are afraid of? You say you are afraid of death. What do we mean by death? Though we have theories, speculations, and there are certain observable facts, death is still the unknown. Whatever we may know about it, death itself cannot be brought into the field of the known; we stretch out a hand to grasp it, but it is not. Association is the known, and the unknown cannot be made familiar; habit cannot capture it, so there is fear.

Can the known, the mind, ever comprehend or contain the unknown? The hand that stretches out can receive only the knowable, it cannot hold the unknowable. To desire experience is to give continuity to thought; to desire experience is to give strength to the past; to desire experience is to further the known. You want to experience death, do you not? Though living, you want to know what death is. But do you know what living is? You know life only as conflict, confusion, antagonism, passing joy and pain. But is that life? Are struggle and sorrow life? In this state which we call life we want to experience something that is not in our own field of consciousness. This pain, this struggle, the hate that is enfolded in joy, is what we call living; and we want to experience something which is the opposite of what we call living. The opposite is the continuation of what *is,* perhaps modified. But death is not the opposite. It is the unknown. The knowable craves to experience death, the unknown; but, do what it will, it cannot experience death, therefore it is fearful. Is that it?

"You have stated it clearly. If I could know or experience what death is while living, then surely fear would cease."

Because you cannot experience death, you are afraid of it. Can the conscious experience that state which is not to be brought into being through the conscious? That which can be experienced is the projection of the conscious, the known. The known can only experience the known; experience is always within the field of the known; the known cannot experience what is beyond its field. Experiencing is utterly different from experience. Experiencing is not within the field of the experiencer; but as experiencing fades, the experiencer and the experience come into being, and then experiencing is brought into the field of the known. The knower, the experiencer, craves for the state of experiencing, the unknown; and as the experiencer, the knower, cannot enter into the state of experiencing, he is afraid. He *is* fear, he is not separate from it. The experiencer of fear is not an observer of it; he is fear itself, the very instrument of fear.

"What do you mean by fear? I know I am afraid of death. I don't feel that I *am* fear, but I am fearful *of* something. I fear and am separate from fear. Fear is a sensation distinct from the 'I' who is looking at it, analysing it. I am the observer, and fear is the observed. How can the observer and the observed be one?"

You say that you are the observer, and fear is the observed. But is that so? Are you an entity separate from your qualities? Are you not identical with your qualities? Are you not your thoughts, emotions, and so on? You are not separate from your qualities, thoughts. You *are* your thoughts. Thought creates the 'you', the supposedly separate entity; without thought, the thinker is not. Seeing the impermanency of itself, thought creates the thinker as the permanent, the enduring; and the thinker then becomes the experiencer, the analyser, the observer separate from the transient. We all crave some kind of permanency, and seeing impermanency about us, thought creates the thinker who is supposed to be permanent. The thinker then proceeds to build up other and higher states of permanency: the soul, the *atman,* the higher self, and so on. Thought is the foundation of this whole structure. But that is another matter. We are concerned with fear. What is fear? Let us see what it is.

You say you are afraid of death. Since you cannot experience it, you are afraid of it. Death is the unknown, and you are afraid of the unknown. Is that it? Now, can you be afraid of that which you do not know? If something is unknown to you, how can you be afraid of it? You are really afraid, not of the unknown, of death, but of loss of the known, because that might cause pain, or take away your pleasure, your gratification. It is the known that causes fear, not the unknown. How can the unknown cause fear?

It is not measurable in terms of pleasure and pain: it is unknown.

Fear cannot exist by itself, it comes in relationship to something. You are actually afraid of the known in its relation to death, are you not? Because you cling to the known, to an experience, you are frightened of what the future might be. But the 'what might be', the future, is merely a reaction, a speculation, the opposite of what *is*. This is so, is it not?

"Yes, that seems to be right."

And do you know what *is*? Do you understand it? Have you opened the cupboard of the known and looked into it? Are you not also frightened of what you might discover there? Have you ever inquired into the known, into what you possess?

"No, I have not. I have always taken the known for granted. I have accepted the past as one accepts sunlight or rain. I have never considered it; one is almost unconscious of it, as one is of one's shadow. Now that you mention it, I suppose I am also afraid to find out what might be there."

Are not most of us afraid to look at ourselves? We might discover unpleasant things, so we would rather not look, we prefer to be ignorant of what *is*. We are not only afraid of what might be in the future, but also of what might be in the present. We are afraid to know ourselves as we are, and this avoidance of what *is* is making us afraid of what *might* be. We approach the so-called known with fear, and also the unknown, death. The avoidance of what *is* is the desire for gratification. We are seeking security, constantly demanding that there shall be no disturbance; and it is this desire not to be disturbed that makes us avoid what *is* and fear what *might* be. Fear is the ignorance of what *is*, and our life is spent in a constant state of fear.

"But how is one to get rid of this fear?"

To get rid of something you must understand it. Is there fear, or only the desire not to see? It is the desire not to see that brings on fear; and when you don't want to understand the full significance of what *is*, fear acts as a preventive. You can lead a gratifying life by deliberately avoiding all inquiry into what *is*, and many do this; but they are not happy, nor are those who amuse themselves with a superficial study of what *is*. Only those who are earnest in their inquiry can be aware of happiness; to them alone is there freedom from fear.

"Then how is one to understand what *is*?"

The what *is* is to be seen in the mirror of relationship, relationship with all things. The what *is* cannot be understood in withdrawal, in isolation; it cannot be understood if there is the interpreter, the translator who denies or accepts. The what *is* can be understood only when the mind is utterly passive, when it is not operating on what *is*.

"Is it not extremely difficult to be passively aware?"

It is, as long as there is thought.

THE FUSION OF THE THINKER AND HIS THOUGHTS

IT WAS A small pond, but very beautiful. Grass covered its banks, and a few steps went down to it. There was a small, white temple at one end, and all around it were tall, slender palms. The temple was well built and well cared for; it was spotlessly clean, and at that hour, when the sun was well behind the palm grove, there was no one there, not even the priest, who treated the temple and its contents with great veneration. This small, decorative temple gave to the pond an atmosphere of peace; the place was so still, and even the birds were silent. The slight breeze that stirred the palms was dying down, and a few clouds floated across the sky, radiant with the evening sun. A snake was swimming across the pond, in and out among the lotus leaves. The water was very clear, and there were pink and violet lotuses. Their delicate scent clung close to the water and to the green banks. There was not a thing stirring now, and the enchantment of the place seemed to fill the earth. But the beauty of those flowers! They were very still, and one or two were beginning to close for the night, shutting out the darkness. The snake had crossed the pond, come up the bank, and was passing close by; its eyes were like bright, black beads, and its forked tongue was playing before it like a small flame, making a path for the snake to follow.

Speculation and imagination are a hindrance to truth. The mind that speculates can never know the beauty of what *is;* it is caught in the net of its own images and words. However far it may wander in its image-making, it is still within the shadow of its own structure and can never see what is beyond itself. The sensitive mind is not an imaginative mind. The faculty to create pictures limits the mind; such a mind is bound to the past, to remembrance, which makes it dull. Only the still mind is sensitive. Accumulation in any form is a burden; and how can a mind be free when it is burdened? Only the free mind is sensitive; the open is the imponderable, the implicit, the unknown. Imagination and speculation impede the open, the sensitive.

He had spent many years, he said, in search of truth. He had been the round of many teachers, many *gurus,* and being still on his pilgrimage, he had stopped here to inquire. Bronzed by the sun and made lean by his wanderings, he was an ascetic who had renounced the world and left his own far-away country. Through the practice of certain disciplines he had with great difficulty learned to concentrate, and had subjugated the appetites. A scholar, with ready quotations, he was good at argument and swift in his conclusions. He had learned Sanskrit, and its resonant phrases were easy for him. All this had given a certain sharpness to his mind; but a mind that is made sharp is not pliable, free.

To understand, to discover, must not the mind be free at the very beginning? Can a mind that is disciplined, suppressed, ever be free? Freedom is not an ultimate goal; it must be at the very beginning, must it not? A mind that is disciplined, controlled, is free within its own pattern; but that is not freedom. The end of discipline is conformity; its path leads to the known, and the known is never the free. Discipline with its fear is the greed of achievement.

"I am beginning to realize that there is something fundamentally wrong with all these disciplines. Though I have spent many years in trying to shape my thoughts to the desired pattern, I find that I am not getting anywhere."

If the means is imitation, the end must be a copy. The means makes the end, does it not? If the mind is shaped in the beginning, it must also be conditioned at the end; and how can a conditioned mind ever be free? The means is the end, they are not two separate processes. It is an illusion to think that through a wrong means the true can be achieved. When the means is suppression, the end also must be a product of fear.

"I have a vague feeling of the inadequacy of disciplines, even when I practise them, as I still do; they are now all but an unconscious habit. From childhood my education has been a process of conformity, and discipline has been almost instinctive with me ever since I first put on this robe. Most of the books I have read, and all the *gurus* I have been to, prescribe control in one form or another, and you have no idea how I went at it. So what you say seems almost a blasphemy; it is really a shock to me, but it is obviously true. Have my years been wasted?"

They would have been wasted if your practices now prevented understanding, the receptivity to truth, that is, if these impediments were not wisely observed and deeply understood. We are so entrenched in our own make-believe that most of us dare not look at it or beyond it. The very urge to understand is the beginning of freedom. So what is our problem?

"I am seeking truth, and I have made disciplines and practices of various kinds the means to that end. My deepest instinct urges me to seek and find, and I am not interested in anything else."

Let us begin near to go far. What do you mean by search? Are you looking for truth? And can it be found by seeking? To seek truth, you must know what it is. Search implies a foreknowledge, something already felt or known, does it not? Is truth something to be known, gathered and held? Is not the intimation of it a projection of the past and so not truth at all, but a remembrance? Search implies an out-going or an inward process, does it not? And must not the mind be still for reality to be? Search is effort to gain the more or the less, it is negative or positive acquisitiveness; and as long as the mind is the concentration, the focus of

65

effort, of conflict, can it ever be still? Can the mind be still through effort? It can be *made* still through compulsion; but what is made can be unmade.

"But is not effort of some kind essential?"

We shall see. Let us inquire into the truth of search. To seek, there must be the seeker, an entity separate from that which he seeks. And is there such a separate entity? Is the thinker, the experiencer, different or separate from his thoughts and experiences? Without inquiring into this whole problem, meditation has no meaning. So we must understand the mind, the process of the self. What is the mind that seeks, that chooses, that is fearful, that denies and justifies? What is thought?

"I have never approached the problem in this way, and I am now rather confused; but please proceed."

Thought is sensation, is it not? Through perception and contact there is sensation; from this arises desire, desire for this and not for that. Desire is the beginning of identification, the 'mine' and the 'not-mine'. Thought is verbalized sensation; thought is the response of memory, the word, the experience, the image. Thought is transient, changing, impermanent, and it is seeking permanency. So thought creates the thinker, who then becomes the permanent; he assumes the role of the censor, the guide, the controller, the moulder of thought. This illusory permanent entity is the product of thought, of the transient. This entity *is* thought; without thought he is not. The thinker is made up of qualities; his qualities cannot be separated from himself. The controller is the controlled, he is merely playing a deceptive game with himself. Till the false is seen as the false, truth is not.

"Then who is the seer, the experiencer, the entity that says, 'I understand'?"

As long as there is the experiencer remembering the experience, truth is not. Truth is not something to be remembered, stored up, recorded, and then brought out. What is accumulated is not truth. The desire to experience creates the experiencer, who then accumulates and remembers. Desire makes for the separation of the thinker from his thoughts; the desire to become, to experience, to be more or to be less, makes for division between the experiencer and the experience. Awareness of the ways of desire is self-knowledge. Self-knowledge is the beginning of meditation.

"How can there be a fusion of the thinker with his thoughts?"

Not through the action of will, nor through discipline, nor through any form of effort, control or concentration, nor through any other means. The use of a means implies an agent who is acting, does it not? As long as there is an actor, there will be a division. The fusion takes place only when the mind is utterly still without trying to be still. There is this stillness, not when the thinker comes to an end, but only when thought itself has come to an end. There must be freedom from the response of conditioning, which is thought. Each problem is solved only when idea, conclusion is not; conclusion, idea, thought, is the agitation of the mind. How can there be understanding when the mind is agitated? Earnestness must be tempered with the swift play of spontaneity. You will find, if you have heard all that has been said, that truth will come in moments when you are not expecting it: If I may say so, be open, sensitive, be fully aware of what *is* from moment to moment. Don't build around yourself a wall of impregnable thought. The bliss of truth comes when the mind is not occupied with its own activities and struggles.

THE PURSUIT OF POWER

THE COW WAS in labour, and the two or three people who regularly attended to her milking, feeding and cleaning were with her now. She was watching them, and if one went away for any reason, she would gently call. At this critical time she wanted all her friends about her; they had come and she was content, but she was labouring heavily. The little calf was born and it was a beauty, a heifer. The mother got up and went round and round her new baby, nudging her gently from time to time; she was so joyous that she would push us aside. She kept this up for a long time till she finally got tired. We held the baby to suckle, but the mother was too excited. At last she calmed down, and then she

67

wouldn't let us go. One of the ladies sat on the ground, and the new mother lay down and put her head in her lap. She had suddenly lost interest in her calf, and her friends were more to her now. It had been very cold, but at last the sun was coming up behind the hills, and it was getting warmer.

He was a member of the government and was shyly aware of his importance. He talked of his responsibility to his people; he explained how his party was superior to and could do things better than the opposition, how they were trying to put an end to corruption and the black market, but how difficult it was to find incorruptible and yet efficient people, and how easy it was for outsiders to criticize and blame the government for the things that were not being done. He went on to say that when people reached his age they should take things more easily; but most people were greedy for power, even the inefficient. Deep down we were all unhappy and out for ourselves, though some of us were clever at hiding our unhappiness and our craving for power. Why was there this urge to power?

What do we mean by power? Every individual and group is after power: power for oneself, for the party, or the ideology. The party and the ideology are an extension of oneself. The ascetic seeks power through abnegation, and so does the mother through her child. There is the power of efficiency with its ruthlessness, and the power of the machine in the hands of a few; there is the domination of one individual by another, the exploitation of the stupid by the clever, the power of money, the power of name and word, and the power of mind over matter. We all want some kind of power, whether over ourselves or over others. This urge to power brings a kind of happiness, a gratification that is not too transient. The power of renunciation is as the power of wealth. It is the craving for gratification, for happiness, that drives us to seek power. And how easily we are satisfied! The ease of achieving some form of satisfaction blinds us. All gratification is blinding. Why do we seek this power?

68

"I suppose primarily because it gives us physical comforts, a social position, and respectability along recognized channels."

Is the craving for power at only one level of our being? Do we not seek it inwardly as well as outwardly? Why? Why do we worship authority, whether of a book, of a person, of the State, or of a belief? Why is there this urge to cling to a person or to an idea? It was once the authority of the priest that held us, and now it is the authority of the expert, the specialist. Have you not noticed how you treat a man with a title, a man of position, the powerful executive? Power in some form seems to dominate our lives: the power of one over many, the using of one by another, or mutual use.

"What do you mean by using another?"

This is fairly simple, is it not? We use each other for mutual gratification. The present structure of society, which is our relationship with each other, is based on need and usage. You need votes to get you into power; you use people to get what you want, and they need what you promise. The woman needs the man, and the man the woman. Our present relationship is based on need and use. Such a relationship is inherently violent, and that is why the very basis of our society is violence. As long as the social structure is based on mutual need and use, it is bound to be violent and disruptive; as long as I use another for my personal gratification, or for the fulfilment of an ideology with which I am identified, there can only be fear, distrust and opposition. Relationship is then a process of self-isolation and disintegration. This is all painfully obvious in the life of the individual and in world affairs.

"But it is impossible to live without mutual need!"

I need the postman, but if I use him to satisfy some inner urge, then the social need becomes a psychological necessity and our relationship has undergone a radical change. It is this psychological need and usage of another that makes for violence and misery. Psychological need creates the search for power, and power is used for gratification at different levels of our being. The man who is ambitious for himself or for his party, or who wants to achieve an ideal, is obviously a disintegrating factor in society.

"Is not ambition inevitable?"

It is inevitable only as long as there is no fundamental transformation in the individual. Why should we accept it as inevitable? Is the cruelty of man to man inevitable? Don't you want to put an end to it? Does not accepting it as inevitable indicate utter thoughtlessness?

"If you are not cruel to others, someone else will be cruel to you, so you have to be on top."

To be on top is what every individual, every group, every ideology is trying to do, and so sustaining cruelty, violence. There can be creation only in peace; and how can there be peace if there is mutual usage? To talk of peace is utter nonsense as long as our relationship with the one or with the many is based on need and use. The need and use of another must inevitably lead to power and dominance. The power of an idea and the power of the sword are similar; both are destructive. Idea and belief set man against man, just as the sword does. Idea and belief are the very antithesis of love.

"Then why are we consciously or unconsciously consumed with this desire for power?"

Is not the pursuit of power one of the recognized and respectable escapes from ourselves, from what *is*? Everyone tries to escape from his own insufficiency, from his inner poverty, loneliness, isolation. The actual is unpleasant, but the escape is glamourous and inviting. Consider what would happen if you were about to be stripped of your power, your position, your hard-earned wealth. You would resist it, would you not? You consider yourself essential to the welfare of society, so you would resist with violence, or with rational and cunning argumentation. If you were able voluntarily to set aside all your many acquisitions at different levels, you would be as nothing, would you not?

"I suppose I would—which is very depressing. Of course I don't want to be as nothing."

So you have all the outer show without the inner substance, the incorruptible inward treasure. You want your outward show, and so does another, and from this conflict arise hate and fear, violence and decay. You with your ideology are as insufficient as the opposition, and so you are destroying each other in the name of peace, sufficiency, adequate employment, or in the name of God. As almost everyone craves to be on top, we have built a society of violence, conflict and enmity.

"But how is one to eradicate all this?"

By not being ambitious, greedy for power, for name, for position; by being what you are, simple and a nobody. Negative thinking is the highest form of intelligence.

"But the cruelty and violence of the world cannot be stopped by my individual effort. And would it not take infinite time for all individuals to change?"

The other is you. This question springs from the desire to avoid your own immediate transformation, does it not? You are saying, in effect, "What is the good of my changing if everyone else does not change?" One must begin near to go far. But you really do not want to change; you want things to go on as they are, especially if you are on top, and so you say it will take infinite time to transform the world through individual transformation. The world is you; you are the problem; the problem is not separate from you; the world is the projection of yourself. The world cannot be transformed till you are. Happiness is in transformation and not in acquisition.

"But I am moderately happy. Of course there are many things in myself which I don't like, but I haven't the time or the inclination to go after them."

Only a happy man can bring about a new social order; but he is not happy who is identified with an ideology or a belief, or who is lost in any social or individual activity. Happiness is not an end in itself. It comes with the understanding of what *is*. Only when the mind is free from its own projections can there be happiness. Happiness that is bought is merely gratification; happiness through action, through power, is only sensation; and as sensation soon withers, there is craving for more and more. As long as the more is a means to happiness, the end is always dissatisfaction, conflict and misery. Happiness is not a remembrance; it is that state which comes into being with truth, ever new, never continuous.

What Is Making You Dull?

HE HAD A small job, with a very poor salary; he came with his wife, who wanted to talk over their problem. They were both quite young, and, though they had been married for some years, they had no children; but that was not the problem. His pay was barely enough to eke out an existence in these difficult times, but as they had no children it was sufficient to survive. What the future held no man knew, though it could hardly be worse than the present. He was disinclined to talk, but his wife pointed out that he must. She had brought him along, almost forcibly it appeared, for he had come very reluctantly; but there he was, and she was glad. He could not talk easily, he said, for he had never talked about himself to anyone but his wife. He had few friends, and even to these he never opened his heart, for they wouldn't have understood him. As he talked he was slowly thawing, and his wife was listening with anxiety. He explained that his work was not the problem; it was fairly interesting, and anyhow it gave them food. They were simple, unassuming people, and both had been educated at one of the universities.

At last she began to explain their problem. She said that for a couple of years now her husband seemed to have lost all interest in life. He did his office work, and that was about all; he went to work in the morning and came back in the evening, and his employers did not complain about him.

"My work is a matter of routine and does not demand too much attention. I am interested in what I do, but it is all somehow a strain. My difficulty is not at the office or with the people with whom I work, but it is within myself. As my wife said, I have lost interest in life, and I don't quite know what is the matter with me."

"He was always enthusiastic, sensitive and very affectionate, but for the past year or more he has become dull and indifferent

72

to everything. He always used to be loving with me, but now life has become very sad for both of us. He doesn't seem to care whether I am there or not, and it has become a misery to live in the same house. He is not unkind or anything of that sort, but has simply become apathetic and utterly indifferent."

Is it because you have no children?

"It isn't that," he said. "Our physical relationship is all right, more or less. No marriage is perfect, and we have our ups and downs, but I don't think this dullness is the result of any sexual maladjustment. Although my wife and I haven't lived together sexually for some time now because of this dullness of mine, I don't think it is the lack of children that has brought it about."

Why do you say that?

"Before this dullness came upon me, my wife and I realized that we couldn't have children. It has never bothered me, though she often cries about it. She wants children, but apparently one of us is incapable of reproduction. I have suggested several things which might make it possible for her to have a child, but she won't try any of them. She will have a child by me or not at all, and she is very deeply upset about it. After all, without the fruit, a tree is merely decorative. We have lain awake talking about all this, but there it is. I realize that one can't have everything in life, and it is not the lack of children that has brought on this dullness; at least, I am pretty sure it is not."

Is it due to your wife's sadness, to her sense of frustration?

"You see, sir, my husband and I have gone into this matter pretty fully. I am more than sad not to have had children, and I pray to God that I may have one some day. My husband wants me to be happy, of course, but his dullness isn't due to my sadness. If we had a child now, I would be supremely happy, but for him it would merely be a distraction, and I suppose it is so with most men. This dullness has been creeping upon him for the past two years like some internal disease. He used to talk to me about everything, about the birds, about his office work, about his ambitions, about his regard and love for me; he would open his heart to me. But now his heart is closed and his mind is somewhere far away. I have talked to him, but it is no good."

73

Have you separated from each other for a time to see how that worked?

"Yes. I went away to my family for about six months, and we wrote to each other; but this separation made no difference. If anything, it made things worse. He cooked his own food, went out very little, kept away from his friends, and was more and more withdrawn into himself. He has never been too social in any case. Even after this separation he showed no quickening spark."

Do you think this dullness is a cover, a pose, an escape from some unfulfilled inner longing?

"I am afraid I don't quite understand what you mean."

You may have an intense longing for something which needs fulfilment, and as that longing has no release, perhaps you are escaping from the pain of it through becoming dull.

"I have never thought about such a thing, it has never occurred to me before. How am I to find out?"

Why hasn't it occurred to you before? Have you ever asked yourself why you have become dull? Don't you want to know?

"It is strange, but I have never asked myself what is the cause of this stupid dullness. I have never put that question to myself."

Now that you are asking yourself that question, what is your response?

"I don't think I have any. But I am really shocked to find how very dull I have become. I was never like this. I am appalled at my own state."

After all, it is good to know in what state one actually is. At least that is a beginning. You have never before asked yourself why you are dull, lethargic; you have just accepted it and carried on, have you not? Do you want to discover what has made you like this, or have you resigned yourself to your present state?

"I am afraid he has just accepted it without ever fighting against it."

You do want to get over this state, don't you? Do you want to talk without your wife?

"Oh, no. There is nothing I cannot say in front of her. I know it is not a lack or an excess of sexual relationship that has brought on this state, nor is there another woman. I couldn't go to another woman. And it is not the lack of children."

Do you paint or write?

"I have always wanted to write, but I have never painted. On my walks I used to get some ideas, but now even that has gone."

Why don't you try to put something on paper? It doesn't matter how stupid it is; you don't have to show it to anyone. Why don't you try writing something?

But to go back. Do you want to find out what has brought on this dullness, or do you want to remain as you are?

"I would like to go away somewhere by myself, renounce everything and find some happiness."

Is that what you want to do? Then why don't you do it? Are you hesitating on account of your wife?

"I am no good to my wife as I am; I am just a wash-out."

Do you think you will find happiness by withdrawing from life, by isolating yourself? Haven't you sufficiently isolated yourself now? To renounce in order to find is no renunciation at all; it is only a cunning bargain, an exchange, a calculated move to gain something. You give up this in order to get that. Renunciation with an end in view is only a surrender to further gain. But can you have happiness through isolation, through dissociation? Is not life association, contact, communion? You may withdraw from one association to find happiness in another, but you cannot completely withdraw from all contact. Even in complete isolation you are in contact with your thoughts, with yourself. Suicide is the complete form of isolation.

"Of course I don't want to commit suicide. I want to live, but I don't want to continue as I am."

Are you sure you don't want to go on as you are? You see, it is fairly clear that there is something which is making you dull, and you want to run away from it into further isolation. To run away from what *is,* is to isolate oneself. You want to isolate yourself, perhaps temporarily, hoping for happiness. But you have already isolated yourself, and pretty thoroughly; further isolation, which you call renunciation, is only a further withdrawal from life. And can you have happiness through deeper and deeper self-isolation? The nature of the self is to isolate itself, its very quality is exclusiveness. To be exclusive is to renounce in order to gain. The more you withdraw from association, the greater the conflict, resistance. Nothing can exist in isolation. However painful relationship may be, it has to be patiently and thoroughly understood. Conflict makes for dullness. Effort to become something only brings problems, conscious or unconscious. You cannot be dull without some cause, for, as you say, you were once alert and keen. You haven't always been dull. What has brought about this change?

"You seem to know, and won't you please tell him?"

I could, but what good would that be? He would either accept or reject it according to his mood and pleasure; but is it not important that he himself should find out? Is it not essential for him to uncover the whole process and see the truth of it? Truth is something that cannot be told to another. He must be able to receive it, and none can prepare him for it. This is not indifference on my part; but he must come to it openly, freely and unexpectedly.

What is making you dull? Shouldn't you know it for yourself? Conflict, resistance, makes for dullness. We think that through struggle we shall understand, through competition we shall be made bright. Struggle certainly makes for sharpness, but what is sharp is soon made blunt; what is in constant use soon wears out. We accept conflict as inevitable, and build our structure of thought and action upon this inevitability. But is conflict inevitable? Is there not a different way of living? There is if we can understand the process and significance of conflict.

Again, why have you made yourself dull?

"Have I made myself dull?"

Can anything make you dull unless you are willing to be made dull? This willingness may be conscious or hidden. Why have you allowed yourself to be made dull? Is there a deep-seated conflict in you?

"If there is, I am totally unaware of it."

But don't you want to know? Don't you want to understand it?

"I am beginning to see what you are driving at," she put in, "but I may not be able to tell my husband the cause of his dullness because I am not quite sure of it myself."

You may or may not see the way this dullness has come upon him; but would you be really helping him if verbally you were to point it out? Is it not essential that he discovers it for himself? Please see the importance of this, and then you will not be impatient or anxious. One can help another, but he alone must undertake the journey of discovery. Life is not easy; it is very complex, but we must approach it simply. We are the problem; the problem is not what we call life. We can understand the problem, which is ourselves, only if we know how to approach it. The approach is all-important, and not the problem.

"But what are we to do?"

You must have listened to all that has been said; if you have, then you will see that truth alone brings freedom. Please don't worry, but let the seed take root.

After some weeks they both came back. There was hope in their eyes and a smile upon their lips.

KARMA

SILENCE IS NOT to be cultivated, it is not to be deliberately brought about; it is not to be sought out, thought of, or meditated upon. The deliberate cultivation of silence is as the enjoyment of some longed-for pleasure; the desire to silence the mind is but the pursuit of sensation. Such silence is only a form of resistance, an isolation which leads to decay. Silence that is bought is a thing of the market in which there is the noise of activity. Silence comes with the absence of desire. Desire is swift, cunning and deep. Remembrance shuts off the sweep of silence, and a mind that is caught in experience cannot be silent. Time, the movement of yesterday flowing into to-day and to-morrow, is not silence. With the cessation of this movement there is silence, and only then can that which is unnamable come into being.

77

"I have come to talk over karma with you. Of course I have certain opinions about it, but I would like to know yours."

Opinion is not truth; we must put aside opinions to find truth. There are innumerable opinions, but truth is not of this or of that group. For the understanding of truth, all ideas, conclusions, opinions, must drop away as the withered leaves fall from a tree. Truth is not to be found in books, in knowledge, in experience. If you are seeking opinions, you will find none here.

"But we can talk about karma and try to understand its significance, can we not?"

That, of course, is quite a different matter. To understand, opinions and conclusions must cease.

"Why do you insist upon that?"

Can you understand anything if you have already made up your mind about it, or if you repeat the conclusions of another? To find the truth of this matter, must we not come to it afresh, with a mind that is not clouded by prejudice? Which is more important, to be free from conclusions, prejudices, or to speculate about some abstraction? Is it not more important to find the truth than to squabble about what truth is? An opinion as to what truth is, is not truth. Is it not important to discover the truth concerning karma? To see the false as the false is to begin to understand it, is it not? How can we see either the true or the false if our minds are entrenched in tradition, in words and explanations? If the mind is tethered to a belief, how can it go far? To journey far, the mind must be free. Freedom is not something to be gained at the end of long endeavour, it must be at the very beginning of the journey.

"I want to find out what karma means to you."

Sir, let us take the journey of discovery together. Merely to repeat the words of another has no deep significance. It is like playing a gramophone record. Repetition or imitation does not bring about freedom. What do you mean by karma?

"It is a Sanskrit word meaning to do, to be, to act, and so on. Karma is action, and action is the outcome of the past. Action cannot be without the conditioning of the background. Through a series of experiences, through conditioning and knowledge, the background of tradition is built up, not only during the present life of the individual and the group, but throughout many incarnations. The constant action and interaction between the background, which is the 'me', and society, life, is karma; and karma binds the mind, the 'me'. What I have done in my past life, or only yesterday, holds and shapes me, giving pain or pleasure in the present. There is group or collective karma, as well as that of the individual. Both the group and the individual are held in the chain of cause and effect. There will be sorrow or joy, punishment or reward, according to what I have done in the past."

You say action is the outcome of the past. Such action is not action at all, but only a reaction, is it not? The conditioning, the background, reacts to stimuli; this reaction is the response of memory, which is not action, but karma. For the present we are not concerned with what action is. Karma is the reaction which arises from certain causes and produces certain results. Karma is this chain of cause and effect. Essentially, the process of time is karma, is it not? As long as there is a past, there must be the present and the future. To-day and to-morrow are the effects of yesterday; yesterday in conjunction with to-day makes to-morrow. Karma, as generally understood, is a process of compensation.

"As you say, karma is a process of time, and mind is the result of time. Only the fortunate few can escape from the clutches of time; the rest of us are bound to time. What we have done in the past, good or evil, determines what we are in the present."

Is the background, the past, a static state? Is it not undergoing constant modification? You are not the same to-day as you were yesterday; both physiologically and psychologically there is a constant change going on, is there not?

"Of course."

So the mind is not a fixed state. Our thoughts are transient, constantly changing; they are the response of the background. If I have been brought up in a certain class of society, in a definite culture, I will respond to challenge, to stimuli, according to my conditioning. With most of us, this conditioning is so deep-rooted that response is almost always according to the pattern. Our thoughts are the response of the background. We *are* the background; that conditioning is not separate or dissimilar from us. With the changing of the background our thoughts also change.

"But surely the thinker is wholly different from the background, is he not?"

Is he? Is not the thinker the result of his thoughts? Is he not composed of his thoughts? Is there a separate entity, a thinker apart from his thoughts? Has not thought created the thinker, given him permanence amidst the impermanency of thoughts? The thinker is the refuge of thought, and the thinker places himself at different levels of permanency.

"I see this is so, but it is rather a shock to me to realize the tricks that thought is playing upon itself."

Thought is the response of the background, of memory; memory is knowledge, the result of experience. This memory, through further experience and response, gets tougher, larger, sharper, more efficient. One form of conditioning can be substituted for another, but it is still conditioning. The response of this conditioning is karma, is it not? The response of memory is called action, but it is only reaction; this 'action' breeds further reaction, and so there is a chain of so-called cause and effect. But is not the cause also the effect? Neither cause nor effect is static. To-day is the result of yesterday, and to-day is the cause of to-morrow; what was the cause becomes the effect, and the effect the cause. One flows into the other. There is no moment when the cause is not also the effect. Only the specialized is fixed in its cause and so in its effect. The acorn cannot become anything but an oak tree. In specialization there is death; but man is not a specialized entity, he can be what he will. He can break through his conditioning—and he must, if he would discover the real. You must cease to be a so-called Brahmin to realize God.

Karma is the process of time, the past moving through the present to the future; this chain is the way of thought. Thought is the result of time, and there can be that which is immeasurable, timeless, only when the process of thought has ceased. Stillness of the mind cannot be induced, it cannot be brought about through any practice or discipline. If the mind is *made* still, then whatever comes into it is only a self-projection, the response of memory. With the understanding of its conditioning, with the choiceless awareness of its own responses as thought and feeling, tranquillity comes to the mind. This breaking of the chain of karma is not a matter of time; for through time, the timeless is not.

Karma must be understood as a total process, not merely as something of the past. The past is time, which is also the present and the future. Time is memory, the word, the idea. When the word, the name, the association, the experience, is not, then only is the mind still, not merely in the upper layers, but completely, integrally.

THE INDIVIDUAL AND THE IDEAL

"OUR LIFE HERE in India is more or less shattered; we want to make something of it again, but we don't know where to begin. I can see the importance of mass action, and also its dangers. I have pursued the ideal of non-violence, but there has been bloodshed and misery. Since the Partition, this country has had blood on its hands, and now we are building up the armed forces. We talk of non-violence and yet prepare for war. I am as confused as the political leaders. In prison I used to read a great deal, but it has not helped me to clarify my own position.

"Can we take one thing at a time and somewhat go into it? First, you lay a great deal of emphasis on the individual; but is not collective action necessary?"

The individual is essentially the collective, and society is the creation of the individual. The individual and society are interrelated, are they not? They are not separate. The individual builds the structure of society, and society or environment shapes the individual. Though environment conditions the individual, he can always free himself, break away from his background. The individual is the maker of the very environment to which he becomes a slave; but he has also the power to break away from it and create an environment that will not dull his mind or spirit. The individual is important only in the sense that he has the capacity to free himself from his conditioning and understand reality. Individuality that is merely ruthless in its own conditioning builds a society whose foundations are based on violence and antagonism. The individual exists only in relationship, otherwise he is not; and it is the lack of understanding of this relationship that is breeding conflict and confusion. If the individual does not understand his relationship to people, to property, and to ideas or beliefs, merely to impose upon him a collective or any other pattern only defeats its own end. To bring about the imposition of a new pattern will require so-called mass action; but the new pattern is the invention of a few individuals, and the mass is mesmerized by the latest slogans, the promises of a new Utopia. The mass is the same as before, only now it has new rulers, new phrases, new priests, new doctrines. This mass is made up of you and me, it is composed of individuals; the mass is fictitious, it is a convenient term for the exploiter and the politician to play with. The many are pushed into action, into war, and so on, by the few; and the few represent the desires and urges of the many. It is the transformation of the individual that is of the highest importance, but not in terms of any pattern. Patterns always condition, and a conditioned entity is always in conflict within himself and so with society. It is comparatively easy to substitute a new pattern of conditioning for the old; but for the individual to free himself from all conditioning is quite another matter.

"This requires careful and detailed thought, but I think I am beginning to understand it. You lay emphasis on the individual, but not as a separate and antagonistic force within society.

"Now the second point. I have always worked for an ideal, and I don't understand your denial of it. Would you mind going into this problem?"

Our present morality is based on the past or the future, on the traditional or the what *ought* to be. The what *ought* to be is the ideal in opposition to what has been, the future in conflict with the past. Non-violence is the ideal, the what *should* be; and the what has been is violence. The what has been projects the what *should* be; the ideal is home-made, it is projected by its own opposite, the actual. The antithesis is an extension of the thesis; the opposite contains the element of its own opposite. Being violent, the mind projects its opposite, the ideal of non-violence. It is said that the ideal helps to overcome its own opposite; but does it? Is not the ideal an avoidance, an escape from the what has been, or from what *is*? The conflict between the actual and the ideal is obviously a means of postponing the understanding of the actual, and this conflict only introduces another problem which helps to cover up the immediate problem. The ideal is a marvellous and respectable escape from the actual. The ideal of non-violence, like the collective Utopia, is fictitious; the ideal, the what *should* be, helps us to cover up and avoid what *is*. The pursuit of the ideal is the search for reward. You may shun the worldly rewards as being stupid and barbarous, which they are; but your pursuit of the ideal is the search for reward at a different level, which is also stupid. The ideal is a compensation, a fictitious state which the mind has conjured up. Being violent, separative, and out for itself, the mind projects the gratifying compensation, the fiction which it calls the ideal, the Utopia, the future, and vainly pursues it. That very pursuit is conflict, but it is also a pleasurable postponement of the actual. The ideal, the what *should* be, does not help in understanding what *is*; on the contrary, it prevents understanding.

"Do you mean to say that our leaders and teachers have been wrong in advocating and maintaining the ideal?"

What do you think?

"If I understand correctly what you say . . ."

Please, it is not a matter of understanding what another may say, but of finding out what is true. Truth is not opinion; truth is not dependent on any leader or teacher. The weighing of opinions only prevents the perception of truth. Either the ideal is a home-made fiction which contains its own opposite, or it is not. There are no two ways about it. This does not depend on any teacher, you must perceive the truth of it for yourself.

"If the ideal is fictitious, it revolutionizes all my thinking. Do you mean to say that our pursuit of the ideal is utterly futile?"

It is a vain struggle, a gratifying self-deception, is it not?

"This is very disturbing, but I am forced to admit that it is. We have taken so many things for granted that we have never allowed ourselves to observe closely what is in our hand. We have deceived ourselves, and what you point out upsets completely the structure of my thought and action. It will revolutionize education, our whole way of living and working. I think I see the implications of a mind that is free from the ideal, from the what *should* be. To such a mind, action has a significance quite different from that which we give it now. Compensatory action is not action at all, but only a reaction—and we boast of action! . . . But without the ideal, how is one to deal with the actual, or with the what has been?"

The understanding of the actual is possible only when the ideal, the what *should* be, is erased from the mind; that is, only when the false is seen as the false. The what *should* be is also the what should *not* be. As long as the mind approaches the actual with either positive or negative compensation, there can be no understanding of the actual. To understand the actual you must be in direct communion with it; your relationship with it cannot be through the screen of the ideal, or through the screen of the past, of tradition, of experience. To be free from the wrong approach is the only problem. This means, really, the understanding of conditioning, which is the mind. The problem is the mind itself, and not the problems it breeds; the resolution of the problems bred by the mind is merely the reconciliation of effects, and that only leads to further confusion and illusion.

"How is one to understand the mind?"

The way of the mind is the way of life—not the ideal life, but the actual life of sorrow and pleasure, of deception and clarity, of conceit and the pose of humility. To understand the mind is to be aware of desire and fear.

"Please, this is getting a bit too much for me. How am I to understand my mind?"

84

To know the mind, must you not be aware of its activities? The mind is only experience, not just the immediate but also the accumulated. The mind is the past in response to the present, which makes for the future. The total process of the mind has to be understood.

"Where am I to begin?"

From the only beginning: relationship. Relationship is life; to be is to be related. Only in the mirror of relationship is the mind to be understood, and you have to begin to see yourself in that mirror.

"Do you mean in my relationship with my wife, with my neighbour, and so on? Is that not a very limited process?"

What may appear to be small, limited, if approached rightly, reveals the fathomless. It is like a funnel, the narrow opens into the wide. When observed with passive watchfulness, the limited reveals the limitless. After all, at its source the river is small, hardly worth noticing.

"So I must begin with myself and my immediate relationships."

Surely. Relationship is never narrow or small. With the one or with the many, relationship is a complex process, and you can approach it pettily, or freely and openly. Again, the approach is dependent on the state of the mind. If you do not begin with yourself, where else will you begin? Even if you begin with some peripheral activity, you are in relationship with it, the mind is the centre of it. Whether you begin near or far, you are there. Without understanding yourself, whatever you do will inevitably bring about confusion and sorrow. The beginning is the ending.

"I have wandered far afield, I have seen and done many things, I have suffered and laughed like so many others, and yet I have had to come back to myself. I am like that *sannyasi* who set out in search of truth. He spent many years going from teacher to teacher, and each pointed out a different way. At last he wearily returned to his home, and in his own house was the jewel! I see how foolish we are, searching the universe for that bliss which is to be found only in our own hearts when the mind is purged of its activities. You are perfectly right. I begin from where I started. I begin with what I am."

To Be Vulnerable Is To Live, To Withdraw Is To Die

THE HURRICANE HAD destroyed the crops, and the sea-water was over the land. The train was crawling along, and on both sides of the line the trees were down, the houses roofless, and the fields utterly deserted. The storm had done a great deal of damage for miles around; living things were destroyed, and the barren earth was open to the sky.

We are never alone; we are surrounded by people and by our own thoughts. Even when the people are distant, we see things through the screen of our thoughts. There is no moment, or it is very rare, when thought is not. We do not know what it is to be alone, to be free of all association, of all continuity, of all word and image. We are lonely, but we do not know what it is to be alone. The ache of loneliness fills our hearts, and the mind covers it with fear. Loneliness, that deep isolation, is the dark shadow of our life. We do everything we can to run away from it, we plunge down every avenue of escape we know, but it pursues us and we are never without it. Isolation is the way of our life; we rarely fuse with another, for in ourselves we are broken, torn and unhealed. In ourselves we are not whole, complete, and the fusion with another is possible only when there is integration within. We are afraid of solitude, for it opens the door to our insufficiency, the poverty of our own being; but it is solitude that heals the deepening wound of loneliness. To walk alone, unimpeded by thought, by the trail of our desires, is to go beyond the reaches of the mind. It is the mind that isolates, separates and cuts off communion. The mind cannot be made whole; it cannot make itself complete, for that very effort is a process of isolation, it is part of the loneliness that nothing can cover. The mind is the product of the many, and what is put together can never be alone. Aloneness is not the result of thought. Only when thought is utterly still is there the flight of the alone to the alone.

The house was well back from the road, and the garden had an abundance of flowers. It was a cool morning, and the sky was very blue; the morning sun was pleasant, and in the shaded, sunken garden the noise of the traffic, the call of the vendors, and the trotting of horses on the road, all seemed very distant. A goat had wandered into the garden; with its short tail wiggling, it nibbled at the flowers till the gardener came and chased it away.

She was saying that she felt very disturbed, but did not want to be disturbed; she wanted to avoid the painful state of uncertainty. Why was she so apprehensive of being disturbed?

What do you mean by being disturbed? And why be apprehensive about it?

"I want to be quiet, to be left alone. I feel disturbed even with you. Though I have seen you only two or three times, the fear of being disturbed by you is coming heavily upon me. I want to find out why I have this fear of being inwardly uncertain. I want to be quiet and at peace with myself, but I am always being disturbed by something or other. Till recently I had managed to be more or less at peace with myself; but a friend brought me along to one of your talks, and now I am strangely upset. I thought you would strengthen me in my peace, but instead you have almost shattered it. I didn't want to come here, as I knew I would make a fool of myself; but still, here I am."

Why are you so insistent that you should be at peace? Why are you making it into a problem? The very demand to be at peace is conflict, is it not? If I may ask, what is it you want? If you want to be left alone, undisturbed and at peace, then why allow yourself to be shaken? It is quite feasible to shut all the doors and windows of one's being, to isolate oneself and live in seclusion. That is what most people want. Some deliberately cultivate isolation, and others, by their desires and activities, both hidden and open, bring about this exclusion. The sincere ones become self-righteous with their ideals and virtues, which are only a defence;

and those who are thoughtless drift into isolation through economic pressure and social influences. Most of us are seeking to build walls around ourselves so as to be invulnerable, but unfortunately there is always an opening through which life creeps in.

"I have generally managed to ward off most of the disturbances, but during the past week or two, because of you, I have been more disturbed than ever. Please tell me why I am disturbed. What is the cause of it?"

Why do you want to know the cause of it? Obviously, by knowing the cause you hope to eradicate the effect. You really do not want to know why you are disturbed, do you? You only want to avoid disturbance.

"I just want to be left alone, undisturbed and at peace; and why am I constantly disturbed?"

You have been defending yourself all your life, have you not? What you are really interested in is to find out how to stop up all the openings, and not how to live without fear, without dependence. From what you have said and left unsaid, it is obvious that you have tried to make your life secure against any kind of inward disturbance; you have withdrawn from any relationship that might cause pain. You have managed fairly well to safeguard yourself against all shock, to live behind closed doors and windows. Some are successful in doing this, and if pushed far enough its ultimate end is the asylum; others fail and become cynical, bitter; and still others make themselves rich in things or in knowledge, which is their safeguard. Most people, including the so-called religious, desire abiding peace, a state in which all conflict has come to an end. Then there are those who praise conflict as the only real expression of life, and conflict is their shield against life.

Can you ever have peace by seeking security behind the walls of your fears and hopes? All your life you have withdrawn, because you want to be safe within the walls of a limited relationship which you can dominate. Is this not your problem? Since you depend, you want to possess that upon which you depend.

You are afraid of and therefore avoid any relationship which you cannot dominate. Isn't that it?

"That is rather a brutal way of putting it, but perhaps that is it."

If you could dominate the cause of your present disturbance, you would be at peace; but since you cannot, you are very concerned. We all want to dominate when we do not understand; we want to possess or be possessed when there is fear of ourselves. Uncertainty of ourselves makes for a feeling of superiority, exclusion and isolation.

If I may ask, of what are you afraid? Are you afraid of being alone, of being left out, of being made uncertain?

"You see, all my life I have lived for others, or so I thought. I have upheld an ideal and been praised for my efficiency in doing the kind of work which is considered good; I have lived a life of self-denial, without security, without children, without a home. My sisters are well-married and socially prominent, and my older brothers are high government officials. When I visit them, I feel I have wasted my life. I have become bitter, and I deeply regret all the things that I haven't had. I now dislike the work I was doing, it no longer brings me any happiness, and I have abandoned it to others. I have turned my back upon it all. As you point out, I have become hard in my self-defence. I have anchored myself in a younger brother who is not well-off and who considers himself a seeker of God. I have tried to make myself inwardly secure, but it has been a long and painful struggle. It is this younger brother who brought me to one of your talks, and the house which I had been so carefully building began to tumble down. I wish to God I had never come to hear you, but I cannot rebuild it, I cannot go through all that suffering and anxiety again. You have no idea what it has been like for me to see my brothers and sisters with position, prestige, and money. But I won't go into all that. I have cut myself off from them, and I rarely see them. As you say, I have gradually shut the door upon all relationships except one or two; but as misfortune would have it, you came to this town, and now everything is wide open again, all the old wounds have come to life, and I am deeply miserable. What am I to do?"

The more we defend, the more we are attacked; the more we seek security, the less of it there is; the more we want peace, the greater is our conflict; the more we ask, the less we have. You have tried to make yourself invulnerable, shock-proof; you have made yourself inwardly unapproachable except to one or two, and have closed all the doors to life. It is slow suicide. Now, why have you done all this? Have you ever asked yourself that question? Don't you want to know? You have come either to find a way to close all the doors, or to discover how to be open, vulnerable to life. Which is it you want—not as a choice, but as a natural, spontaneous thing?

"Of course I see now that it is really impossible to shut all the doors, for there is always an opening. I realize what I have been doing; I see that my own fear of uncertainty has made for dependence and domination. Obviously I could not dominate every situation, however much I might like to, and that is why I limited my contacts to one or two which I could dominate and hold. I see all that. But how am I to be open again, free and without this fear of inward uncertainty?"

Do you see the necessity of being open and vulnerable? If you do not see the truth of that, then you will again surreptitiously build walls around yourself. To see the truth in the false is the beginning of wisdom; to see the false as the false is the highest comprehension. To see that what you have been doing all these years can only lead to further strife and sorrow—actually to experience the truth of it, which is not mere verbal acceptance—will put an end to that activity. You cannot voluntarily make yourself open; the action of will cannot make you vulnerable. The very desire to be vulnerable creates resistance. Only by understanding the false as the false is there freedom from it. Be passively watchful of your habitual responses; simply be aware of them without resistance; passively watch them as you would watch a child, without the pleasure or distaste of identification. Passive watchfulness itself is freedom from defence, from closing the door. To be vulnerable is to live, and to withdraw is to die.

Despair and Hope

THE LITTLE DRUM was beating out a gay rhythm, and presently it was joined by a reed instrument; together they filled the air. The drum dominated, but it followed the reed. The latter would stop, but the little drum would go on, sharp and clear, until it was again joined by the song of the reed. The dawn was still far away and the birds were quiet, but the music filled the silence. There was a wedding going on in the little village. During the previous evening there had been much gaiety; the songs and laughter had gone on late into the night, and now the parties were being awakened by music. Presently the naked branches began to show against the pale sky; the stars were disappearing one by one, and the music had come to an end. There were the shouts and calling of children, and noisy quarrelling around the only water tap in the village. The sun was still below the horizon, but the day had begun.

To love is to experience all things, but to experience without love is to live in vain. Love is vulnerable, but to experience without this vulnerability is to strengthen desire. Desire is not love and desire cannot hold love. Desire is soon spent and in its spending is sorrow. Desire cannot be stopped; the ending of desire by will, by any means that the mind can devise, leads to decay and misery. Only love can tame desire, and love is not of the mind. The mind as the observer must cease for love to be. Love is not a thing that can be planned and cultivated; it cannot be bought through sacrifice or through worship. There is no means to love. The search for a means must come to an end for love to be. The spontaneous shall know the beauty of love, but to pursue it ends freedom. To the free alone is there love, but freedom never directs, never holds. Love is its own eternity.

She spoke easily, and words came naturally to her. Though still young, there was sadness about her; she smiled with distant remembrance, and her smile was strained. She had been married but had no children, and her husband had recently died. It was not one of those arranged marriages, nor one of mutual desire. She did not want to use the word 'love', for it was in every book and on every tongue; but their relationship had been something extraordinary. From the day they were married till the day of his death, there had never been so much as a cross word or a gesture of impatience, nor were they ever separated from each other, even for a day. A fusion had taken place between them, and everything else—children, money, work, society—had become of secondary importance. This fusion was not romantic sentimentalism or a thing imagined after his death, but it had been a reality from the very first. Their joy had not been of desire, but of something that went beyond and above the physical. Then suddenly, a couple of months ago, he was killed in an accident. The bus took a curve too fast, and that was that.

"Now I am in despair; I have tried to commit suicide, but somehow I can't. To forget, to be numb, I have done everything short of throwing myself into the river, and I haven't had a good night's sleep these two months. I am in complete darkness; it is a crisis beyond my control which I cannot understand, and I am lost."

She covered her face with her hands. Presently she continued.

"It is not a despair that can be remedied or wiped away. With his death, all hope has come to an end. People have said I will forget and remarry, or do something else. Even if I could forget, the flame has gone out; it cannot be replaced, nor do I want to find a substitute for it. We live and die with hope, but I have none. I have no hope, therefore I am not bitter; I am in despair and darkness, and I do not want light. My life is a living death, and I do not want anyone's sympathy, love, or pity. I want to remain in my darkness, without feeling, without remembering."

Is that why you have come, to be made more dull, to be confirmed in your despair? Is that what you want? If it is, then you will have what you desire. Desire is as pliable and as swift as the mind; it will adjust itself to anything, mould itself to any circumstances, build walls that will keep out light. Its very despair is its delight. Desire creates the image it will worship. If you desire to live in darkness, you will succeed. Is this why you have come, to be strengthened in your own desire?

"You see, a friend of mine told me about you, and I came impulsively. If I had stopped to think, probably I wouldn't have come. I have always acted rather impulsively, and it has never led me into mischief. If you ask me why I have come, all I can say is that I don't know. I suppose we all want some kind of hope; one cannot live in darkness forever."

What is fused cannot be pulled apart; what is integrated cannot be destroyed; if the fusion is there, death cannot separate. Integration is not with another, but with and in oneself. The fusion of the different entities in oneself is completeness with the other; but completeness with the other is incompleteness in oneself. Fusion with the other is still incompleteness. The integrated entity is not made whole by another; because he is complete, there is completeness in all his relationships. What is incomplete cannot be made complete in relationship. It is illusion to think we are made complete by another.

"I was made complete by him. I knew the beauty and the joy of it."

But it has come to an end. There is always an ending to that which is incomplete. The fusion with the other is always breakable; it is always ceasing to be. Integration must begin within oneself, and only then is fusion indestructible. The way of integration is the process of negative thinking, which is the highest comprehension. Are you seeking integration?

"I don't know what I am seeking, but I would like to understand hope, because hope seems to play an important part in our life. When he was alive, I never thought of the future, I never thought of hope or happiness; to-morrow did not exist as far as I was concerned. I just lived, without a care."

Because you were happy. But now unhappiness, discontent, is creating the future, the hope—or its opposite, despair and hopelessness. It is strange, is it not? When one is happy, time is non-existent, yesterday and to-morrow are wholly absent; one has no

93

thought for the past or the future. But unhappiness makes for hope and despair.

"We are born with hope and we take it with us to death."

Yes, that is just what we do; or rather, we are born in misery, and hope takes us to death. What do you mean by hope?

"Hope is to-morrow, the future, the longing for happiness, for the betterment of to-day, for the advancement of oneself; it is the desire to have a nicer home, a better piano or radio; it is the dream of social improvement, a happier world, and so on."

Is hope only in the future? Is there not hope also in the what has been, in the hold of the past? Hope is in both the forward and the backward movement of thought. Hope is the process of time, is it not? Hope is the desire for the continuation of that which has been pleasant, of that which can be improved, made better; and its opposite is hopelessness, despair. We swing between hope and despair. We say that we live because there is hope; and hope is in the past, or, more frequently, in the future. The future is the hope of every politician, of every reformer and revolutionary, of every seeker after virtue and what we call God. We say that we live by hope; but do we? Is it living when the future or the past dominates us? Is living a movement of the past to the future? When there is concern for to-morrow, are you living? It is because to-morrow has become so important that there is hopelessness, despair. If the future is all-important and you live for it and by it, then the past is the means of despair. For the hope of to-morrow, you sacrifice to-day; but happiness is ever in the now. It is the unhappy who fill their lives with concern for to-morrow, which they call hope. To live happily is to live without hope. The man of hope is not a happy man, he knows despair. The state of hopelessness projects hope or resentment, despair or the bright future.

"But are you saying that we must live without hope?"

Is there not a state which is neither hope nor hopelessness, a state which is bliss? After all, when you considered yourself happy, you had no hope, had you?

"I see what you mean. I had no hope because he was beside me and I was happy to live from day to day. But now he is gone, and . . . We are free of hope only when we are happy. It is when we are unhappy, disease-ridden, oppressed, exploited, that to-morrow becomes important; and if to-morrow is impossible, we are in complete darkness, in despair. But how is one to remain in the state of happiness?"

First see the truth of hope and hopelessness. Just see how you have been held by the false, by the illusion of hope, and then by despair. Be passively watchful of this process—which is not as easy as it sounds. You ask how to remain in the state of happiness. Is not this very question based essentially on hope? You wish to regain what you have lost, or through some means to possess it again. This question indicates the desire to gain, to become, to arrive, does it not? When you have an objective, an end in view, there is hope; so again you are caught in your own unhappiness. The way of hope is the way of the future, but happiness is never a matter of time. When there was happiness, you never asked how to continue in it; if you had asked, you would have already tasted unhappiness.

"You mean this whole problem arises only when one is in conflict, in misery. But when one is miserable one wants to get out of it, which is natural."

The desire to find a way out only brings another problem. By not understanding the one problem, you introduce many others. Your problem is unhappiness, and to understand it there must be freedom from all other problems. Unhappiness is the only problem you have; don't become confused by introducing the further problem of how to get out of it. The mind is seeking a hope, an answer to the problem, a way out. See the falseness of this escape, and then you will be directly confronted with the problem. It is this direct relationship with the problem that brings a crisis, which we are all the time avoiding; but it is only in the fullness and intensity of the crisis that the problem comes to an end.

"Ever since the fatal accident I have felt that I must get lost in my own despair, nourish my own hopelessness; but somehow it has been too much for me. Now I see that I must face it without fear, and without the feeling of disloyalty to him. You see, I felt deep down that I would in some way be disloyal to him if I continued to be happy; but now the burden is already lifting, and I sense a happiness which is not of time."

THE MIND AND THE KNOWN

THE DAILY PATTERN of life was repeating itself around the only water tap in the village; the water was running slowly, and a group of women were awaiting their turn. Three of them were noisily and bitterly quarrelling; they were completely absorbed in their anger and paid not the slightest attention to anyone else, nor was anyone paying attention to them. It must have been a daily ritual. Like all rituals, it was stimulating, and these women were enjoying the stimulation. An old woman helped a young one to lift a big, brightly-polished brass pot onto her head. She had a little pad of cloth to bear the weight of the pot, which she held lightly with one hand. Her walk was superb, and she had great dignity. A little girl came quietly, slipped her pot under the tap, and carried it away without saying a word. Other women came and went, but the quarrel went on, and it seemed as though it would never end. Suddenly the three stopped, filled their vessels with water, and went away as though nothing had happened. By now the sun was getting strong, and smoke was rising above the thatched roofs of the village. The day's first meal was being cooked. How suddenly peaceful it was! Except for the crows, almost everything was quiet. Once the vociferous quarrel was over, one could hear the roar of the sea beyond the houses, the gardens and the palm groves.

We carry on like machines with our tiresome daily routine. How eagerly the mind accepts a pattern of existence, and how tenaciously it clings to it! As by a driven nail, the mind is held together by idea, and around the idea it lives and has its being. The mind is never free, pliable, for it is always anchored; it moves within the radius, narrow or wide, of its own centre. From its centre it dare not wander; and when it does, it is lost in fear. Fear is not of the unknown, but of the loss of the known. The unknown does not incite fear, but dependence on the known does. Fear is always with desire, the desire for the more or for the less. The mind, with its incessant weaving of patterns, is the maker of time; and with time there is fear, hope and death. Hope leads to death.

He said he was a revolutionary; he wanted to blast every social structure and start all over again. He had eagerly worked for the extreme left, for the proletarian revolution, and that too had failed. Look what had happened in the country where that revolution was so gloriously accomplished! Dictatorship, with its police and its army, had inevitably bred new class distinctions, and all within a few years; what had been a glorious promise had come to nothing. He wanted a deeper and wider revolution to be started all over again, taking care to avoid all the pitfalls of the former revolution.

What do you mean by revolution?

"A complete change of the present social structure, with or without bloodshed, according to a clear-cut plan. To be effective, it must be well thought out, organized in every detail and scrupulously executed. Such a revolution is the only hope, there is no other way out of this chaos."

But won't you have the same results again—compulsion and its officers?

"It may at first result in that, but we will break through it. There will always be a separate and united group outside the government to watch over and guide it."

You want a revolution according to a pattern, and your hope is in to-morrow, for which you are willing to sacrifice yourself and others. Can there be a fundamental revolution if it is based on idea? Ideas inevitably breed further ideas, further resistance and suppression. Belief engenders antagonism; one belief gives rise to many, and there are hostility and conflict. Uniformity of belief is not peace. Idea or opinion invariably creates opposition, which those in power must always seek to suppress. A revolution

97

based on idea brings into being a counter-revolution, and the revolutionary spends his life fighting other revolutionaries, the better-organized liquidating the weaker. You will be repeating the same pattern, will you not? Would it be possible to talk over the deeper significance of revolution?

"It would have little value unless it led to a definite end. A new society must be built, and revolution according to a plan is the only way to achieve it. I don't think I will change my views, but let us see what you have to say. What you will say has probably already been said by Buddha, Christ, and other religious teachers, and where has it got us? Two thousand years and more of preaching about being good, and look at the mess the capitalists have made!"

A society based on idea, shaped according to a particular pattern, breeds violence and is in a constant state of disintegration. A patterned society functions only within the frame of its self-projected belief. Society, the group, can never be in a state of revolution; only the individual can. But if he is revolutionary according to a plan, a well-authenticated conclusion, he is merely conforming to a self-projected ideal or hope. He is carrying out his own conditioned responses, modified perhaps, but limited all the same. A limited revolution is no revolution at all; like reform, it is a retrogression. A revolution based on idea, on deduction and conclusions, is but a modified continuity of the old pattern. For a fundamental and lasting revolution we must understand the mind and idea.

"What do you mean by idea? Do you mean knowledge?"

Idea is the projection of the mind; idea is the outcome of experience, and experience is knowledge. Experience is always interpreted according to the conscious or unconscious conditioning of the mind. The mind is experience, the mind is idea; the mind is not separate from the quality of thought. Knowledge, accumulated and accumulating, is the process of the mind. Mind is experience, memory, idea, it is the total process of response. Till we understand the working of the mind, of consciousness, there cannot be a fundamental transformation of man and his relationships, which constitute society.

"Are you suggesting that the mind as knowledge is the real enemy of revolution, and that the mind can never produce the new plan, the new State? If you mean that because the mind is still linked with the past it can never comprehend the new, and that whatever it may plan or create is the outcome of the old, then how can there ever be any change at all?"

Let us see. Mind is held in a pattern; its very existence is the frame within which it works and moves. The pattern is of the past or the future, it is despair and hope, confusion and Utopia, the what has been and the what *should* be. With this we are all familiar. You want to break the old pattern and substitute a 'new' one, the new being the modified old. You call it the new for your own purposes and manoeuvres, but it is still the old. The so-called new has its roots in the old: greed, envy, violence, hatred, power, exclusion. Embedded in these, you want to produce a new world. It is impossible. You may deceive yourself and others, but unless the old pattern is broken completely there cannot be a radical transformation. You may play around with it, but you are not the hope of the world. The breaking of the pattern, both the old and the so-called new, is of the utmost importance if order is to come out of this chaos. That is why it is essential to understand the ways of the mind. The mind functions only within the field of the known, of experience, whether conscious or unconcious, collective or superficial. Can there be action without a pattern? Until now we have known action only in relation to a pattern, and such action is always an approximation to what *has* been or what *should* be. Action so far has been an adjustment to hope and fear, to the past or to the future.

"If action is not a movement of the past to the future, or between the past and the future, then what other action can there possibly be? You are not inviting us to inaction, are you?"

It would be a better world if each one of us were aware of true inaction, which is not the opposite of action. But that is another matter. Is it possible for the mind to be without a pattern, to be free of this backward and forward swing of desire? It is definitely possible. Such action is living in the now. To live is to be without hope, without the care of to-morrow; it is not hopelessness or indifference. But we are *not* living, we are always pursuing death, the past or the future. Living is the greatest revolution. Living has no pattern, but death has: the past or the future, the what has been or the Utopia. You are living for the Utopia, and so you are inviting death and not life.

"That is all very well, but it leads us nowhere. Where is your revolution? Where is action? Where is there a new manner of living?"

Not in death but in life. You are pursuing the ideal, the hope, and this pursuit you call action, revolution. Your ideal, your hope is the projection of the mind away from what *is*. The mind, being the result of the past, is bringing out of itself a pattern for the new, and this you call revolution. Your new life is the same old one in different clothes. The past and the future do not hold life; they have the remembrance of life and the hope of life, but they are not the living. The action of the mind is not living. The mind can act only within the frame of death, and revolution based on death is only more darkness, more destruction and misery.

"You leave me utterly empty, almost naked. It may be spiritually good for me, there is a lightness of heart and mind, but it is not so helpful in terms of collective revolutionary action."

CONFORMITY AND FREEDOM

THE STORM BEGAN early in the morning with thunder and lightning, and now it was raining very steadily; it hadn't stopped all day, and the red earth was soaking it up. The cattle were taking shelter under a large tree, where there was also a small white temple. The base of the tree was enormous, and the surrounding field was bright green. There was a railway line on the other side of the field, and the trains would labour up the slight incline, giving a triumphant hoot at the top. When one walked along the railway line one would occasionally come upon a large cobra, with beautiful markings, cut in two by a recent train. The birds would soon get at the dead pieces, and in a short time there wouldn't be a sign of the snake.

To live alone needs great intelligence; to live alone and yet be pliable is arduous. To live alone, without the walls of self-enclosing gratifications, needs extreme alertness; for a solitary life encourages sluggishness, habits that are comforting and hard to break. A single life encourages isolation, and only the wise can live alone without harm to themselves and to others. Wisdom is alone, but a lonely path does not lead to wisdom. Isolation is death, and wisdom is not found in withdrawal. There is no path to wisdom, for all paths are separative, exclusive. In their very nature, paths can only lead to isolation, though these isolations are called unity, the whole, the one, and so on. A path is an exclusive process; the means is exclusive, and the end is as the means. The means is not separate from the goal, the what *should* be. Wisdom comes with the understanding of one's relationship with the field, with the passer-by, with the fleeting thought. To withdraw, to isolate oneself in order to find, is to put an end to discovery. Relationship leads to an aloneness that is not of isolation. There must be an aloneness, not of the enclosing mind, but of freedom. The complete is the alone, and incompleteness seeks the way of isolation.

She had been a writer, and her books had quite a wide circulation. She said she had managed to come to India only after many years. When she first started out she had no idea where she would end up; but now, after all this time, her destination had become clear. Her husband and her whole family were interested in religious matters, not casually but quite seriously; nevertheless she had made up her mind to leave them all, and had come in the hope of finding some peace. She hadn't known a soul in this country when she came, and it was very hard the first year. She went first to a certain *ashrama* or retreat about which she had read. The *guru* there was a mild old man who had had certain religious experiences on which he now lived, and who constantly repeated some Sanskrit saying which his disciples understood. She was welcomed at this retreat, and she found it easy to adjust herself to its rules. She remained there for several months, but found no peace, so one day she announced her departure. The disciples were horrified that she could even think of leaving such a master of wisdom; but she left. Then she went to an *ashrama* among the mountains and stayed there for some time, happily at first, for it was beautiful with trees, streams, and wild life. The discipline was rather rigourous, which she didn't mind; but again the living were the dead. The disciples were worshipping dead knowledge, dead tradition, a dead teacher. When she left they also were shocked, and threatened her with spiritual darkness. She then went to a very well-known retreat where they repeated various religious assertions and regularly practised prescribed meditations; but gradually she found that she was being entrapped and destroyed. Neither the teacher nor the disciples wanted freedom, though they talked about it. They were all concerned with maintaining the centre, with holding the disciples in the name of the *guru*. Again she broke away and went elsewhere; again the same story with a slightly different pattern.

"I assure you, I have been to most of the serious *ashramas,* and they all want to hold one, to grind one down to fit the pattern of thought which they call truth. Why do they all want one to conform to a particular discipline, to the mode of life laid down by the teacher? Why is it that they never give freedom but only promise freedom?"

Conformity is gratifying; it assures security to the disciple, and gives power to the disciple as well as to the teacher. Through conformity there is the strengthening of authority, secular or religious; and conformity makes for dullness, which they call peace. If one wants to avoid suffering through some form of resistance, why not pursue that path, though it involves a certain amount of pain? Conformity anaesthetizes the mind to conflict. We want to be made dull, insensitive; we try to shut off the ugly, and thereby we also make ourselves dull to the beautiful. Conformity to the authority of the dead or the living gives intense satisfaction. The teacher knows and you don't know. It would be foolish for you to try to find out anything for yourself when your comforting teacher already knows; so you become his slave, and slavery is better than confusion. The teacher and the disciple thrive on mutual exploitation. You really don't go to an *ashrama* for freedom, do you? You go there to be comforted, to live a life of enclosing discipline and belief, to worship and in turn be worshipped —all of which is called the search for truth. They cannot offer freedom, for it would be their own undoing. Freedom cannot be found in any retreat, in any system or belief, nor through the conformity and fear called discipline. Disciplines cannot offer freedom; they may promise, but hope is not freedom. Imitation as a means to freedom is the very denial of freedom, for the means is the end; copy makes for more copy, not for freedom. But we like to deceive ourselves, and that is why compulsion or the promise of reward exists in different and subtle forms. Hope is the denial of life.

"I am now avoiding all *ashramas* like the very plague. I went to them for peace and I was given compulsions, authoritarian doctrines and vain promises. How eagerly we accept the *guru's* promise! How blind we are! At last, after these many years, I am completely denuded of any desire to pursue their promised rewards. Physically I am worn out, as you can see; for, very foolishly, I really did try their formulas. At one of these places, where the teacher is on the rise and very popular, when I told them that I was coming to see you, they threw up their hands, and some had tears in their eyes. That was the last straw! I have come here because I want to talk over something that is gripping my heart. I hinted at it to one of the teachers, and his reply was that I must control my thought. It is this. The ache of solitude is more than I can bear; not the physical solitude, which is welcome, but the deep inner pain of being alone. What am I to do about it? How am I to regard this void?"

When you ask the way, you become a follower. Because there is this ache of solitude, you want help, and the very demand for guidance opens the door to compulsion, imitation and fear. The 'how' is not at all important, so let us understand the nature of this pain rather than try to overcome it, avoid it, or go beyond it. Till there is complete understanding of this ache of solitude, there can be no peace, no rest, but only incessant struggle; and whether we are aware of it or not, most of us are violently or subtly trying to escape from its fear. This ache is only in relation to the past, and not in relation to what *is*. What *is* has to be discovered, not verbally, theoretically, but directly experienced. How can there be discovery of what actually *is* if you approach it with a sense of pain or fear? To understand it, must you not come to it freely, denuded of past knowledge concerning it? Must you not come with a fresh mind, unclouded by memories, by habitual responses? Please do not ask how the mind is to be free to see the new, but listen to the truth of it. Truth alone liberates, and not your desire to be free. The very desire and effort to be free is a hindrance to liberation.

To understand the new, must not the mind, with all its conclusions, safeguards, cease its activities? Must it not be still, without seeking a way of escape from this solitude, a remedy for it? Must not the ache of solitude be observed, with its movement of despair and hope? Is it not this very movement that makes for solitude and its fear? Is not the very activity of the mind a process of isolation, resistance? Is not every form of relationship of the mind a way of separation, withdrawal? Is not experience itself a process of self-isolation? So the problem is not the ache of solitude, but the mind which projects the problem. The understanding of the mind is the beginning of freedom. Freedom is not something in the future, it is the very first step. The activity of the mind can be understood only in the process of response to every kind of stimulation. Stimulation and response are relationship at all levels. Accumulation in any form, as knowledge, as experience, as belief, prevents freedom; and it is only when there is freedom that truth can be.

"But is not effort necessary, the effort to understand?"

Do we understand anything through struggle, through conflict? Does not understanding come when the mind is utterly still, when the action of effort has ceased? The mind that is *made* still is not a tranquil mind; it is a dead, insensitive mind. When desire is, the beauty of silence is not.

TIME AND CONTINUITY

THE EVENING LIGHT was on the water, and the dark trees were against the setting sun. A crowded bus went by, followed by a big car with smart people in it. A child passed rolling a hoop. A woman with a heavy load stopped to adjust it, then continued on her weary way. A boy on a bicycle saluted someone, and was intent on getting home. Several women walked by, and a man stopped, lit a cigarette, threw the match in the water, looked around, and went on. No one seemed to notice the colours on the water and the dark trees against the sky. A girl came along carrying a baby, talking and pointing to the darkening waters to amuse and distract it. Lights were appearing in the houses, and the evening star was beginning to sail the heavens.

There is a sadness of which we are so little aware. We know the ache and sorrow of personal strife and confusion; we know futility and the misery of frustration; we know the fullness of joy and its transiency. We know our own sorrow, but we are not aware of the sadness of the other. How can we be when we are enclosed in our own misfortunes and trials? When our hearts are weary and dull, how can we feel the weariness of another? Sadness is so exclusive, isolating and destructive. How quickly the smile fades! Everything seems to end in sorrow, the ultimate isolation.

She was very well-read, capable and direct. She had studied sciences and religion, and had carefully followed modern psychology. Though still quite young, she had been married—with the usual miseries of marriage, she added. Now she was foot-loose and eager to find something more than the usual conditioning, to feel her way beyond the limits of the mind. Her studies had opened her mind to possibilities beyond the conscious and the collective gatherings of the past. She had attended several of the talks and discussions, she explained, and had felt that a source common to all the great teachers was active; she had listened with care and had understood a great deal, and had now come to discuss the inexhaustible and the problem of time.

"What is the source beyond time, that state of being which is not within the reasoning of the mind? What is the timeless, that creativity of which you have spoken?"

Is it possible to be aware of the timeless? What is the test of knowing or being aware of it? How would you recognize it? By what would you measure it?

"We can only judge by its effects."

But judging is of time; and are the effects of the timeless to be judged by the measurement of time? If we can understand what we mean by time, perhaps it may be possible for the timeless to be; but is it possible to discuss what that timeless is? Even if both of us are aware of it, can we talk about it? We may talk about it, but our experience will not be the timeless. It can never be talked about or communicated except through the means of time; but the word is not the thing, and through time the timeless obviously cannot be understood. Timelessness is a state which comes only when time is not. So let us rather consider what we mean by time.

"There are different kinds of time: time as growth, time as distance, time as movement."

Time is chronological and also psychological. Time as growth is the small becoming the large, the bullock cart evolving into the jet plane, the baby becoming the man. The heavens are filled with growth, and so is the earth. This is an obvious fact, and it would be stupid to deny it. Time as distance is more complex.

"It is known that a human being can be in two different places at the same time—at one place for several hours, and at another for a few minutes during the same period."

Thought can and does wander far afield while the thinker remains in one place.

"I am not referring to that phenomenon. A person, a physical entity, has been known to be in two widely separated places simultaneously. However, our point is time."

Yesterday using to-day as a passage to to-morrow, the past flowing through the present to the future, is one movement of time, not three separate movements. We know time as chronological and psychological, growth and becoming. There is the growth of the seed into the tree, and there is the process of psychological becoming. Growth is fairly clear, so let us put that aside for the time being. Psychological becoming implies time. I am *this* and I shall become *that,* using time as a passage, as a means; the what has been is becoming the what will be. We are very familiar with this process. So thought is time, the thought that has been and the thought that will be, the what *is* and the ideal. Thought is the product of time, and without the thinking process, time is not. The mind is the maker of time, it *is* time.

"That is obviously true. Mind is the maker and user of time. Without the mind-process, time is not. But is it possible to go beyond the mind? Is there a state which is not of thought?"

Let us together discover whether there is such a state or not. Is love thought? We may think of someone we love; when the other is absent, we think of him, or we have an image, a photograph of him. The separation makes for thought.

"Do you mean that when there is oneness, thought ceases and there is only love?"

Oneness implies duality, but that is not the point. Is love a thought-process? Thought is of time; and is love time-binding? Thought is bound by time, and you are asking if it is possible to be free from the binding quality of time.

"It must be, otherwise there could be no creation. Creation is possible only when the process of continuity ceases. Creation is the new, the new vision, the new invention, the new discovery, the new formulation, not the continuity of the old."

Continuity is death to creation.

"But how is it possible to put an end to continuity?"

What do we mean by continuity? What makes for continuity?

What is it that joins moment to moment, as the thread joins the beads in a necklace? The moment is the new, but the new is absorbed into the old and so the chain of continuity is formed. Is there ever the new, or only recognition of the new by the old? If the old recognizes the new, is it the new? The old can recognize only its own projection; it may call it the new, but it is not. The new is not recognizable; it is a state of non-recognition, non-association. The old gives itself continuity through its own projections; it can never know the new. The new may be translated into the old, but the new cannot be with the old. The experiencing of the new is the absence of the old. The experience and its expression is thought, idea; thought translates the new in terms of the old. It is the old that gives continuity; the old is memory, the word, which is time.

"How is it possible to put an end to memory?"

Is it possible? The entity that desires to put an end to memory is himself the forger of memory; he is not apart from memory. That is so, is it not?

"Yes, the maker of effort is born of memory, of thought; thought is the outcome of the past, conscious or unconscious. Then what is one to do?"

Please listen, and you will do naturally, without effort, what is essential. Desire is thought; desire forges the chain of memory. Desire is effort, the action of will. Accumulation is the way of desire; to accumulate is to continue. Gathering experience, knowledge, power, or things, makes for continuity, and to deny these is to continue negatively. Positive and negative continuance are similar. The gathering centre is desire, the desire for the more or the less. This centre is the self, placed at different levels according to one's conditioning. Any activity of this centre only brings about the further continuity of itself. Any movement of the mind is time-binding; it prevents creation. The timeless is not with the time-binding quality of memory. The limitless is not to be measured by memory, by experience. There is the unnamable only when experience, knowledge, has wholly ceased. Truth alone frees the mind from its own bondage.

THE FAMILY AND THE DESIRE FOR SECURITY

WHAT AN UGLY thing it is to be satisfied! Contentment is one thing and satisfaction another. Satisfaction makes the mind dull and the heart weary; it leads to superstition and sluggishness, and the edge of sensitivity is lost. It is those who are seeking gratification and those who have it that bring confusion and misery; it is they who breed the smelly village and the noisy town. They build temples for the graven image and perform satisfying rituals; they foster class segregation and war; they are forever multiplying the means of gratification; money, politics, power and religious organizations are their ways. They burden the earth with their respectability and its lamentations.

But contentment is another matter. It is arduous to be content. Contentment cannot be searched out in secret places; it is not to be pursued, as pleasure is; it is not to be acquired; it cannot be bought at the price of renunciation; it has no price at all; it is not reached by any means; it is not to be meditated upon and gathered. The pursuit of contentment is only the search for greater satisfaction. Contentment is the complete understanding of what *is* from moment to moment; it is the highest form of negative understanding. Gratification knows frustration and success, but contentment knows no opposites with their empty conflict. Contentment is above and beyond the opposites; it is not a synthesis, for it has no relation to conflict. Conflict can only produce more conflict, it breeds further illusion and misery. With contentment comes action that is not contradictory. Contentment of the heart frees the mind from its activities of confusion and distraction. Contentment is a movement that is not of time.

She explained that she had taken her master's degree in science, with honours, had taught, and had done some social work. In the short time since her graduation she had travelled about the country doing various things: teaching mathematics in one place, doing social work in another, helping her mother, and organizing for a society to which she belonged. She was not in politics, because she considered it the pursuit of personal ambition and a stupid waste of time. She had seen through all that, and was now about to be married.

Have you made up your own mind whom to marry, or are your parents arranging the matter?

"Probably my parents. Perhaps it is better that way."

Why, if I may ask?

"In other countries the boy and girl fall in love with each other; it may be all right at the beginning, but soon there is contention and misery, the quarrelling and making up, the tedium of pleasure and the routine of life. The arranged marriage in this country ends the same way, the fun goes out of it, so there isn't much to choose between the two systems. They are both pretty terrible, but what is one to do? After all, one must marry, one can't remain single all one's life. It is all very sad, but at least the husband gives a certain security and children are a joy; one can't have one without the other."

But what happens to all the years that you spent in acquiring your master's degree?

"I suppose one will play with it, but children and the household work will take most of one's time."

Then what good has your so-called education done? Why spend so much time, money and effort to end up in the kitchen? Don't you want to do any kind of teaching or social work after your marriage?

"Only when there is time. Unless one is well-to-do, it is impossible to have servants and all the rest of it. I am afraid all those days will be over once I get married—and I want to get married. Are you against marriage?"

Do you regard marriage as an institution to establish a family? Is not the family a unit in opposition to society? Is it not a centre from which all activity radiates, an exclusive relationship that dominates every other form of relationship? Is it not a self-enclosing activity that brings about division, separation, the high and the low, the powerful and the weak? The family as a system appears to resist the whole; each family opposes other families, other groups. Is not the family with its property one of the causes of war?

"If you are opposed to the family, then you must be for the collectivization of men and women in which their children belong to the State."

Please don't jump to conclusions. To think in terms of formulas and systems only brings about opposition and contention. You have your system, and another his; the two systems fight it out, each seeking to liquidate the other, but the problem still remains.

"But if you are against the family, then what are you for?"

Why put the question that way? If there is a problem, is it not stupid to take sides according to one's prejudice? Is it not better to understand the problem than to breed opposition and enmity, thereby multiplying our problems?

The family as it is now is a unit of limited relationship, self-enclosing and exclusive. Reformers and so-called revolutionaries have tried to do away with this exclusive family spirit which breeds every kind of anti-social activity; but it is a centre of stability as opposed to insecurity, and the present social structure throughout the world cannot exist without this security. The family is not a mere economic unit, and any effort to solve the issue on that level must obviously fail. The desire for security is not only economic, but much more profound and complex. If man destroys the family, he will find other forms of security through the State, through the collective, through belief and so on, which will in turn breed their own problems. We must understand the desire for inward, psychological security and not merely replace one pattern of security with another.

So the problem is not the family, but the desire to be secure. Is not the desire for security, at any level, exclusive? This spirit of exclusiveness shows itself as the family, as property, as the State, the religion, and so on. Does not this desire for inward security build up outward forms of security which are always exclusive? The very desire to be secure destroys security. Exclusion, separation, must inevitably bring about disintegration; nationalism, class-antagonism and war, are its symptoms. The family as a means of inward security is a source of disorder and social catastrophe.

"Then how is one to live, if not as a family?"

Is it not odd how the mind is always looking for a pattern, a blue-print? Our education is in formulas and conclusions. The 'how' is the demand for a formula, but formulas cannot resolve the problem. Please understand the truth of this. It is only when we do not seek inward security that we can live outwardly secure. As long as the family is a centre of security, there will be social disintegration; as long as the family is used as a means to a self-protective end, there must be conflict and misery. Please do not look puzzled, it is fairly simple. As long as I use you or another for my inner, psychological security, I must be exclusive; *I* am all-important, *I* have the greatest significance; it is *my* family, *my* property. The relationship of utility is based on violence; the family as a means of mutual inward security makes for conflict and confusion.

"I understand intellectually what you say, but is it possible to live without this inward desire to be secure?"

To understand intellectually is not to understand at all. You mean you hear the words and grasp their meaning, and that is all; but this will not produce action. Using another as a means of satisfaction and security is not love. Love is never security; love is a state in which there is no desire to be secure; it is a state of vulnerability; it is the only state in which exclusiveness, enmity and hate are impossible. In that state a family may come into being, but it will not be exclusive, self-enclosing.

"But we do not know such love. How is one . . . ?"

It is good to be aware of the ways of one's own thinking. The inward desire for security expresses itself outwardly through exclusion and violence, and as long as its process is not fully understood there can be no love. Love is not another refuge in the search for security. The desire for security must wholly cease for love to be. Love is not something that can be brought about through compulsion. Any form of compulsion, at any level, is the very denial of love. A revolutionary with an ideology is not a revolutionary at all; he only offers a substitute, a different kind of security, a new hope; and hope is death. Love alone can bring about a radical revolution or transformation in relationship; and love is not a thing of the mind. Thought can plan and formulate magnificent structures of hope, but thought will only lead to further conflict, confusion and misery. Love is when the cunning, self-enclosing mind is not.

THE 'I'

"MEDITATION IS OF the greatest importance to me; I have been meditating very regularly twice a day for more than twenty-five years. At the beginning it was all very difficult, I had no control over my thoughts and there were far too many distractions; but I gradually cut them out pretty thoroughly. More and more I gave my time and energy to the final end. I have been to various teachers and have followed several different systems of meditation, but somehow I was never satisfied with any of them—perhaps 'satisfaction' is not the right word. They all led to a certain point, depending on the particular system, and I found myself becoming a mere result of the system, which was not the final end. But from all these experimentations I have learned to master my thoughts completely, and my emotions also are entirely under control. I have practised deep breathing to quiet the body and the mind. I have repeated the sacred word and fasted for long periods; morally I have been upright, and worldly things have no attraction for me. But after all these years of struggle and effort, of discipline and denial, there is not the peace, the bliss of which the Great Ones speak. On rare occasions there have been enlightening moments of deep ecstasy, the intuitive promise of greater things; but I seem unable to pierce the illusion of my own mind, and I am endlessly caught in it. A cloud of confusing despair is descending upon me and there is increasing sorrow."

We were sitting on the bank of a wide river, close to the water. The town was up the river, some distance away. A boy was singing on the other bank. The sun was setting behind us and there were heavy shadows on the water. It was a beautiful, still evening, with masses of clouds towards the east, and the deep river seemed hardly to be flowing. To all this expanding beauty he was completely oblivious; he was wholly absorbed in his problem. We were silent, and he had closed his eyes; his stern face was calm, but inwardly there was an intense struggle going on. A flock of birds settled down at the water's edge; their cries must have carried across the river, for presently another flock came from the other shore and joined them. There was a timeless silence covering the earth.

During all these years, have you ever stopped striving after the final end? Do not will and effort make up the 'I', and can the process of time lead to the eternal?

"I have never consciously stopped striving after that for which my heart, my whole being longs. I dare not stop; if I did, I would fall back, I would deteriorate. It is the very nature of all things to struggle ever upwards, and without will and effort there would be stagnation; without this purposive striving, I could never go beyond and above myself."

Can the 'I' ever free itself from its own bondage and illusions? Must not the 'I' cease for the nameless to be? And does not this constant striving after the final end only strengthen the self, however concentrated its desire may be? You struggle after the final end, and another pursues worldly things; your effort may be more ennobling, but it is still the desire to gain, is it not?

"I have overcome all passion, all desire, except this one, which is more than desire; it is the only thing for which I live."

Then you must die to this too, as you are dead to other longings and desires. Through all these years of struggle and constant elimination, you have strengthened yourself in this one purpose, but it is still within the field of the 'I'. And you want to experience the unnamable—that is your longing, is it not?

"Of course. Beyond a shadow of doubt I want to know the final end, I want to experience God."

The experiencer is ever being conditioned by his experience. If the experiencer is aware that he is experiencing, then the experience is the outcome of his self-projected desires. If you know you are experiencing God, then that God is the projection of your hopes and illusions. There is no freedom for the experiencer, he is forever caught in his own experiences; he is the maker of time and he can never experience the eternal.

"Do you mean to say that that which I have diligently built up, with considerable effort and through wise choice, must be destroyed? And must I be the instrument of its destruction?"

Can the 'I' positively set about abnegating itself? If it does, its motive, its intention is to gain that which is not to be possessed. Whatever its activity, however noble its aim, any effort on the part of the 'I' is still within the field of its own memories, idiosyncrasies and projections, whether conscious or unconscious. The 'I' may divide itself into the organic 'I', and the 'non-I' or transcendental self; but this dualistic separation is an illusion in which the mind is caught. Whatever may be the movement of the mind, of the 'I', it can never free itself; it may go from level to level, from stupid to more intelligent choice, but its movement will always be within the sphere of its own making.

"You seem to cut off all hope. What is one to do?"

You must be completely denuded, without the weight of the past or the enticement of a hopeful future—which does not mean despair. If you are in despair, there is no emptiness, no nakedness. You cannot 'do' anything. You can and must be still, without any hope, longing, or desire; but you cannot determine to be still, suppressing all noise, for in that very effort there is noise. Silence is not the opposite of noise.

"But in my present state, what is to be done?"

If it may be pointed out, you are so eager to get on, so impatient to have some positive direction, that you are not really listening.

The evening star was reflected in the peaceful river.

* * *

Early next morning he came back. The sun was just showing itself above the tree-tops, and there was a mist over the river. A boat with wide sails, heavily laden with firewood, was lazily floating down the river; except for the one at the rudder, the men were all asleep on different parts of the boat. It was very still, and the daily human activities along the river had not yet begun.

"In spite of my outward impatience and anxiety, inwardly I must have been alert to what you were saying yesterday, for when I woke up this morning there was a certain sense of freedom and a clarity that comes with understanding. I did my usual morning meditation for an hour before sunrise, and I am not at all sure that my mind isn't caught in a number of widening illusions. May we proceed from where we left off?"

We cannot begin exactly where we left off, but we can look at our problem afresh. The outward and inward mind is ceaselessly active, receiving impressions; caught in its memories and re-actions, it is an aggregate of many desires and conflicts. It functions only within the field of time, and in that field there is contradiction, the opposition of will or desire, which is effort. This psychological activity of the 'I', of the 'me' and the 'mine', must cease, for such activity causes problems and brings about various forms of agitation and disorder. But any effort to stop this activity only makes for greater activity and agitation.

"That is true, I have noticed it. The more one tries to make the mind still, the more resistance there is, and one's effort is spent in overcoming this resistance; so it becomes a vicious and unbreakable circle."

If you are aware of the viciousness of this circle and realize that *you* cannot break it, then with this realization the censor, the observer, ceases to be.

"That seems to be the most difficult thing to do: to suppress the observer. I have tried, but so far I have never been able to succeed. How is one to do it?"

Are you not still thinking in terms of the 'I' and the 'non-I'? Are you not maintaining this dualism within the mind by word, by the constant repetition of experience and habit? After all, the thinker and his thought are not two different processes, but we make them so in order to attain a desired end. The censor comes into being with desire. Our problem is not how to suppress the censor, but to understand desire.

"There must be an entity which is capable of understanding, a state which is apart from ignorance."

The entity which says, 'I understand', is still within the field of the mind; it is still the observer, the censor, is it not?

"Of course it is; but I do not see how this observer can be eradicated. And *can* it be?"

Let us see. We were saying that it is essential to understand desire. Desire can and does divide itself into pleasure and pain, wisdom and ignorance; one desire opposes another, the more profitable conflicts with the less profitable, and so on. Though for various reasons it may separate itself, desire is in fact an indivisible process, is it not?

"This is a difficult thing to grasp. I am so used to opposing one desire by another, to suppressing and transforming desire, that I cannot as yet be fully aware of desire as a single, unitary process; but now that you have pointed it out, I am beginning to feel that it is so."

Desire may break itself up into many opposing and conflicting urges, but it is still desire. These many urges go to make up the 'I', with its memories, anxieties, fears, and so on, and the entire activity of this 'I' is within the field of desire; it has no other field of activity. That is so, is it not?

"Please go on. I am listening with my whole being, trying to go beyond the words, deeply and without effort."

Our problem, then, is this: is it possible for the activity of desire to come to an end voluntarily, freely, without any form of compulsion? It is only when this happens that the mind can be still. If you are aware of this as a fact, does not the activity of desire come to an end?

"Only for a very brief period; then once again the habitual activity begins. How can this be stopped? . . . But as I ask, I see the absurdity of asking!"

You see how greedy we are; we want ever more and more. The demand for the cessation of the 'I' becomes the new activity of the 'I'; but it is not new, it is merely another form of desire. Only when the mind is spontaneously still can the other, that which is not of the mind, come into being.

THE NATURE OF DESIRE

IT WAS A calm evening, but many white sails were on the lake. In the far distance a snow-covered peak hung as though suspended from the skies. The evening breeze from the north-east was not yet blowing, but there were ripples on the water towards the north and more boats were putting out. The water was very blue and the skies were very clear. It was a wide lake, but on sunny days the towns could be seen on the other side. In this little bay, secluded and forgotten, it was very peaceful; there were no tourists, and the steamboat that went round the lake never came here. Nearby was a village of fishermen; and as the weather promised to be clear, there would be small boats, with lanterns, fishing late into the night. In the enchantment of evening they were preparing their nets and their boats. The valleys were in deep shadow, but the mountains still held the sun.

We had been walking for some time and we sat down by the path, for he had come to talk things over.

"As far back as I can remember, I have had endless conflict, mostly within myself, though sometimes it manifests outwardly. I am not greatly worried by any outward conflict, as I have learnt to adjust myself to circumstances. This adjustment has been painful, however, for I am not easily persuaded or dominated. Life has been difficult, but I am efficient enough to make a good living. But all this is not my problem. What I cannot understand is this inward conflict which I am unable to control. I often wake up in the middle of the night from violent dreams, and I never seem to have a moment's respite from my conflict; it goes on beneath the everyday occupations, and frequently explodes in my more intimate relationships."

What do you mean by conflict? What is the nature of it?

"Outwardly I am a fairly busy man, and my work demands concentration and attention. When my mind is thus occupied, my inward conflicts are forgotten; but as soon as there is a lull in my work, I am back in my conflicts. These conflicts are of varying nature and at different levels. I want to be successful in my work, to be at the top of my profession, with plenty of money and all the rest of it, and I know I can be. At another level, I am aware of the stupidity of my ambition. I love the good things of life, and opposed to that, I want to lead a simple, almost an ascetic existence. I hate a number of people, and yet I want to forget and forgive. I can go on giving you instances, but I am sure you can understand the nature of my conflicts. Instinctively I am a peaceful person, yet anger is easy for me. I am very healthy—which may be a misfortune, at least in my case. Outwardly I give the appearance of being calm and steady, but I am agitated and confused by my inward conflicts. I am well over thirty, and I really want to break through the confusion of my own desires. You see, another of my difficulties is that I find it almost impossible to talk these things over with anybody. This is the first time in many years that I have opened up a little. I am not secretive, but I hate to talk about myself, and I could not possibly do so with any psychologist. Knowing all this, can you tell me whether it is possible for me to have some kind of inward serenity?"

Instead of trying to do away with conflict, let us see if we can understand this agglomeration of desire. Our problem is to see the nature of desire, and not merely to overcome conflict; for it is desire that causes conflict. Desire is stimulated by association and remembrance; memory is part of desire. The recollection of the pleasant and the unpleasant nourishes desire and breaks it up into opposing and conflicting desires. The mind identifies itself with the pleasant as opposed to the unpleasant; through the choice of pain and pleasure the mind separates desire, dividing it into different categories of pursuits and values.

"Though there are many conflicting and opposing desires, all desires are one. Is that it?"

That is so, is it not? And it is really important to understand this, otherwise the conflict between opposing desires is endless. The dualism of desire, which the mind has brought about, is an illusion. There is no dualism in desire, but merely different types of desire. There is dualism only between time and eternity. Our concern is to see the unreality of the dualism of desire. Desire does divide itself into want and non-want, but the avoidance of the one and the pursuit of the other is still desire. There is no escape from conflict through any of the opposites of desire, for desire itself breeds its own opposition.

"I see rather vaguely that what you say is a fact, but it is also a fact that I am still torn between many desires."

It is a fact that all desire is one and the same, and we cannot alter that fact, twist it to suit our convenience and pleasure, or use it as an instrument to free ourselves from the conflicts of desire; but if we see it to be true, then it has the power to set the mind free from breeding illusion. So we must be aware of desire breaking itself up into separate and conflicting parts. We *are* these opposing and conflicting desires, we are the whole bundle of them, each pulling in a different direction.

"Yes, but what can we do about it?"

Without first catching a glimpse of desire as a single unit, whatever we may or may not do will be of very little significance, for desire only multiplies desire and the mind is trapped in this conflict. There is freedom from conflict only when desire, which makes up the 'I' with its remembrances and recognitions, comes to an end.

"When you say that conflict ceases only with the cessation of desire, does this imply an end to one's active life?"

It may or it may not. It is foolish on our part to speculate about what kind of life it will be without desire.

"You surely do not mean that organic wants must cease."

Organic wants are moulded and expanded by psychological desires; we are talking of these desires.

"Can we go more deeply into the functioning of these inner cravings?"

Desires are both open and hidden, conscious and concealed. The concealed are of far greater significance than the obvious;

but we cannot become familiar with the deeper if the superficial are not understood and tamed. It is not that the conscious desires must be suppressed, sublimated, or moulded to any pattern, but they must be observed and quieted. With the calming of superficial agitation, there is a possibility that the deeper desires, motives and intentions will come to the surface.

"How is one to quiet the surface agitation? I see the importance of what you are saying, but I do not quite see how to approach the problem, how to experiment with it."

The experimenter is not separate from that with which he is experimenting. The truth of this must be seen. You who are experimenting with your desires are not an entity apart from those desires, are you? The 'I' who says, 'I will suppress this desire and go after that', is himself the outcome of all desire, is he not?

"One can feel that it is so, but actually to realize it, is quite another matter."

If as each desire arises there is an awareness of this truth, then there is freedom from the illusion of the experimenter as a separate entity, unrelated to desire. As long as the 'I' exerts itself to be free from desire, it is only strengthening desire in another direction and so perpetuating conflict. If there is an awareness of this fact from moment to moment, the will of the censor ceases; and when the experiencer is the experience, then you will find that desire with its many varying conflicts comes to an end.

"Will all this help one to a calmer and fuller life?"

Certainly not at the beginning. It is sure to arouse more disturbances, and deeper adjustments may have to be made; but the deeper and wider one goes into this complex problem of desire and conflict, the simpler it becomes.

THE PURPOSE OF LIFE

THE ROAD IN front of the house went down to the sea, weaving its way past many small shops, great flats, garages, temples, and a dusty, neglected garden. When it reached the sea, the road became a big thoroughfare, with taxis, rattling buses, and all the noise of a modern city. Leading off this thoroughfare there was a peaceful, sheltered avenue overhung with huge rain-trees, but in the morning and evening it was busy with cars on their way to a smart club, with its golf-course and lovely gardens. As I walked along this avenue there were various types of beggars lying on the pavement; they were not noisy, and did not even stretch out their hands to the passer-by. A girl about ten years old was lying with her head on a tin can, resting with wide-open eyes; she was dirty, with matted hair, but she smiled as I smiled at her. Further along, a little girl, hardly three, came forward with outstretched hand and an enchanting smile. The mother was watching from behind a nearby tree. I took the outstretched hand and we walked together for a few paces, returning her to her mother. As I had no coin, I returned with one the next day, but the little girl would not take it, she wanted to play; so we played, and the coin was given to the mother. Whenever I walked along that avenue the little girl was always there, with a shy smile and bright eyes.

Opposite the entrance to the fashionable club a beggar was seated on the ground; he was covered with a filthy gunny-sack, and his matted hair was full of dust. Some days, as I went by, he would be lying down, his head in the dust, his naked body covered with the gunny-sack; on other days he would be sitting up, perfectly still, looking without seeing, with the massive rain-trees over him. One evening there was gaiety at the club; it was all lit up, and sparkling cars full of laughing people were driving in, tooting their horns. From the club-house came light music, loud and air-filling. Many policemen were at the entrance, where a large crowd had gathered to watch the smartly-dressed and well-fed people pass by in their cars. The beggar had turned his back on all this. One man was offering him something to eat, and another a cigarette, but he silently refused both without making a movement. He was slowly dying, day by day, and the people passed by.

Those rain-trees were massive against the darkening sky, and of fantastic shape. They had very small leaves, but their branches seemed huge, and they had a strange majesty and aloofness in that over-crowded city of noise and pain. But the sea was there, everlastingly in motion, restless and infinite. There were white sails, mere specks in that infinitude, and on the dancing waters the moon made a path of silver. The rich beauty of the earth, the distant stars, and deathless humanity. Immeasurable vastness seemed to cover all things.

He was a youngish man, and had come from the other side of the country, a tiresome journey. He had taken a vow not to marry till he had found the meaning and purpose of life. Determined and aggressive, he worked in some office from which he had taken leave for a certain period to try to find the answer to his search. He had a busy and argumentative mind, and was so taken up with his own and other people's answers that he would hardly listen. His words could not come fast enough, and he quoted endlessly what the philosophers and teachers had said concerning the purpose of life. He was tormented and deeply anxious.

"Without knowing the purpose of life, my very existence has no meaning, and all my action is destructive. I earn a livelihood just to carry on; I suffer, and death awaits me. This is the way of life, but what is the purpose of it all? I do not know. I have been to the learned, and to the various *gurus;* some say one thing, some another. What do you say?"

Are you asking in order to compare what is said here with what has been said elsewhere?

"Yes. Then I can choose, and my choice will depend on what I consider to be true."

Do you think that the understanding of what is true is a matter of personal opinion and dependent on choice? Through choice will you discover what is true?

"How else can one find the real if not through discrimination, through choice? I shall listen to you very carefully, and if. what you say appeals to me, I shall reject what the others have said and pattern my life after the goal you have set. I am most earnest in my desire to find out what is the true purpose of life."

Sir, before going any further, is it not important to ask yourself if you are capable of seeking out the true? This is suggested with respect, and not in a derogatory spirit. Is truth a matter of opinion, of pleasure, of gratification? You say that you will accept what appeals to you, which means that you are not interested in truth, but are after that which you find most gratifying. You are prepared to go through pain, through compulsion, in order to gain that which in the end is pleasurable. You are seeking pleasure, not truth. Truth must be something beyond like and dislike, must it not? Humility must be the beginning of all search.

"That is why I have come to you, sir. I am really seeking; I look to the teachers to tell me what is true, and I shall follow them in a humble and contrite spirit."

To follow is to deny humility. You follow because you desire to succeed, to gain an end. An ambitious man, however subtle and hidden his ambition, is never humble. To pursue authority and set it up as a guide is to destroy insight, understanding. The pursuit of an ideal prevents humility, for the ideal is the glorification of the self, the ego. How can he who in different ways gives importance to the 'me', ever be humble? Without humility, reality can never be.

"But my whole concern in coming here is to find out what is the *true* purpose of life."

If one may be permitted to say so, you are just caught up in an idea, and it is becoming a fixation. This is something of which one has to be constantly watchful. Wanting to know the true purpose of life, you have read many philosophers and sought out many teachers. Some say this, some say that, and you want to know the truth. Now, do you want to know the truth of what they say, or the truth of your own inquiry?

"When you ask a straight question like that, I feel rather hesitant in my reply. There are people who have studied and experienced more than I ever can, and it would be absurd conceit on my part to discard what they say, which may help me to uncover the significance of life. But each one speaks according to his own experience and understanding, and they sometimes contradict each other. The Marxists say one thing, and the religious people say something quite different. Please help me to find the truth in all this."

To see the false as the false, and the truth in the false, and the true as the true, is not easy. To perceive clearly, there must be freedom from desire, which twists and conditions the mind. You are so eager to find the true significance of life that your very eagerness becomes a hindrance to the understanding of your own inquiry. You want to know the truth of what you have read and of what your teachers have said, do you not?

"Yes, most definitely."

Then you must be able to find out for yourself what is true in all these statements. Your mind must be capable of direct perception; if it is not, it will be lost in the jungle of ideas, opinions and beliefs. If your mind has not the capacity to see what is true, you will be like a driven leaf. So what is important is not the conclusions and assertions of others, whoever they be, but for you to have insight into what is true. Is this not most essential?

"I think it is, but how am I going to have this gift?"

Understanding is not a gift reserved for the few, but it comes to those who are earnest in their self-knowledge. Comparison does not bring about understanding; comparison is another form of distraction, as judgment is evasion. For the truth to be, the mind must be without comparison, without evaluation. When the mind is comparing, evaluating, it is not quiet, it is occupied. An occupied mind is incapable of clear and simple perception.

"Does it mean, then, that I must strip myself of all the values that I have built up, the knowledge that I have gathered?"

Must not the mind be free to discover? Does knowledge, information—the conclusions and experiences of oneself and others, this vast, accumulated burden of memory—bring freedom? Is there freedom as long as there is the censor who is judging, condemning, comparing? The mind is never quiet if it is always acquiring and calculating; and must not the mind be still for truth to be?

"I see that, but aren't you asking too much of a simple and ignorant mind like mine?"

Are you simple and ignorant? If you really were, it would be a great delight to begin with true inquiry; but unfortunately you are not. Wisdom and truth come to a man who truly says, "I am ignorant, I do not know". The simple, the innocent, not those who are burdened with knowledge, will see the light, for they are humble.

"I want only one thing, to know the true purpose of life, and you shower me with things that are beyond me. Can you not please tell me in simple words what is the true significance of life?"

Sir, you must begin very near to go far. You want the immense without seeing what is close by. You want to know the significance of life. Life has no beginning and no end; it is both death and life; it is the green leaf, and the withered leaf that is driven by the wind; it is love and its immeasurable beauty; it is the sorrow of solitude and the bliss of aloneness. It cannot be measured, nor can the mind discover it.

VALUING AN EXPERIENCE

ON THE HOT rock in the burning sun the village women were spreading the paddy that had been kept in the storehouse. They had carried large bundles of it to the flat, sloping rock, and the two oxen that were tied to the tree would presently tread on the paddy to release the grain. The valley was far from any town, and the huge tamarind trees gave deep shadows. Through the valley a dusty road made its way to the village and beyond. Cattle and innumerable goats covered the hillsides. The rice-fields were deep in water, and the white rice-birds flew with lazy wings from one field to another; they seemed without fear, but they were shy and would not let one get near them. The mango trees were beginning to bloom, and the river made a cheerful noise with its clear running water. It was a pleasant land, and yet poverty hung over it like a plague. Voluntary poverty is one thing, but compulsory poverty is quite another. The villagers were poor and diseased, and although there was now a medical dispensary and food was distributed, the damage wrought by centuries of privation could not be wiped away in a few years. Starvation is not the problem of one community or of one country, but of the whole world.

With the setting sun, a gentle breeze came from the east, and from the hills came strength. These hills were not high, but high enough to give to the air a soft coolness, so different from the plains. The stars seemed to hang down very close to the hills, and occasionally one would hear the cough of a leopard. That evening the light behind the darkening hills seemed to give greater meaning and beauty to all the things about one. As one sat on the bridge, the villagers going by on their way home suddenly stopped talking, and only resumed their conversation as they disappeared into the darkness. The visions that the mind can conjure up are so empty and dull; but when the mind does not build out of its own materials—memory and time—, there is that without name.

A bullock-cart, with a hurricane lamp burning, was coming up the road; slowly every part of the steel-bound wheel touched the hard ground. The driver was asleep, but the oxen knew their way home; they went by, and then they too were swallowed up in the darkness. It was intensely still now. The evening star was on the hill, but soon she would drop from sight. In the distance an owl was calling, and all about one the insect world of the night was alive and busy; yet the stillness was not broken. It held everything in it, the stars, the lonely owl, the myriad insects. If one listened to it, one lost it; but if one were of it, it welcomed one. The watcher can never be of this stillness; he is an outsider looking in, but he is not of it. The observer only experiences, he is never the experience, the thing itself.

He had travelled all over the world, knew several languages, and had been a professor and a diplomat. In his youth he had been at Oxford, and having made his way through life rather strenuously, he had retired before the usual age. He was familiar with Western music, but liked the music of his own country best. He had studied the different religions, and had been particularly impressed with Buddhism; but after all, he added, stripped of their superstitions, dogmas and rituals, they all essentially said the

127

same thing. Some of the rituals had beauty in them, but finance and romance had taken over most religions, and he himself was free of all rituals and dogmatic accretions. He had played around with thought-transference and hypnosis, and was acquainted with clairvoyance, but he had never looked upon them as an end in themselves. One could develop extended faculties of observation, greater control over matter, and so on, but all this seemed to him rather primitive and obvious. He had taken certain drugs, including the very latest, which for the time being had given him an intensity of perception and experience beyond the superficial sensations; but he had not given great importance to these experiences, for they did not in any way reveal the significance of that which he felt was beyond all ephemeral things.

"I have tried various forms of meditation," he said, "and for a whole year I withdrew from all activity to be by myself and meditate. At different times I have read what you say about meditation, and was greatly struck by it. Right through from boyhood the very word 'meditation', or its Sanskrit equivalent, has had a very strange effect upon me. I have always found an extraordinary beauty and delight in meditation, and it is one of the few things that I have really enjoyed in life—if one may use such a word with regard to so profound a thing as meditation. That enjoyment has not gone from me, but has deepened and widened through the years, and what you said about meditation has opened new heavens to me. I don't want to ask you anything more about meditation, because I have read almost everything that you have so far said about it, but I would like to talk over with you, if I may, an event that happened quite recently." He paused for a moment, and then went on.

"From what I have told you, you can see that I am not the kind of person to create symbolic images and worship them. I have scrupulously avoided any identification with self-projected religious concepts or figures. One has read or heard that some of the saints—or at least some of those whom people have called saints—have had visions of Krishna, Christ, the Mother as Kali, the Virgin Mary, and so on. I can see how easily one could hypnotize oneself through a belief and evoke some vision which might radically alter the conduct of one's life. But I do not wish to be under any delusion; and having said all this, I want to describe something that took place a few weeks ago.

"A group of us had been meeting fairly often to talk things over seriously, and one evening we were discussing rather heatedly the remarkable similarity between Communism and Catholicism, when suddenly there appeared in the room a seated figure, with yellow robe and shaven head. I was quite startled. I rubbed my eyes and looked at the faces of my friends. They were completely oblivious of the figure, and were so occupied with their discussion that they did not notice my silence. I shook my head, coughed, and again rubbed my eyes, but the figure was still there. I cannot convey to you what a beautiful face it had; its beauty was not merely of form, but of something infinitely greater. I could not take my eyes off that face; and as it was getting to be too much for me, and not wanting my friends to notice my silence and my astonished absorption, I got up and went out on the veranda. The night air was fresh and cold. I walked up and down, and presently went in again. They were still talking; but the atmosphere of the room had changed, and the figure was still where it had been before, seated on the floor, with its extraordinary head cleanly shaven. I could not go on with what we had been discussing, and presently all of us left. As I walked home the figure went before me. That was several weeks ago, and it has still not left me, though it has lost that forceful immanence. When I close my eyes, it is there, and something very strange has happened to me. But before I go into that, what *is* this experience? Is it a self-projection from the unconscious past, without my cognizance and conscious volition, or is it something wholly independent of me, without any relation to my consciousness? I have thought a great deal about the matter, and I have not been able to find the truth of it."

Now that you have had this experience, do you value it? Is it important to you, if one may ask, and do you hold on to it?

"In a way, I suppose I do, if I am to answer honestly. It has given me a creative release—not that I write poems or paint, but this experience has brought about a deep sense of freedom and peace. I value it because it has caused a profound transformation in myself. It is, indeed, vitally important to me, and I would not lose it at any price."

Are you not afraid of losing it? Do you consciously pursue that figure, or is it an ever-living thing?

"I suppose I am apprehensive of losing it, for I do constantly dwell on that figure and am always using it to bring about a desired state. I had never before thought of it in this way, but now that you ask, I see what I am doing."

Is it a living figure, or the memory of a thing that has come and gone?

"I am almost afraid to answer that question. Please do not think me sentimental, but this experience has meant a very great deal to me. Although I came here to talk the matter over with you and see the truth of it, I now feel rather hesitant and unwilling to inquire into it; but I must. Sometimes it is a living figure, but more often it is the recollection of a past experience."

You see how important it is to be aware of what *is* and not be caught in what one would *like* it to be. It is easy to create an illusion and live in it. Let us go patiently into the matter. Living in the past, however pleasant, however edifying, prevents the experiencing of what *is*. The what *is* is ever new, and the mind finds it extremely arduous and difficult not to live in the thousand yesterdays. Because you are clinging to that memory, the living experience is denied. The past has an ending, and the living is the eternal. The memory of that figure is enchanting you, inspiring you, giving you a sense of release; it is the dead that is giving life to the living. Most of us never know what it is to live because we are living with the dead.

May I point out, sir, that apprehension of losing something very precious has crept in. Fear has arisen in you. Out of that one experience you have brought into being several problems: acquisitiveness, fear, the burden of experience, and the emptiness of your own being. If the mind can free itself from all acquisitive urges, experiencing will have quite a different significance, and then fear totally disappears. Fear is a shadow, and not a thing in itself.

"I am really beginning to see what I have been doing. I am not excusing myself, but as the experience was intense, so has been the desire to hold on to it. How difficult it is not to be caught in a deep emotional experience! The memory of an experience is as invitingly forceful as the experience itself."

It is most difficult to differentiate between experiencing and memory, is it not? When does experiencing become memory, a thing of the past? Wherein does the subtle difference lie? Is it a matter of time? Time is not when experiencing is. Every experience becomes a movement into the past; the present, the state of experiencing, is imperceptibly flowing into the past. Every living experience, a second later, has become a memory, a thing of the past. This is the process we all know, and it seems to be inevitable. But is it?

"I am following very keenly what you are unfolding, and I am more than delighted that you are talking of this, because I am aware of myself only as a series of memories, at whatever level of my being. I am memory. Is it possible to be, to exist in the state of experiencing? That is what you are asking, is it not?"

Words have subtle meanings to all of us, and if for a moment we can go beyond these references and their reactions, perhaps we shall get at the truth. With most of us, experiencing is always becoming memory. Why? Is it not the constant activity of the mind to take in or absorb, and to push away or deny? Does it not hold on to what is pleasurable, edifying, significant, and try to eliminate all that is not useful to itself? And can it ever be without this process? Surely, that is a vain question, as we shall find out in the very asking of it.

Now let us go further. This positive or negative accumulation, this evaluating process of the mind, becomes the censor, the watcher, the experiencer, the thinker, the ego. At the moment of experiencing, the experiencer is not; but the experiencer comes into being when choice begins, that is, when the living is over and there is the beginning of accumulation. The acquisitive urge blots out the living, the experiencing, making of it a thing of the past, of memory. As long as there is the observer, the experiencer, there must inevitably be acquisitiveness, the gathering-in process; as long as there is a separate entity who is watching and choosing, experience is always a process of becoming. Being or experiencing is, when the separate entity is not.

"How is the separate entity to cease?"

Why are you asking that question? The 'how' is a new way to acquire. We are now concerned with acquisitiveness, and not with how to attain freedom from it. Freedom *from* something is no freedom at all; it is a reaction, a resistance, which only breeds further opposition.

But let us go back to your original question. Was the figure self-projected, or did it come into being uninfluenced by you? Was it independent of you? Consciousness is a complicated affair, and it would be foolish to give a definite answer, would it not? But one can see that recognition is based on a conditioning of the mind. You had studied Buddhism, and as you said, it had impressed you more than any other religion, so the conditioning process had taken place. That conditioning may have projected the figure, even though the conscious mind was occupied with a wholly different matter. Also, your mind being made acute and sensitive by the way of your life, and by the discussion you were having with your friends, perhaps you 'saw' thought clothed in a Buddhist form, as another might 'see' it in a Christian form. But whether it was self-projected or otherwise, is not of vital importance, is it?

"Perhaps not, but it has shown me a great deal."

Has it? It did not reveal to you the working of your own mind, and you became a prisoner to that experience. All experience has significance when with it there comes self-knowledge, which is the only releasing or integrating factor; but without self-knowledge, experience is a burden leading to every kind of illusion.

This Problem of Love

A SMALL DUCK was coming up the wide canal like a ship under sail, alone and full of quacking importance. The canal wound in and out through the town. There were no other ducks in sight, but this one made enough noise for many ducks. The few who heard him paid no attention, but that didn't matter to the duck. He wasn't frightened, but he felt himself to be a very prominent person on that canal; he owned it. Beyond the town the countryside was pleasant with green pastures and fat black and white cows. There were masses of clouds on the horizon and the skies seemed low, close to the earth, with that light which only this part of the world seems to have. The land was as flat as one's palm, and the road climbed only to pass over the bridges that crossed the high canals. It was a lovely evening; the sun was setting over the North Sea, and the clouds took on the colouring of the setting sun. Great streaks of light, blue and rose, shot across the sky.

She was the wife of a well-known man who was very high up in the government, almost at the top, but not quite. Well-dressed and quiet in manner, she had that peculiar atmosphere of power and wealth, the assurance of one long accustomed to being obeyed and getting things done. From one or two things she said, it was evident that her husband had the brains and she the drive. Together they had risen high, but just when much greater power and position were almost theirs, he had fallen desperately ill. At this point in her narrative she could hardly continue, and tears rolled down her cheeks. She had come in with smiling assurance, but it had rapidly disappeared. Sitting back, she was silent for a time, and then continued.

"I have read some of your talks and have attended one or two of them. While I was listening to you, what you said meant a great deal. But these things quickly escape one, and now that I am really in great trouble I thought I would come and see you. I am sure you understand what has happened. My husband is fatally ill, and all the things we lived and worked for are falling to pieces. The party and its work will go on, but . . . Though there are nurses and doctors, I have been looking after him myself, and for months I have had very little sleep. I can't bear to lose him, though the doctors say there is little chance of his recovery. I have thought and thought about all this, and I am almost sick with anxiety. We have no children, as you know; and we have meant a great deal to each other. And now . . ."

Do you really want to talk seriously and go into things?

"I feel so desperate and confused, I don't believe I am capable of serious thinking; but I must come to some kind of clarity within myself."

Do you love your husband, or do you love the things which came about through him?

"I love . . ." She was too shocked to continue.

Please do not think the question brutal, but you will have to find the true answer to it, otherwise sorrow will always be there. In uncovering the truth of that question there may be the discovery of what love is.

"In my present state I cannot think it all out."

But has not this problem of love passed through your mind?

"Once, perhaps, but I quickly got away from it. I always had so much to do before he was ill; and now, of course, all thinking is pain. Did I love him because of the position and power that went with him, or did I simply love him? I am already talking of him as though he were not! I really don't know in what way I love him. At present I am too confused, and my brain refuses to work. If I may, I would like to come back another time, perhaps after I have accepted the inevitable."

If I may point out, acceptance is also a form of death.

* * *

Several months passed before we met again. The papers had been full of his death, and now he too was forgotten. His death had left marks on her face, and soon bitterness and resentment were showing themselves in her talk.

"I haven't talked to anyone about all these things," she explained. "I just withdrew from all my past activities and buried myself in the country. It has been terrible, and I hope you won't mind if I just talk a little. All my life I have been tremendously ambitious, and before marrying I indulged in good works of every kind. Soon after I married, and largely because of my husband, I left all the petty wrangling of good works and plunged into politics with my whole heart. It was a much wider field of struggle and I enjoyed every minute of it, the ups and the downs, the intrigues and the jealousies. My husband was brilliant in his quiet way, and with my driving ambition we were always moving up. As we had no children, all my time and thought were given over to furthering my husband. We worked together splendidly, complementing each other in an extraordinary way. Everything was going as we had planned, but I always had a gnawing fear that it was all going too well. Then one day, two years ago, when my husband was being examined for some minor trouble, the doctor said there was a growth which must be examined immediately. It was malignant. For a time we were able to keep the whole thing a dead secret; but six months ago it all began again, and it has been a pretty terrible ordeal. When I last came to see you I was too distressed and miserable to think, but perhaps I can now look at things with a little more clarity. Your question disturbed me more than I can tell you. You may remember that you asked me if I loved my husband, or the things that went with him. I have thought a great deal about it; but is it not too complex a problem to be answered by oneself?"

Perhaps; but unless one finds out what love is, there will always be pain and sad disappointments. And it is difficult to discover where love ends and confusion begins, is it not?

"You are asking if my love for my husband was unmixed with my love for position and power. Did I love my husband because he gave me the means for the fulfilment of my ambition? It is partly this, and also the love of the man. Love is a mixture of so many things."

Is it love when there is complete identification with another? And is not this identification a round-about way of giving importance to oneself? Is it love when there is the sorrow of loneliness, the pain of being deprived of the things that seemingly gave significance to life? To be cut off from the ways of self-fulfilment, from the things that the self has lived on, is the denial of self-importance, and this brings about disenchantment, bitterness, the misery of isolation. And is this misery love?

"You are trying to tell me, are you not, that I did not love my husband at all? I am really appalled at myself when you put it that way. And there is no other way to put it, is there? I had never thought about all this, and only when the blow struck was there any real sorrow in my life. Of course, to have had no children was a great disappointment, but it was tempered by the fact that I had my husband and the work. I suppose they became my children. There is a fearful finality about death. Suddenly I find myself alone, without anything to work for, put aside and forgotten. I now realize the truth of what you say; but if you had said these things to me three or four years ago, I would not have listened to you. I wonder if I have been listening to you even now, or merely seeking out reasons to justify myself! May I come and talk to you again?"

WHAT IS THE TRUE FUNCTION OF A TEACHER?

THE BANYANS and the tamarinds dominated the small valley, which was green and alive after the rains. In the open the sun was strong and biting, but in the shade it was pleasantly cool. The shadows were deep, and the old trees were shapely against the blue sky. There was an astonishing number of birds in that valley, birds of many different kinds, and they would come to these trees and so quickly disappear in them. There would probably be no more rain for several months, but now the countryside lay green and peaceful, the wells were full, and there was hope in the land. The corrupting towns were far beyond the hills, but the nearby villages were filthy and the people were starving. The government only promised, and the villagers seemed to care so little. There was beauty and gladness all about them, but they had no eyes for it nor for their own inward riches. Amidst so much loveliness the people were dull and empty.

He was a teacher with little pay and a large family, but he was interested in education. He said he had a difficult time making ends meet, but he managed somehow, and poverty was not a disturbing factor. Though food was not in abundance, they had enough to eat, and as his children were being educated freely in the school where he was teaching, they could scrape along. He was proficient in his subject and taught other subjects too, which he said any teacher could do who was at all intelligent. He again stressed his deep interest in education.

"What is the function of a teacher?" he asked.

Is he merely a giver of information, a transmitter of knowledge?

"He has to be at least that. In any given society, boys and girls must be prepared to earn a livelihood, depending on their capacities, and so on. It is part of the function of a teacher to impart knowledge to the student so that he may have a job when the time comes, and may also, perhaps, help to bring about a better social structure. The student must be prepared to face life."

That is so, sir, but aren't we trying to find out what is the function of a teacher? Is it merely to prepare the student for a successful career? Has the teacher no greater and wider significance?

"Of course he has. For one thing, he can be an example. By the way of his life, by his conduct, attitude and outlook, he can influence and inspire the student."

Is it the function of a teacher to be an example to the student? Are there not already enough examples, heroes, leaders, without adding another to the long list? Is example the way of education? Is it not the function of education to help the student to be free, to be creative? And is there freedom in imitation, in conformity, whether outward or inward? When the student is encouraged to follow an example, is not fear sustained in a deep and subtle form? If the teacher becomes an example, does not that very example mould and twist the life of the student, and are you not then encouraging the everlasting conflict between what he is and what he should be? Is it not the function of a teacher to help the student to understand what he is?

"But the teacher must guide the student towards a better and nobler life."

guide, you must know; but do you? What do you know? You know only what you have learnt through the screen of your prejudices, which is your conditioning as a Hindu, a Christian, or a Communist; and this form of guidance only leads to greater misery and bloodshed, as is being shown throughout the world. Is it not the function of a teacher to help the student to free himself intelligently from all these conditioning influences so that he will be able to meet life deeply and fully, without fear, without aggressive discontent? Discontent is part of intelligence, but not the easy pacification of discontent. Acquisitive discontent is soon pacified, for it pursues the well-worn pattern of acquisitive action. Is it not the function of a teacher to dispel the gratifying illusion of guides, examples and leaders?

"Then at least the teacher can inspire the student to greater things."

Again, are you not approaching the problem wrongly, sir? If you as a teacher infuse thought and feeling into the student, are you not making him psychologically dependent on you? When you act as his inspiration, when he looks up to you as he would to a leader or to an ideal, surely he is depending on you. Does not dependence breed fear? And does not fear cripple intelligence?

"But if the teacher is not to be either an inspirer, an example, or a guide, then what in heaven's name is his true function?"

The moment you are none of these things, what are you? What is your relationship with the student? Did you previously have any relationship with the student at all? Your relationship with him was based on an idea of what was good for him, that he ought to be this or that. You were the teacher and he was the pupil; you acted upon him, you influenced him according to your particular conditioning, so, consciously or unconsciously you moulded him in your own image. But if you cease to act upon him, then he becomes important in himself, which means that you have to understand him and not demand that he should understand you or your ideals, which are phony anyway. Then you have to deal with what *is* and not with what *should* be.

Surely, when the teacher regards each student as a unique individual and therefore not to be compared with any other, he is then not concerned with system or method. His sole concern is with 'helping' the student to understand the conditioning influences about him and within himself, so that he can face intelligently, without fear, the complex process of living and not add more problems to the already existing mess.

"Are you not asking of the teacher a task that is far beyond him?"

If you are incapable of this, then why be a teacher? Your question has meaning only if teaching is a mere career to you, a job like any other, for I feel that nothing is impossible for the true educator.

Your Children and Their Success

It was an enchanted evening. The hill-tops were aglow with the setting sun, and in the sand on the path that led across the valley, four woodpeckers were taking a bath. With their longish beaks they would pull the sand under them, their wings would flutter as they pushed their bodies deeper into it, and then they would begin all over again, the tufts on their heads bobbing up and down. They were calling to each other and enjoying themselves thoroughly. Not to disturb them, we stepped off the path onto the short, thick grass of recent rains; and there, a few feet away, was a large snake, yellowish and powerful. Its head was sleek, painted, and cruelly shaped. It was too intent on those birds to be disturbed, its black eyes watching without movement and its black, forked tongue darting in and out. Almost imperceptibly it was moving towards the birds, its scales making no noise on the grass. It was a cobra, and there was death about it. Dangerous but beautiful, it was shiny in the darkening light, and it must recently have shed its old skin. Suddenly the four birds took to the air with a cry, and then we saw an extraordinary thing take place: a cobra relax. It had been so eager, so tense, and now it seemed almost lifeless, part of the earth—but in a second, fatal. It moved with ease and only lifted its head when we made a slight noise, but with it went a peculiar stillness, the stillness of fear and death.

She was a small, elderly lady with white hair, but was well preserved. Though gentle of speech, her figure, her walk, her gestures and the way she held her head, all showed a deep-rooted aggressiveness which her voice did not conceal. She had a large family, several sons and daughters, but her husband had been dead for some time and she alone had had to bring them up. One of her sons, she said with evident pride, was a successful doctor with a large practice, and also a good surgeon. One of her daughters was a clever and successful politician, and without too much difficulty was getting her own way; she said this with a smile which implied, "You know what women are". She went on to explain that this political lady had spiritual aspirations.

What do you mean by spiritual aspirations?

"She wants to be the head of some religious or philosophical group."

To have power over others through an organization is surely evil, is it not? That is the way of all politicians, whether they are in politics or not. You may hide it under pleasant and deceptive words, but is not the desire for power always evil?

She listened, but what was being said had no meaning to her. It was written on her face that she was concerned about something, and what it was would presently emerge. She went on to tell of the activities of her other children, all of whom were vigorous and doing well except the one she really loved.

"What is sorrow?" she suddenly asked. "Somewhere in the background I seem to have had it all my life. Though all but one of my children are well-off and contented, sorrow has been constantly with me. I can't put my finger on it, but it has pursued me, and I often lie awake at night wondering what it is all about. I am also concerned about my youngest son. You see, he is a failure. Whatever he touches goes to pieces: his marriage, his relationship with his brothers and sisters, and with his friends. He almost never has a job, and when he does get one, something happens and he's out. He seems incapable of being helped. I worry about him, and though he adds to my sorrow, I don't think he is the root of it. What is sorrow? I have had anxieties, disappointments and physical pain, but this pervading sorrow is something beyond all that, and I have not been able to find its cause. Could we talk about it?"

You are very proud of your children and especially of their success, are you not?

"I think any parent would be, as they have all made good except the last one. They are prosperous and happy. But why are you asking that question?"

It may have something to do with your sorrow. Are you sure that your sorrow has nothing to do with their success?

"Of course; on the contrary, I am very happy about it."

What do you think is the root of your sorrow? If one may ask, did the death of your husband affect you very deeply? Are you still affected by it?

"It was a great shock and I was very lonely after his death, but I soon forgot my loneliness and sorrow as there were the children to be seen to and I had no time to think about myself."

Do you think that time wipes away loneliness and sorrow? Are they not still there, buried in the deeper layers of your mind, even though you may have forgotten them? May it not be that these are the cause of your conscious sorrow?

"As I say, the death of my husband was a shock, but somehow it was to be expected, and with tears I accepted it. As a girl, before I married, I saw my father's death, and some years later that of my mother also; but I have never been interested in official religion, and all this clamour for explanations of death and the hereafter has never bothered me. Death is inevitable, and let us accept it with as little noise as possible."

That may be the way you regard death, but is loneliness to be so easily reasoned away? Death is something of to-morrow, to be faced, perhaps, when it comes; but is not loneliness ever present? You may deliberately shut it out, but it is still there behind the door. Should you not invite loneliness and look at it?

"I don't know about that. Loneliness is most unpleasant, and I

141

doubt if I can go so far as to invite that awful feeling. It is really quite frightening."

Must you not understand it fully, since that may be the cause of your sorrow?

"But how am I to understand it when it is the very thing that gives me pain?"

Loneliness does not give you pain, but the idea of loneliness causes fear. You have never experienced the state of loneliness. You have always approached it with apprehension, dread, with the urge to get away from it or to find a way to overcome it; so you have avoided it, have you not? You have really never come directly into contact with it. To put loneliness away from you, you have escaped into the activities of your children and their success. Their success has become yours; but behind this worship of success, is there not some deep concern?

"How do you know?"

The thing you escape into—the radio, social activity, a particular dogma, so-called love, and so on—becomes all-important, as necessary to you as drink to the drunkard. One may lose oneself in the worship of success, or in the worship of an image, or in some ideal; but all ideals are illusory, and in the very losing of oneself there is anxiety. If one may point out, your children's success has been to you a source of pain, for you have a deeper concern about them and about yourself. In spite of your admiration of their success and of the applause they have received from the public, is there not behind it a sense of shame, of disgust, or disappointment? Please forgive me for asking, but are you not deeply distressed about their success?

"You know, sir, I have never dared to acknowledge, even to myself, the nature of this distress, but it is as you say."

Do you want to go into it?

"Now, of course, I do want to go into it. You see, I have always been religious without belonging to any religion. Here and there I have read about religious matters, but I have never been caught in any so-called religious organization. Organized religion has seemed too distant and not sufficiently intimate. Beneath my worldly life, however, there has always been a vague religious groping, and when I began to have children, this groping took the form of a deep hope that one of my children would be religiously inclined. And not one of them is; they have all become prosperous and worldly, except the last one, who is a mixture of everything. All of them are really mediocre, and that is what hurts. They are engrossed in their worldliness. It all seems so superficial and silly, but I haven't discussed it with any of them, and even if I did, they wouldn't understand what I was talking about. I thought that at least one of them would be different, and I am horrified at their mediocrity and my own. It is this, I suppose, that is causing my sorrow. What can one do to break up this stupid state?"

In oneself or in another? One can only break up mediocrity in oneself, and then perhaps a different relationship with others may arise. To know that one is mediocre is already the beginning of change, is it not? But a petty mind, becoming aware of itself, frantically tries to change, to improve, and this very urge is mediocre. Any desire for self-improvement is petty. When the mind knows that it is mediocre and does not act upon itself, there is the breaking up of mediocrity.

"What do you mean by 'act upon itself'?"

If a petty mind, realizing it is petty, makes an effort to change itself, is it not still petty? The effort to change is born of a petty mind, therefore that very effort is petty.

"Yes, I see that, but what can one do?"

Any action of the mind is small, limited. The mind must cease to act, and only then is there the ending of mediocrity.

THE URGE TO SEEK

TWO GOLDEN-GREEN birds with long tails used to come to that garden every morning and sit on a particular branch, playing and calling to each other. They were so restless, always on the move, their bodies quivering, but they were lovely things, and they never seemed to tire in their flight and play. It was a

sheltered garden, and many other birds constantly cam
Two young mongooses, sleek and swift, their yellowi
kling in the sun, would chase each other along the to
wall, and then, slipping through a hole, would come i   he garden; but how cautious and observant they were even in their play,
keeping close to the wall, their red eyes alert and watchful. Occasionally an old mongoose, comfortably fat, would come slowly
into the garden through the same hole. It must have been their
father or mother, for once the three of them were together. Coming into the garden one after another through the hole, they
crossed the whole length of the lawn in single file and disappeared
among the bushes.

"Why do we seek?" asked P. "What is the purpose of our
search? How weary one gets of this everlasting seeking! Is there
no end to it?"

"We search for what we want to find," answered M., "and
after finding what we seek, we move on to further discovery. If
we did not seek, all living would come to an end, life would
stagnate and have no meaning."

" 'Seek and ye shall find'," quoted R. "We find what we want,
what we consciously or unconsciously crave for. We have never
questioned this urge to seek; we have always sought, and apparently we shall always go on seeking."

"The desire to seek is inevitable," stated L. "You might just
as well ask why we breathe, or why the hair grows. The urge to
seek is as inevitable as day and night."

When you assert so definitely that the urge to seek is inevitable,
the discovery of the truth of the matter is blocked, is it not? When
you accept anything as final, determined, does not all inquiry
come to an end?

"But there are certain fixed laws, like gravity, and it is wiser
to accept than to batter one's head vainly against them," replied L.

We accept certain dogmas and beliefs for various psychological
reasons, and through the process of time what is thus accepted
becomes 'inevitable', a so-called necessity for man.

144

"If L. accepts as inevitable the urge to seek, then he will go on seeking, and for him it is not a problem," said M.

The scientist, the cunning politician, the unhappy, the diseased —each is seeking in his own way and changing the object of his search from time to time. We are all seeking, but we have never, it seems, asked ourselves why we seek. We are not discussing the object of our search, whether noble or ignoble, but we are trying to find out, aren't we, why we seek at all? What is this urge, this everlasting compulsion? Is it inevitable? Has it an unending continuity?

"If we do not seek," asked Y., "will we not become lazy and just stagnate?"

Conflict in one form or another appears to be the way of life, and without it we think that life would have no meaning. To most of us, the cessation of struggle is death. Search implies struggle, conflict, and is this process essential to man, or is there a different 'way' of life in which search and struggle are not? Why and what do we seek?

"I seek ways and means to assure, not my own survival, but that of my nation," said L.

Is there such a vast difference between national and individual survival? The individual identifies himself with the nation, or with a particular form of society, and then wants that nation or society to survive. The survival of this or that nation is also the survival of the individual. Is not the individual ever seeking to survive, to have continuity, by being identified with something greater or nobler than himself?

"Is there not a point or a moment at which we suddenly find ourselves without search, without struggle?" asked M.

"That moment may be merely the result of weariness," replied R., "a brief pause before plunging again into the vicious circle of search and fear."

"Or it may be outside of time," said M.

Is the moment we are talking about outside of time, or is it only a point of rest before starting to seek again? Why do we seek, and is it possible for this search to come to an end? Unless we discover for ourselves why we seek and struggle, the state in

145

which search has come to an end will remain for us an illusion, without significance.

"Is there no difference between the various objects of search?" asked B.

Of course there are differences, but in all seeking the urge is essentially the same, is it not? Whether we seek to survive individually or as a nation; whether we go to a teacher, a *guru*, a saviour; whether we follow a particular discipline, or find some other means of bettering ourselves, is not each one of us, in his own limited or extensive way, seeking some form of satisfaction, continuity, permanency? So we are now asking ourselves, not what we seek, but why do we seek at all? And is it possible for all search to come to an end, not through compulsion or frustration, or because one has found, but because the urge has wholly ceased?

"We are caught in the habit of search, and I suppose it is the outcome of our dissatisfaction," said B.

Being discontented, dissatisfied, we seek contentment, satisfaction. As long as there is this urge to be satisfied, to fulfil, there must be search and struggle. With the urge to fulfil there is always the shadow of fear, is there not?

"How can we escape from fear?" asked B.

You want to fulfil without the sting of fear; but is there ever an enduring fulfilment? Surely, the very desire to fulfil is itself the cause of frustration and fear. Only when the significance of fulfilment is seen is there an ending of desire. Becoming and being are two widely different states, and you cannot go from one to the other; but with the ending of becoming, the other is.

LISTENING

THE FULL MOON was just coming up over the river; there was a haze which made her red, and smoke was rising from the many villages, for it was cold. There was not a ripple on the river, but the current was hidden, strong and deep. The swallows were flying low, and one or two wing-tips touched the water, disturbing ever so little the placid surface. Up the river the evening star was just visible over a minaret in the distant, crowded town. The parrots were coming back to be near human habitation, and their flight was never straight. They would drop with a screech, pick up a grain, and fly sideways, but they were always moving forward towards a leafy tree, where they were gathering by the hundreds; then off they would fly again to a more sheltering tree, and as darkness came there would be silence. The moon was now well over the tops of the trees, and she made a silvery pathway on the still waters.

"I see the importance of listening, but I wonder if I ever really listen to what you say," he remarked. "Somehow I have to make a great effort to listen."

When you make an effort to listen, are you listening? Is not that very effort a distraction which prevents listening? Do you make an effort when you listen to something that gives you delight? Surely, this effort to listen is a form of compulsion. Compulsion is resistance, is it not? And resistance breeds problems, so listening becomes one of them. Listening itself is never a problem.

"But to me it is. I want to listen correctly because I feel that what you are saying has deep significance, but I can't go beyond its verbal meaning."

If I may say so, you are not listening now to what is being said. You have made listening into a problem, and this problem is preventing you from listening. Everything we touch becomes a problem, one issue breeds many other issues. Perceiving this, is it possible not to breed problems at all?

"That would be marvellous, but how is one to come to that happy state?"

Again, you see, the question of 'how', the manner of achieving a certain state, becomes still another problem. We are talking of not giving birth to problems. If it may be pointed out, you must be aware of the manner in which the mind is creating the problem. You want to achieve the state of perfect listening; in other words, you are not listening, but you want to achieve a state, and you need time and interest to gain that or any other state. The need for time and interest generates problems. You are not simply aware that you are not listening. When you are aware of it, the very fact that you are not listening has its own action; the truth of that fact acts, you do not act upon the fact. But you want to act upon it, to change it, to cultivate its opposite, to bring about a desired state, and so on. Your effort to act upon the fact breeds problems, whereas seeing the truth of the fact brings its own liberating action. You are not aware of the truth, nor do you see the false as the false, as long as your mind is occupied in any way with effort, with comparison, with justification or condemnation.

"All this may be so, but with all the conflicts and contradictions that go on within oneself, it still seems to me that it is almost impossible to listen."

Listening itself is a complete act; the very act of listening brings its own freedom. But are you really concerned with listening, or with altering the turmoil within? If you would listen, sir, in the sense of being aware of your conflicts and contradictions without forcing them into any particular pattern of thought, perhaps they might altogether cease. You see, we are constantly trying to be this or that, to achieve a particular state, to capture one kind of experience and avoid another, so the mind is everlastingly occupied with something; it is never still to listen to the noise of its own struggles and pains. Be simple, sir, and don't try to become something or to capture some experience.

THE FIRE OF DISCONTENT

IT HAD BEEN raining quite heavily for several days, and the streams were swollen and noisy. Brown and dirty, they came from every gully and joined a wider stream that ran through the middle of the valley, and this in turn joined the river that went down to the sea some miles away. The river was high and fast-flowing, winding through orchards and open country. Even in summer the river was never dry, though all the streams that fed it showed their barren rocks and dry sands. Now the river was flowing faster than a man could walk, and on both banks people were watching the muddy waters. It was not often that the river was so high. The people were excited, their eyes sparkled, for the fast-moving waters were a delight. The town near the sea might suffer, the river might overflow its banks, inundating the fields and the groves, and damaging the houses; but here, under the lonely bridge, the brown waters were singing. A few people were fishing, but they could not have caught much, for the current was too strong, carrying with it the debris of all the neighbouring streams. It began to rain again, yet the people stayed to watch and to take delight in simple things.

"I have always been a seeker," she said. "I have read, oh, so many books on many subjects. I was a Catholic, but left that church to join another; leaving that too, I joined a religious society. I have recently been reading oriental philosophy, the teachings of the Buddha, and added to all this, I have had myself psycho-analysed; but even that hasn't stopped me from seeking, and now here I am talking to you. I nearly went to India in search of a Master, but circumstances prevented me from going."

She went on to say that she was married and had a couple of children, bright and intelligent, who were in college; she wasn't worried about them, they could look after themselves. Social interests meant nothing any more. She had been seriously trying to meditate but got nowhere, and her mind was as silly and vagrant as before.

"What you say about meditation and prayer is so different from what I have read and thought, that it has greatly puzzled me," she added. "But through all this wearisome confusion, I really want to find truth and understand its mystery."

Do you think that by seeking truth you will find it? May it not be that the so-called seeker can never find truth? You have never fathomed this urge to seek, have you? Yet you keep on seeking, going from one thing to another in the hope of finding what you want, which you call truth and make a mystery of.

"But what's wrong with going after what I want? I have always gone after what I wanted, and more often than not I have got it."

That may be; but do you think that you can collect truth as you would money or paintings? Do you think it is another ornament for one's vanity? Or must the mind that is acquisitive wholly cease for the other to be?

"I suppose I am too eager to find it."

Not at all. You will find what you seek in your eagerness, but it will not be the real.

"Then what am I supposed to do, just lie down and vegetate?"

You are jumping to conclusions, are you not? Is it not important to find out why you are seeking?

"Oh, I know why I am seeking. I am thoroughly discontented with everything, even with the things I have found. The pain of discontent returns again and again; I think I have got hold of something, but it soon fades away and once again the pain of discontent overwhelms me. I have tried in every way I can think of to overcome it, but somehow it is too strong within me, and I must find something—truth, or whatever it is—that will give me peace and contentment."

Should you not be thankful that you have not succeeded in smothering this fire of discontent? To overcome discontent has been your problem, has it not? You have sought contentment, and fortunately you have not found it; to find it is to stagnate, vegetate.

"I suppose that is really what I am seeking: an escape from this gnawing discontent."

Most people are discontented, are they not? But they find satisfaction in the easy things of life, whether it is mountain-climbing or the fulfilment of some ambition. The restlessness of discontent is superficially turned into achievements that gratify. If we are shaken in our contentment, we soon find ways to overcome the pain of discontent, so we live on the surface and never fathom the depths of discontent.

"How is one to go below the surface of discontent?"

Your question indicates that you still desire to escape from discontent, does it not? To live with that pain, without trying to escape from it or to alter it, is to penetrate the depths of discontent. As long as we are trying to get somewhere, or to be something, there must be the pain of conflict, and having caused the pain, we then want to escape from it; and we do escape into every kind of activity. To be integrated with discontent, to remain with and be part of discontent, without the observer forcing it into grooves of satisfaction or accepting it as inevitable, is to allow that which has no opposite, no second, to come into being.

"I follow what you are saying, but I have fought discontent for so many years that it is now very difficult for me to be part of it."

The more you fight a habit, the more life you give to it. Habit is a dead thing, do not fight it, do not resist it; but with the perception of the truth of discontent, the past will have lost its significance. Though painful, it is a marvellous thing to be discontented without smothering that flame with knowledge, with tradition, with hope, with achievement. We get lost in the mystery of man's achievement, in the mystery of the church, or of the jet plane. Again, this is superficial, empty, leading to destruction and misery. There is a mystery that is beyond the capacities and powers of the mind. You cannot seek it out or invite it; it must come without your asking, and with it comes a benediction for man.

AN EXPERIENCE OF BLISS

IT WAS A very hot and humid day. In the park many people were stretched out on the grass or sitting on benches in the shade of the heavy trees; they were taking cool drinks and gasping for clean, fresh air. The sky was grey, there was not the slightest breeze, and the fumes of this vast mechanized city filled the air. In the country it must have been lovely, for spring was just turning into summer. Some trees would just be putting forth their leaves, and along the road which ran beside the wide, sparkling river, every kind of flower would be out. Deep in the woods there would be that peculiar silence in which you can almost hear things being born, and the mountains, with their deep valleys, would be blue and fragrant. But here in the city . . . !

Imagination perverts the perception of what *is;* and yet how proud we are of our imagination and speculation. The speculative mind, with its intricate thoughts, is not capable of fundamental transformation; it is not a revolutionary mind. It has clothed itself with what *should* be and follows the pattern of its own limited and enclosing projections. The good is not in what *should* be, it lies in the understanding of what *is*. Imagination prevents the perception of what *is,* as does comparison. The mind must put aside all imagination and speculation for the real to be.

He was quite young, but he had a family and was a business man of some repute. He looked very worried and miserable, and was eager to say something.

"Some time ago I had a most remarkable experience, and as I have never before talked about it to anyone, I wonder if I am capable of explaining it to you; I hope so, for I cannot go to anybody else. It was an experience which completely ravished my heart; but it has gone, and now I have only the empty memory of it. Perhaps you can help me to get it back. I will tell you, as fully as I can, what that blessing was. I have read of these things, but they were always empty words and appealed only to my senses; but what happened to me was beyond all thought, beyond imagination and desire, and now I have lost it. Please do help me to get it back." He paused for a moment, and then continued.

"I woke up one morning very early; the city was still asleep, and its murmur had not yet begun. I felt I had to get out, so I dressed quickly and went down to the street. Even the milk truck was not yet on its rounds. It was early spring, and the sky was pale blue. I had a strong feeling that I should go to the park, a mile or so away. From the moment I came out of my front door I had a strange feeling of lightness, as though I were walking on air. The building opposite, a drab block of flats, had lost all its ugliness; the very bricks were alive and clear. Every little object which ordinarily I would never have noticed seemed to have an extraordinary quality of its own, and strangely, everything seemed to be a part of me. Nothing was separate from me; in fact, the 'me' as the observer, the perceiver, was absent, if you know what I mean. There was no 'me' separate from that tree, or from that paper in the gutter, or from the birds that were calling to each other. It was a state of consciousness that I had never known.

"On the way to the park," he went on, "there is a flower-shop. I have passed it hundreds of times, and I used to glance at the flowers as I went by. But on this particular morning I stopped in front of it. The plate glass window was slightly frosted with the heat and damp from inside, but this did not prevent me from seeing the many varieties of flowers. As I stood looking at them, I found myself smiling and laughing with a joy I had never before experienced. Those flowers were speaking to me, and I was speaking to them; I was among them, and they were part of me. In saying this, I may give you the impression that I was hysterical, slightly off my head; but it was not so. I had dressed very carefully, and had been aware of putting on clean things, looking at my watch, seeing the names of the shops, including that of my tailor, and reading the titles of the books in a bookshop window. Everything was alive, and I loved everything. I was the scent of those flowers, but there was no 'me' to smell the flowers, if you know what I mean. There was no separation between them and me. That flower-shop was fantastically alive with colours, and the beauty of it all must have been stunning, for time and its measurement had ceased. I must have stood there for over twenty minutes, but I assure you there was no sense of time. I could hardly tear myself away from those flowers. The world of struggle, pain and sorrow was there, and yet it was not. You see, in that state, words have no meaning. Words are descriptive, separative, comparative, but in that state there were no words; 'I' was not experiencing, there was only that state, that experience. Time had stopped; there was no past, present or future. There was only—oh, I don't know how to put it into words, but it doesn't matter. There was a Presence—no, not that word. It was as though the earth, with everything in it and on it, were in a state of benediction, and I, walking towards the park, were part of it. As I drew near the park I was absolutely spell-bound by the beauty of those familiar trees. From the pale yellow to the almost black-green, the leaves were dancing with life; every leaf stood out, separate, and the whole richness of the earth was in a single leaf. I was conscious that my heart was beating fast; I have a very good heart, but I could hardly breathe as I entered the park, and I thought I was going to faint. I sat down on a bench, and tears were rolling down my cheeks. There was a silence that was utterly unbearable, but that silence was cleansing all things of pain and sorrow. As I went deeper into the park, there was music in the air. I was surprised, as there was no house nearby, and no one would have a radio in the park at that hour of the morning. The music was part of the whole thing. All the goodness, all the compassion of the world was in that park, and God was there.

"I am not a theologian, nor much of a religious person," he continued. "I have been a dozen times or so inside a church, but it has never meant anything to me. I cannot stomach all that nonsense that goes on in churches. But in that park there was a Being, if one may use such a word, in whom all things lived and had their being. My legs were shaking and I was forced to sit down again, with my back against a tree. The trunk was a living thing, as I was, and I was part of that tree, part of that Being, part of the world. I must have fainted. It had all been too much for me: the vivid, living colours, the leaves, the rocks, the flowers, the incredible beauty of everything. And over all was the benediction of . . .

"When I came to, the sun was up. It generally takes me about twenty minutes to walk to the park, but it was nearly two hours since I had left my house. Physically I seemed to have no strength to walk back; so I sat there, gathering strength and not daring to think. As I slowly walked back home, the whole of that experience was with me; it lasted two days, and faded away as suddenly as it had come. Then my torture began. I didn't go near my office for a week. I wanted that strange living experience back again, I wanted to live once again and forever in that beatific world. All this happened two years ago. I have seriously thought of giving up everything and going away into some lonely corner of the world, but I know in my heart that I cannot get it back that way. No monastery can offer me that experience, nor can any candle-lit church, which only deals with death and darkness. I considered making my way to India, but that too I put aside. Then I tried a certain drug; it made things more vivid, and so on, but an opiate is not what I want. That is a cheap way of experiencing, it is a trick but not the real thing.

"So here I am," he concluded. "I would give everything, my life and all my possessions, to live again in that world. What am I to do?"

It came to you, sir, uninvited. You never sought it. As long as you are seeking it, you will never have it. The very desire to live again in that ecstatic state is preventing the new, the fresh experience of bliss. You see what has happened: you have had that experience, and now you are living with the dead memory of yesterday. What has been is preventing the new.

"Do you mean to say that I must put away and forget all that has been, and carry on with my petty life, inwardly starving from day to day?"

If you do not look back and ask for more, which is quite a task, then perhaps that very thing over which you have no control may act as it will. Greed, even for the sublime, breeds sorrow; the urge for the more opens the door to time. That bliss cannot be bought through any sacrifice, through any virtue, through any drug. It is not a reward, a result. It comes when it will; do not seek it.

"But was that experience real, was it of the highest?"

We want another to confirm, to make us certain of what has been, and so we find shelter in it. To be made certain or secure in that which has been, even if it were the real, is to strengthen the unreal and breed illusion. To bring over to the present what is past, pleasurable or painful, is to prevent the real. Reality has no continuity. It is from moment to moment, timeless and measureless.

A Politician Who Wanted To Do Good

IT HAD RAINED during the night, and the perfumed earth was still damp. The path led away from the river among ancient trees and mango groves. It was a path of pilgrimage trodden by thousands, for it had been the tradition for over twenty centuries that all good pilgrims must tread that path. But it was not the right time of the year for pilgrims, and on this particular morning only the villagers were walking there. In their gaily-coloured clothes, with the sun behind them and with loads of hay, vegetables and firewood on their heads, they were a beautiful sight; they walked with grace and dignity, laughing and talking over village affairs. On both sides of the path, stretching as far as the eye could see, there were green, cultivated fields of winter wheat, with wide patches of peas and other vegetables for the market. It was a lovely morning, with clear blue skies, and there was a blessing on the land. The earth was a living thing, bountiful, rich and sacred. It was not the sacredness of man-made things, of temples, priests and books; it was the beauty of complete peace and complete silence. One was bathed in it; the trees, the grass, and the big bull, were part of it; the children playing in the dust were aware of it, though they knew it not. It was not a passing thing; it was there without a beginning, without an ending.

He was a politician and he wanted to do good. He felt himself to be unlike other politicians, he said, for he really was concerned with the welfare of the people, with their needs, their health, and their growth. Of course he was ambitious, but who was not? Ambition helped him to be more active, and without it he would be lazy, incapable of doing much good to others. He wanted to become a member of the cabinet, and was well on his way to it, and when he got there he would see that his ideas were carried out. He had travelled the world over, visiting various countries and studying the schemes of different governments, and after careful thought he had been able to work out a plan that would really benefit his country.

"But now I don't know if I can put it through," he said with evident pain. "You see, I have not been at all well lately. The doctors say that I must take it easy, and I may have to undergo a very serious operation; but I cannot bring myself to accept this situation."

If one may ask, what is preventing you from taking it easy?

"I refuse to accept the prospect of being an invalid for the rest of my life and not being able to do what I want to do. I know, verbally at least, that I cannot keep up indefinitely the pace I have been used to, but if I am laid up my plan may never go through. Naturally there are other ambitious people, and it is a matter of dog eat dog. I was at several of your meetings, so I thought I would come and talk things over with you."

Is your problem, sir, that of frustration? There is a possibility of long illness, with a decline of usefulness and popularity, and you find that you cannot accept this, because life would be utterly barren without the fulfilment of your schemes; is that it?

"As I said, I am as ambitious as the next man, but I also want to do good. On the other hand, I am really quite ill, and I simply can't accept this illness, so there is a bitter conflict going on within me, which I am quite aware is making me still more ill. There is another fear too, not for my family, who are all well provided for, but the fear of something that I have never been able to put into words, even to myself."

You mean the fear of death?

"Yes, I think that is it; or rather, of coming to an end without fulfilling what I have set out to do. Probably this is my greatest fear, and I do not know how to assuage it."

Will this illness totally prevent your political activities?

"You know what it is like. Unless I am in the centre of things, I shall be forgotten and my schemes will have no chance. It will virtually mean a withdrawal from politics, and I am loath to do that."

So, you can either voluntarily and easily accept the fact that you must withdraw, or equally happily go on doing your political work, knowing the serious nature of your illness. Either way, disease may thwart your ambitions. Life is very strange, is it not? If I may suggest, why not accept the inevitable without bitterness? If there is cynicism or bitterness, your mind will make the illness worse.

"I am fully aware of all this, and yet I cannot accept—least of all happily, as you suggest—my physical condition. I could perhaps carry on with a bit of my political work, but that is not enough."

Do you think that the fulfilment of your ambition to do good is the only way of life for you, and that only through you and your schemes will your country be saved? You are the centre of all this supposedly good work, are you not? You are really not deeply concerned with the good of the people, but with good as manifested through you. *You* are important, and not the good of the people. You have so identified yourself with your schemes and with the so-called good of the people, that you take your own fulfilment to be their happiness. Your schemes may be excellent, and they may, by some happy chance, bring good to the people; but you want your name to be identified with that good. Life is strange; disease has come upon you, and you are thwarted in furthering your name and your importance. This is what is causing conflict in you, and not anxiety lest the people should not be helped. If you loved the people and did not indulge in mere lip-service, it would have its own spontaneous effect which would be of significant help; but you do not love the people, they are merely the tools of your ambition and your vanity. Doing good is on the way to your own glory. I hope you don't mind my saying all this?

"I am really happy that you have expressed so openly the things that are deeply concealed in my heart, and it has done me good. I have somehow felt all this, but have never allowed myself to face it directly. It is a great relief to hear it so plainly stated, and I hope I shall now understand and calm my conflict. I shall see how things turn out, but already I feel a little more detached from my anxieties and hopes. But sir, what of death?"

This problem is more complex and it demands deep insight,

does it not? You can rationalize death away, saying that all things die, that the fresh green leaf of spring is blown away in the autumn, and so on. You can reason and find explanations for death, or try to conquer by will the fear of death, or find a belief as a substitute for that fear; but all this is still the action of the mind. And the so-called intuition concerning the truth of re-incarnation, or life after death, may be merely a wish for survival. All these reasonings, intuitions, explanations, are within the field of the mind, are they not? They are all activities of thought to overcome the fear of death; but the fear of death is not to be so tamely conquered. The individual's desire to survive through the nation, through the family, through name and idea, or through beliefs, is still the craving for his own continuity, is it not? It is this craving, with its complex resistances and hopes, that must voluntarily, effortlessly and happily come to an end. One must die each day to all one's memories, experiences, knowledge and hopes; the accumulations of pleasure and repentance, the gather-ing of virtue, must cease from moment to moment. These are not just words, but the statement of an actuality. What continues can never know the bliss of the unknown. Not to gather, but to die each day, each minute, is timeless being. As long as there is the urge to fulfil, with its conflicts, there will always be the fear of death.

THE COMPETITIVE WAY OF LIFE

THE MONKEYS WERE on the road, and in the middle of the road a baby monkey was playing with its tail, but the mother was keeping an eye on it. They were all well aware that someone was there, at a safe distance. The adult males were large, heavy and rather vicious, and most of the other monkeys avoided them. They were all eating some kind of berries that had fallen on the road from a large, shady tree with thick leaves. The recent rains had filled the river, and the stream under the narrow bridge was gurgling. The monkeys avoided the water and the puddles on the road, and when a car appeared, splattering mud as it came, they were off the road in a second, the mother taking the baby with her. Some climbed the tree and others went down the bank on each side of the road, but they were back on it as soon as the car had sped by. They had now got quite used to the human presence. They were as restless as the human mind, and up to all kinds of tricks.

The rice-fields on either side of the road were a luscious, sparkling green in the warm sun, and against the blue hills beyond the fields the rice-birds were white and slow-winged. A long, brownish snake had crawled out of the water and was resting in the sun. A brilliantly blue kingfisher had alighted on the bridge and was readying itself for another dive. It was a lovely morning, not too hot, and the solitary palms scattered over the fields told of many things. Between the green fields and the blue hills there was communion, a song. Time seemed to pass so quickly. In the blue sky the kites were wheeling; occasionally they would alight on a branch to preen themselves, and then off they would go again, calling and circling. There were also several eagles, with white necks and golden-brown wings and bodies. Among the newly-sprouted grass there were large red ants; they would race jerkily forward, suddenly stop, and then go off in the opposite direction. Life was so rich, so abundant—and unnoticed, which was perhaps what all these living things, big and little, wanted.

A young ox with bells around its neck was drawing a light cart which was delicately made, its two large wheels connected by a thin steel bar on which a wooden platform was mounted. On this platform a man was sitting, proud of the fast-trotting ox and the turnout. The ox, sturdy and yet slender, gave him importance; everyone would look at him now, as the passing villagers did. They stopped, looked with admiring eyes, made comments, and passed on. How proud and erect the man sat, looking straight ahead! Pride, whether in little things or in great achievements, is essentially the same. What one does and what one has gives one importance and prestige; but man in himself, as a total being, seems to have hardly any significance at all.

He came with two of his friends. Each of them had a good college degree, and they were doing well, they said, in their various professions. They were all married and had children, and they seemed pleased with life, yet they were disturbed too.

"If I may," he said, "I would like to ask a question to set the ball rolling. It is not an idle question, and it has somewhat disturbed me since hearing you a few evenings ago. Among other things you said that competition and ambition were destructive urges which man must understand and so be free of, if he is to live in a peaceful society. But are not struggle and conflict part of the very nature of existence?"

Society as at present constituted is based on ambition and conflict, and almost everyone accepts this fact as inevitable. The individual is conditioned to its inevitability; through education, through various forms of outward and inward compulsion, he is made to be competitive. If he is to fit into this society at all, he must accept the conditions it lays down, otherwise he has a pretty bad time. We seem to think that we have to fit into this society; but why should one?

"If we don't, we will just go under."

I wonder if that would happen if we saw the whole significance of the problem? We might not live according to the usual pattern, but we would live creatively and happily, with a wholly different outlook. Such a state cannot be brought about if we accept the present social pattern as inevitable. But to get back to your point: do ambition, competition and conflict constitute a predestined and inevitable way of life? You evidently assume that they do. Now let us begin from there. Why do you take this competitive way of life to be the only process of existence?

"I am competitive, ambitious, like all those around me. It is a fact which often gives me pleasure, and sometimes pain, but I just accept it without struggle, because I don't know any other way of living; and even if I did, I suppose I would be afraid to try it. I have many responsibilities, and I would be gravely concerned about the future of my children if I broke away from the usual thoughts and habits of life."

You may be responsible for others, sir, but have you not also the responsibility to bring about a peaceful world? There can be no peace, no enduring happiness for man as long as we—the individual, the group and the nation—accept this competitive existence as inevitable. Competitiveness, ambition, implies conflict within and without, does it not? An ambitious man is not a peaceful man, though he may talk of peace and brotherhood. The politician can never bring peace to the world, nor can those who belong to any organized belief, for they all have been conditioned to a world of leaders, saviours, guides and examples; and when you follow another you are seeking the fulfilment of your own ambition, whether in this world or in the world of ideation, the so-called spiritual world. Competitiveness, ambition, implies conflict, does it not?

"I see that, but what is one to do? Being caught in this net of competition, how is one to get out of it? And even if one does get out of it, what assurance is there that there will be peace between man and man? Unless all of us see the truth of the matter at the same time, the perception of that truth by óne or two will have no value whatever."

You want to know how to get out of this net of conflict, fulfilment, frustration. The very question 'how?' implies that you want to be assured that your endeavour will not be in vain. You still want to succeed, only at a different level. You do not see that all ambition, all desire for success in any direction, creates conflict both within and without. The 'how?' is the way of ambition and conflict, and that very question prevents you from seeing the truth of the problem. The 'how?' is the ladder to further success. But we are not now thinking in terms of success or failure, rather in terms of the elimination of conflict; and does it follow that without conflict, stagnation is inevitable? Surely, peace comes into being, not through safeguards, sanctions and guarantees, but it is there when *you* are not—you who are the agent of conflict with your ambitions and frustrations.

Your other point, sir, that all must see the truth of this problem at the same time, is an obvious impossibility. But it is possible for *you* to see it; and when you do, that truth which you have seen, and which brings freedom, will affect others. It must begin with you, for you are the world, as the other is.

Ambition breeds mediocrity of mind and heart; ambition is superficial, for it is everlastingly seeking a result. The man who wants to be a saint, or a successful politician, or a big executive, is concerned with personal achievement. Whether identified with an idea, a nation, or a system, religious or economic, the urge to be successful strengthens the ego, the self, whose very structure is brittle, superficial and limited. All this is fairly obvious if one looks into it, is it not?

"It may be obvious to you, sir, but to most of us conflict gives a sense of existence, the feeling that we are alive. Without ambition and competition, our lives would be drab and useless."

Since you are maintaining this competitive way of life, your children and your children's children will breed further antagonism, envy and war; neither you nor they will have peace. Having been conditioned to this traditional pattern of existence, you are in turn educating your children to accept it; so the world goes on in this sorrowful way.

"We want to change, but . . ." He was aware of his own futility and stopped talking.

MEDITATION—EFFORT—CONSCIOUSNESS

THE SEA WAS beyond the mountains to the east of the valley, and through the centre of the valley a river made its way leisurely to the sea. The river flowed full all the year round, and it was beautiful even where it passed by the town, which was quite large. The townspeople used the river for everything—for fishing, for bathing, for drinking water, for sewage disposal, and the wastes of a factory went into it. But the river threw off all the filth of man, and its waters were once again clear and blue soon after it had passed his habitations.

A wide road went along the river to the west, leading up to tea plantations in the mountains; it curved in and out, sometimes losing the river, but most of the time in sight of it. As the road climbed, following the river, the plantations became bigger, and here and there were factories to dry and process the tea. Soon the estates became vast, and the river was noisy with waterfalls. In the morning one would see brightly-dressed women, their bodies bent, their skin turned dark by the blazing sun, picking the delicate leaves of the tea bushes. It all had to be picked before a certain time in the morning and carried to the nearest factory before the sun became too hot. At that altitude the sun was strong and painfully penetrating, and though they were used to it, some of the women had their heads covered with part of the cloth they wore. They were gay, fast and skilful in their work, and soon that particular task would be over for the day; but most of them were wives and mothers, and they would still have to cook and look after the children. They had a union, and the planters treated them decently, for it would be disastrous to have a strike and allow the tender leaves to grow to their normal size.

The road continued up and up, and the air became quite cold. At eight thousand feet there were no more tea plantations, but men were working the soil and cultivating many things to be sent down to the towns along the sea. From that altitude the view over the forests and plains was magnificent, with the river, silver now, dominating everything. Going back another way, the road wound through green, sparkling rice-fields and deep woods. There were many palms and mangoes, and flowers were everywhere. The people were cheerful, and along the roadside they were setting out many things, from trinkets to luscious fruit. They were lazy and easy-going, and seemed to have enough to eat, unlike those in the lowland, where life was hard, meagre and crowded.

He was a *sannyasi,* a monk, but not of any particular order, and he spoke of himself as of a third person. While still young he had renounced the world and its ways and had wandered all over the country, staying with some of the well-known religious teachers, talking with them and following their peculiar disciplines and rituals. He had fasted for many a day, lived in solitude among the mountains, and done most of the things that *sannyasis* are supposed to do. He had damaged himself physically through excessive ascetic practices, and although that was long ago, his body still suffered from it. Then one day he had decided to abandon all these practices, rituals and disciplines as being vain and without much significance, and had gone off into some far-away mountain village, where he had spent many years in deep contemplation. The usual thing had happened, he said with a smile, and he in his turn had become well-known and had had a large following of disciples to whom he taught simple things. He had read the ancient Sanskrit literature, and now that too he had put away. Although it was necessary to describe briefly what his life had been, he added, that was not the thing for which he had come.

"Above all virtue, sacrifice, and the action of dispassionate help, is meditation," he stated. "Without meditation, knowledge and action become a wearisome burden with very little meaning; but few know what meditation is. If you are willing, we must talk this over. In meditation it has been the experience of the speaker to reach different states of consciousness; he has had the experiences that all aspiring human beings sooner or later go through, the visions embodying Krishna, Christ, Buddha. They are the outcome of one's own thought and education, and of what may be called one's culture. There are visions, experiences and powers of many different varieties. Unfortunately, most seekers are caught in the net of their own thought and desire, even some of the greatest exponents of truth. Having the power of healing and the gift of words, they become prisoners to their own capacities and experiences. The speaker himself has passed through these experiences and dangers, and to the best of his ability has understood and gone beyond them—at least, let us hope so. What then is meditation?"

Surely, in considering meditation, effort and the maker of effort must be understood. Good effort leads to one thing, and bad to another, but both are binding, are they not?

"It is said that you have not read the *Upanishads* or any of the sacred literature, but you sound like one who has read and knows."

It is true that I have read none of those things, but that is not important. Good effort and wrong effort are both binding, and it is this bondage that must be understood and broken. Meditation is the breaking of all bondage; it is a state of freedom, but not *from* anything. Freedom *from* something is only the cultivation of resistance. To be conscious of being free is not freedom. Consciousness is the experiencing of freedom or of bondage, and that consciousness is the experiencer, the maker of effort. Meditation is the breaking down of the experiencer, which cannot be done consciously. If the experiencer is broken down consciously, then there is a strengthening of the will, which is also a part of consciousness. Our problem, then, is concerned with the whole process of consciousness, and not with one part of it, small or great, dominant or subservient.

"What you say seems to be true. The ways of consciousness are profound, deceptive and contradictory. It is only through dispassionate observation and careful study that this tangle can be unravelled and order can prevail."

But, sir, the unraveller is still there; one may call him the higher self, the *atman,* and so on, but he is still part of consciousness, the maker of effort who is everlastingly trying to get somewhere. Effort is desire. One desire can be overcome by a greater desire, and that desire by still another, and so on endlessly. Desire breeds deception, illusion, contradiction, and the visions of hope. The all-conquering desire for the ultimate, or the will to reach that which is nameless, is still the way of consciousness, of the experiencer of good and bad, the experiencer who is waiting, watching, hoping. Consciousness is not of one particular level, it is the totality of our being.

"What has been heard so far is excellent and true; but if one may inquire, what is it that will bring peace, stillness to this consciousness?"

Nothing. Surely, the mind is ever seeking a result, a way to some achievement. Mind is an instrument that has been put together, it is the fabric of time, and it can only think in terms of result, of achievement, of something to be gained or avoided.

"That is so. It is being stated that as long as the mind is active, choosing, seeking, experiencing, there must be the maker of effort who creates his own image, calling it by different names, and this is the net in which thought is caught."

Thought itself is the maker of the net; thought is the net. Thought is binding; thought can only lead to the vast expanse of time, the field in which knowledge, action, virtue, have importance. However refined or simplified, thinking cannot break down all thought. Consciousness as the experiencer, the observer, the chooser, the censor, the will, must come to an end, voluntarily and happily, without any hope of reward. The seeker ceases. This is meditation. Silence of the mind cannot be brought about through the action of will. There is silence when will ceases. This is meditation. Reality cannot be sought; it is when the seeker is not. Mind is time, and thought cannot uncover the measureless.

PSYCHO-ANALYSIS AND THE HUMAN PROBLEM

THE BIRDS AND the goats were all somewhere else, and it was strangely quiet and far away under the wide-spreading tree which stood alone in an expanse of fields, well-cultivated and richly green. The hills were at some distance, harsh and uninviting in the mid-day sun, but under the tree it was dark, cool and pleasant. This tree, huge and impressive, had gathered great strength and symmetry in its solitude. It was a vital thing, alone, and yet it seemed to dominate all its surroundings, even the distant hills. The villagers worshipped it; against its vast trunk there was a carved stone on which someone had placed bright yellow flowers. In the evening no one came to the tree; its solitude was too overpowering, and it was better to worship it during the day when there were rich shadows, chattering birds, and the sound of human voices. But at this hour all the villagers were around their huts, and under the tree it was very peaceful. The sun never penetrated to the base of the tree, and the flowers would last till the next day, when new offerings would be made. A narrow path led to the tree, and then continued on through the green fields. The goats were carefully herded along this path until they were near the hills, and then they ran wild, eating everything within reach. The full glory of the tree was towards evening. As the sun set behind the hills, the fields became more intensely green, and only the top of the tree caught the last rays, golden and transparent. With the coming of darkness the tree appeared to withdraw from all its surroundings and close upon itself for the night; its mystery seemed to grow, entering into the mystery of all things.

A psychologist and an analyst, he had been in practice for a number of years and had many cures to his credit. He worked in a hospital as well as in his private office. His many prosperous patients had made him prosperous too, with expensive cars, a country house, and all the rest of it. He took his work seriously, it was not just a money-making affair, and he used different methods of analysis depending upon the patient. He had studied mesmerism, and tentatively practised hypnosis on some of his patients.

"It is a very curious thing," he said, "how, during the hypnotic state, people will freely and easily speak of their hidden compulsions and responses, and every time a patient is put under hypnosis I feel the strangeness of it. I have myself been scrupulously honest, but I am fully aware of the grave dangers of hypnotism, especially in the hands of unscrupulous people, medical or otherwise. Hypnosis may or may not be a short cut, and I don't feel it is justified except in certain stubborn cases. It takes a long period to cure a patient, generally several months, and it is a pretty tiring business.

"Some time ago," he went on, "a patient whom I had been treating for a number of months came to see me. By no means a stupid woman, she was well-read and had wide interests; and with considerable excitement and a smile which I had not seen for a long time, she told me that she had been persuaded by a friend to attend some of your talks. It appeared that during the talks she felt herself being released from her depressions, which were rather serious. She said that the first talk had quite bewildered her. The thoughts and the words were new to her and seemed contradictory, and she did not want to attend the second talk; but her friend explained that this often happened, and that she should listen to several talks before making up her mind. She finally went to all of them, and as I say, she felt a sense of release. What you said seemed to touch certain points in her consciousness, and without making any effort to be free from her frustrations and depressions, she found that they were gone; they had simply ceased to exist. This was some months ago. I saw her again the other day, and those depressions have certainly cleared up; she is normal and happy, especially in her relationship with her family, and things seem to be all right.

"This is all just preliminary," he continued. "You see, thanks to this patient, I have read some of your teachings, and what I really want to talk over with you is this: is there a way or a method by which we can quickly get at the root of all this human misery? Our present techniques take time and require a considerable amount of patient investigation."

Sir, if one may ask, what is it that you are trying to do with your patients?

"Stated simply, without psycho-analytical jargon, we try to help them to overcome their difficulties, depressions, and so on, in order that they may fit into society."

Do you think it is very important to help people to fit into this corrupt society?

"It may be corrupt, but the reformation of society is not our business. Our business is to help the patient to adjust himself to his surroundings and be a more happy and useful citizen. We are dealing with abnormal cases and are not trying to create supernormal people. I don't think that is our function."

Do you think you can separate yourself from your function? If I may ask, is it not also your function to bring about a totally new order, a world in which there will be no wars, no antagonism, no urge to compete, and so on? Do not all these urges and compulsions bring about a social environment which develops abnormal people? If one is only concerned with helping the individual to conform to the existing social pattern, here or elsewhere, is one not maintaining the very causes that make for frustration, misery and destruction?

"There is certainly something in what you say, but as analysts I don't think we are prepared to go so deeply into the whole causation of human misery."

Then it seems, sir, that you are concerned, not with the total development of man, but only with one particular part of his total consciousness. Healing a certain part may be necessary, but without understanding the total process of man, we may cause other forms of disease. Surely, this is not a matter for argumentation or speculation; it is an obvious fact that must be taken into consideration, not merely by specialists, but by each one of us.

"You are leading into very deep issues to which I am not accustomed, and I find myself beyond my depth. I have thought only vaguely about these things, and about what we are actually trying to accomplish with our patients apart from the usual procedure. You see, most of us have neither the inclination nor the necessary time to study all this; but I suppose we really ought to if we want to free ourselves and help our patients to be free from the confusion and misery of the present western civilization."

The confusion and misery are not only in the West, for human beings the world over are in the same plight. The problem of the individual is also the world's problem, they are not two separate and distinct processes. We are concerned, surely, with the human problem, whether the human being is in the Orient or in the Occident, which is an arbitrary geographical division. The whole consciousness of man is concerned with God, with death, with right and happy livelihood, with children and their education, with war and peace. Without understanding all this, there can be no healing of man.

"You are right, sir, but I think very few of us are capable of such wide and deep investigation. Most of us are educated wrongly. We become specialists, technicians, which has its uses, but unfortunately that is the end of us. Whether his speciality is the heart or the complex, each specialist builds his own little heaven, as the priest does, and though he may occasionally read something on the side, there he remains till he dies. You are right, but there it is.

"Now, sir, I would like to return to my question: is there a method or technique by which we can go directly to the root of our miseries, especially those of the patient, and thereby eradicate them quickly?"

Again, if one may ask, why are you always thinking in terms of methods and techniques? Can a method or technique set man free, or will it merely shape him to a desired end? And the desired end, being the opposite of man's anxieties, fears, frustrations, pressures, is itself the outcome of these. The reaction of the opposite is not true action, either in the economic or the psychological world. Apart from technique or method, there may be a factor which will really help man.

"What is that?"

Perhaps it is love.

CLEANSED OF THE PAST

A WELL-KEPT ROAD led up to the foot of the hill, and a path continued from there. On top of the hill were the ruins of a very ancient stronghold. Thousands of years ago it was a formidable place, a fortress of gigantic rocks, of proud pillared halls with mosaic floors, of marble baths and chambers. The closer one approached this citadel, the higher and thicker its walls became, and the more vigorously it must have been defended; yet it was conquered, destroyed, and built again. The outer walls were made of enormous blocks of rock placed one on top of the other without any mortar to bind them. Within the walls there was an ancient well, many feet deep, with steps leading down to it. The steps were smooth and slippery, and the sides of the well were glistening with moisture. It was all in ruins now, but the marvellous view from the top of the hill remained. Away to the left was the sparkling sea, bordering wide open plains with hills behind them. In the near distance there were two smaller hills which in those far-off days had also been fortresses, but nothing comparable to this lofty citadel that looked down on these neighbouring hills and on the plains. It was a lovely morning, with the breeze from the sea stirring the bright flowers among the ruins. These flowers were very beautiful, their colours rich and deep, and they grew in extraordinary places, on rocks, in the crevices of broken walls, and in the courtyards. They had grown there, wild and free, for untold centuries, and it seemed a sacrilege to tread on them, for they crowded the path; it was their world, and we were strangers, but they did not make one feel that way.

The view from this hilltop was not breath-taking, like those which are seen occasionally, and which obliterate consciousness with grandeur and silence. Here it was not like that. Here there was peaceful enchantment, gentle and expansive; here you could live timelessly, without a past and a future, for you were one with this whole rapturous world. You were not a human being, a stranger from a different land, but you were those hills, those goats, and the goatherd. You were the sky and the blossoming earth; you were not apart from it, you were of it. But you were not conscious that you were of it, any more than those flowers were. You *were* those smiling fields, the blue sea, and the distant train with its passengers. You didn't exist, you who choose, compare, act and seek; you were with everything.

Someone said that it was late and we must be going, so we went down the path on the other side of the hill, and then along the road leading to the sea.

We were sitting under a tree, and he was telling how, as a young and middle-aged man, he had worked in different parts of Europe throughout the two world wars. During the last one he had no home, often went hungry, and was nearly shot for something or other by this or that conquering army. He had spent sleepless and tortured nights in prison, for in his wanderings he had lost his passport, and none would believe his simple statement as to where he was born and to what country he belonged. He spoke several languages, had been an engineer, then in some sort of business, and was now painting. He now had a passport, he said with a smile, and a place to live.

"There are many like me, people who were destroyed and have come back to life again," he went on. "I don't regret it, but somehow I have lost the intimate contact with life, at least with what one calls life. I am fed up with armies and kings, flags and politics. They have caused as much mischief and sorrow as our official religion, which has shed more blood than any other; not even the Moslem world can compete with us in violence and horror, and now we are all at it again. I used to be very cynical, but that too has passed. I live alone, for my wife and child died during the war, and any country, as long as it is warm, is good enough for me. I don't care much one way or the other, but I sell my paintings now and then, which keeps me going. At times it is rather difficult to make ends meet, but something always turns up, and as my wants are very simple I am not greatly bothered about money. I am a monk at heart, but outside the prison of a monastery. I am telling you all this, not just to ramble on about myself, but to give you a sketch of my background, for in talking things over with you I may get to understand something which has become very vital to me. Nothing else interests me, not even my painting.

"One day I set out for those hills with my painting things, for I had seen something over there which I wanted to paint. It was fairly early in the morning when I got to the place, and there were a few clouds in the sky. From where I was I could see across the valley to the bright sea. I was enchanted to be alone, and began to paint. I must have been painting for some time, and it was coming along beautifully, without any strain or effort, when I became aware that something was taking place inside my head, if I can put it that way. I was so absorbed in my painting that for a while I did not notice what was happening to me, and then suddenly I was aware of it. I could not go on with my painting, but I sat very still." After a moment's pause, he continued.

"Don't think me crazy, for I am not, but sitting there I was aware of an extraordinarily creative energy. It wasn't I that was creative, but something in me, something that was also in those ants and in that restless squirrel. I don't think I am explaining this very well, but surely you understand what I mean. It was not the creativeness of some Tom, Dick or Harry writing a poem, or of myself painting a silly picture; it was just creation, pure and simple, and the things produced by the mind or by the hand were on the outer fringes of this creation, with little significance. I seemed to be bathed in it; there was a sacredness about it, a benediction. If I were to put it in religious words, I would say . . . But I won't. Those religious words stick in my mouth, they no longer have any meaning. It was the centre of Creation, God himself . . . Again these words! But I tell you, it was holy, not the man-made holiness of churches, incense and hymns, which is all immature nonsense. This was something uncontaminated, unthought-of, and tears were rolling down my cheeks; I was being washed clean of all my past. The squirrel had stopped fretting about its next meal, and there was an astonishing silence—not the silence of the night when all things sleep, but a silence in which everything was awake.

"I must have sat there, motionless, for a very long time, for the sun was in the west; I was a little stiff, one leg had gone to sleep, and I could stand up only with difficulty. I am not exaggerating, sir, but time seemed to have stopped—or rather, there was no time. I had no watch, but several hours must have passed from the moment I put my brush down to the moment I got up. I was not hysterical, nor had I been unconscious, as some might conclude; on the contrary, I was fully alert, aware of everything that was happening around me. Picking up all my things and carefully putting them in my knapsack, I left, and in that extraordinary state I walked back to my house. All the noises of a small town did not in any way disturb that state, and it lasted for several hours after I got home. When I awoke the next morning, it was completely gone. I looked at my painting; it was good, but nothing outstanding.

"Sorry to have talked so long," he concluded, "but it has been bottled up in me, and I could not have talked to anyone else. If I did, they would call in a priest, or suggest one of those analysts. Now I am not asking for an explanation, but how does this thing come into being? What are the circumstances necessary for it to be?"

You are asking this question because you want to experience it again, are you not?

"I suppose that is the motive behind my question, but . . ."

Please, let us go on from there. What is important is not that it happened, but that you should not go after it. Greed breeds arrogance, and what is necessary is humility. You cannot cultivate humility; if you do, it is no longer humility but another acquisition. It is important, not that you should have another such experience, but that there should be innocence, freedom from the memory of experience, good or bad, pleasant or painful.

"Good Lord, you are telling me to forget something which has become of total importance to me. You are asking the impossible. I cannot forget it, nor do I want to."

Yes, sir, that is the difficulty. Please listen with patience and insight. What have you now? A dead memory. While it was happening it was a living thing and there was no 'me' to experience that living thing, no memory clinging to what had been. Your mind was then in a state of innocency, without seeking, asking, or holding; it was free. But now you are seeking and clinging to the dead past. Oh, yes, it is dead; your remembrance has destroyed it and is creating the conflict of duality, the conflict between what has been and what you hope for. Conflict is death, and you are living with darkness. This thing does happen when the self is absent; but the memory of it, the craving for more, strengthens the self and prevents the living reality.

"Then how am I to wipe away this exciting memory?"

Again, your very question indicates the desire to recapture that state, does it not? You want to wipe away the memory of that state in order to experience it further, so craving still remains, though you are willing to forget what has been. Your craving for that extraordinary state is similar to that of a man who is addicted to drink or to a drug. What is all-important is not the further experiencing of that reality, but that this craving should be understood and should voluntarily dissolve without resistance, without the action of will.

"Do you mean that the very remembering of that state, and my intense urge to experience it again, are preventing something of a similar or perhaps a different nature from happening? Must I do nothing, consciously or unconsciously, to bring it about?"

If you really understand, that is so.

"You are asking an almost impossible thing, but one never knows."

AUTHORITY AND CO-OPERATION

SHE HAD BEEN secretary to a big business executive, she explained, and had worked with him for many years. She must have been very efficient, for it showed in her bearing and in her words. Having put away some money, she had given up that job a couple of years ago because she desired to help the world. Still quite young and vigorous, she wanted to devote the rest of her years to something worth while, so she considered the various spiritual organizations. Before going to college she had been educated in a convent, but the things they had taught her there now seemed limited, dogmatic and authoritarian, and naturally she could not belong to such a religious institution. After studying several others, she had at last landed in one which seemed to be broader and have greater significance than most, and now she was active at the very centre of that organization, helping one of its chief workers.

"At last I have found something that gives a satisfactory explanation of the whole business of existence," she went on. "Of course they have their authority in the Masters, but one doesn't have to believe in them. I happen to, but that is neither here nor there. I belong to the inner group, and as you know, we practise certain forms of meditation. Very few are now told of their initiation by the Masters, not as many as before. They are more cautious these days."

If one may ask, why are you explaining all this?

"I was present at your discussion the other afternoon when it was stated that all following is evil. I have since attended several more of these discussions, and naturally I am disturbed by all that was said. You see, working for the Masters does not necessarily mean following them. There is authority, but it is we who need authority. They do not ask obedience of us, but we give it to them, or to their representatives."

If, as you say, you took part in the discussions, don't you think that what you are saying now is rather immature? Taking shelter in the Masters or in their representatives, whose authority must be based on their own self-chosen duty and pleasure, is essentially the same as taking shelter in the authority of the church, is it not? One may be considered narrow and the other wide, but both are obviously binding. When one is confused one seeks guidance, but that which one finds will invariably be the outcome of one's own confusion. The leader is as confused as the follower who, out of his conflict and misery, has chosen the leader. Following another, whether it be a leader, a saviour, or a Master, does not bring about clarity and happiness. Only with the understanding of confusion and the maker of it, is there freedom from conflict and misery. This seems fairly obvious, does it not?

"It may be to you, sir, but I still don't understand. We need to work along the right lines, and those who know can and do lay down certain plans for our guidance. This does not imply blind following."

There is no enlightened following; all following is evil. Authority corrupts, whether in high places or among the thoughtless. The thoughtless are not made thoughtful by following another, however great and noble he may be.

"I like co-operating with my friends in working for something which has world-wide significance. To work together, we need some kind of authority over us."

Is it co-operation when there is the compelling influence, pleasant or unpleasant, of authority? Is it co-operation when you are working for a plan laid down by another? Are you not then consciously or unconsciously conforming through fear, through hope of reward, and so on? And is conformity co-operation? When there is authority over you, benevolent or tyrannical, can there be co-operation? Surely, co-operation comes into being only when there is the love of the thing for itself without the fear of punishment or failure, and without the hunger for success or recognition. Co-operation is possible only when there is freedom from envy, acquisitiveness, and from the craving for personal or collective dominance, power.

"Aren't you much too drastic in these matters? Nothing would ever be achieved if we were to wait until we had freed ourselves from all those inward causes which are obviously evil."

But what are you achieving now? There must be deep earnestness and inward revolution if there is to be a different world; there must be at least some who are not consciously or unconsciously perpetuating conflict and misery. Personal ambition, and ambition for the collective, must drop away, for ambition in any form prevents love.

"I am too disturbed by all that you have said, and I hope I may come back another day when I am a little more calm."

She came back many days later.

"After I had seen you I went away by myself to think all this over objectively and clearly, and I spent several sleepless nights. My friends warned me not to be too disturbed by what you said, but I was disturbed, and I had to settle certain things for myself. I have been reading some of your talks more thoughtfully, without putting up resistance, and things are becoming clear. There is no going back, and I am not dramatizing. I have resigned from the organization, with all that it means. My friends are naturally upset, and they think I will come back; but I am afraid not. I have done this because I see the truth of what has been said. We shall see what happens now."

MEDIOCRITY

THE STORM HAD lasted for several days, with high winds and torrential rains. The earth was soaking up the water, and the dust of many summers was being washed from the trees. In this part of the country it hadn't really rained for several years, but now it was making up for it, at least everyone hoped so, and there was gladness in the noise of the rain and the running waters. It was still raining when we all went to bed, and the patter of rain was very strong on the roof. It had a rhythm, a dance, and there was the murmur of many streams. Then what a lovely morning it was! The clouds were gone, and the hills all around were sparkling in the early-morning sun; they had all been washed clean, and there was a benediction in the air. Nothing was yet stirring, and only the high hilltops were aglow. In a few minutes the noises of the day would begin; but now there was a deep peace in the valley, though the streams were gurgling and far away a cock had begun to crow. All the colours had come to life; everything was so vivid, the new grass and that enormous tree which seemed to dominate the valley. There was new life with abundance, and now the gods would receive their offering, gladly and freely given; now the fields would be made rich for the coming rice, and there would be no lack of fodder for the cows and the goats; now the wells would be full, and marriages could be performed with gladness. The earth was red, and there would be rejoicing.

"I am well aware of the state of my mind," he explained. "I have been to college and received a so-called education, and I have read fairly extensively. Politically I have been of the extreme left, and I am quite familiar with their literature. The party has become like any organized religion; it is what Catholicism was and continues to be, with the excommunications, the threats and deprivations. For a time I worked ambitiously in

179

politics, hoping for a better world; but I have seen through that game, though I could have gone ahead in it. Long ago I saw that real reformation doesn't come through politics; politics and religion don't mix. I know it is the thing to say that we must bring religion into politics; but the moment we do, it is no longer religion, it becomes just nonsense. God doesn't talk to us in political terms, but we make our own god in terms of our politics or economic conditioning.

"But I haven't come to talk politics with you, and you are quite right to refuse to discuss it. I have come to talk over something that is really eating me up. The other evening you said something about mediocrity. I listened but couldn't take it in, for I was too disturbed; but as you were talking, that word 'mediocrity' struck me very forcibly. I had never thought of myself as being mediocre. I am not using that word in the social sense, and as you pointed out, it has nothing to do with class and economic differences, or with birth."

Of course. Mediocrity is entirely outside the field of arbitrary social divisions.

"I see it is. You also said, if I remember rightly, that the truly religious person is the only revolutionary, and such a person is not mediocre. I am talking of the mediocrity of the mind, not of job or position. Those who are in the highest and most powerful positions, and those who have marvellously interesting occupations, may still be mediocre. I have neither an exalted position nor a particularly interesting occupation, and I am aware of the state of my own mind. It is just mediocre. I am a student of both western and eastern philosophy, and am interested in many other things, but in spite of this my mind is quite ordinary; it has some capacity for co-ordinated thinking, but it is still mediocre and uncreative."

Then what is the problem, sir?

"First, I am really quite ashamed of the state I am in, of my own utter stupidity, and I am saying this without any self-pity. Deep down in myself, in spite of all my learning, I find that I am not creative in the most profound sense of that word. It must be possible to have that creativeness of which you spoke the other day; but how is one to set about it? Is this too blunt a question?"

Can we think of this problem very simply? What is it that makes the mind-heart mediocre? One may have encyclopaedic knowledge, great capacity, and so on; but beyond all these superficial acquisitions and gifts, what makes the mind deeply stupid? Can the mind be, at any time, other than what it has always been?

"I am beginning to see that the mind, however clever, however capable, can also be stupid. It cannot be made into something else, for it will always be what it is. It may be infinitely capable of reasoning, speculation, design, calculation; but however expansible, it will always remain in the same field. I have just caught the significance of your question. You are asking whether the mind, which is capable of such astonishing feats, can transcend itself by its own will and effort."

That is one of the questions that arise. If, however clever and capable, the mind is still mediocre, can it through its own volition ever go beyond itself? Mere condemnation of mediocrity, with its wide scope of eccentricities, will in no way alter the fact. And when condemnation, with all its implications, has ceased, is it possible to find out what it is that brings about the state of mediocrity? We now understand the significance of that word, so let us stick to it. Is not one of the factors of mediocrity the urge to achieve, to have a result, to succeed? And when we want to become creative, we are still dealing with the matter superficially, are we not? I am *this*, which I want to change into *that*, so I ask how; but when creativeness is something to be striven after, a result to be achieved, the mind has reduced it to its own condition. This is the process that we have to understand, and not attempt to change mediocrity into something else.

"Do you mean that any effort on the part of the mind to change what it is, merely leads to the continuation of itself in another form, and so there is no change at all?"

That is so, is it not? The mind has brought about its present state through its own effort, through its desires and fears, through its hopes, joys and pains; and any attempt on its part to change that state is still in the same direction. A petty mind trying *not* to be, is still petty. Surely, the problem is the cessation of all effort on the part of the mind to be something, in whatever direction.

"Of course. But this does not imply negation, a state of vacuity, does it?"

If one merely hears the words without catching their significance, without experimenting and experiencing, then conclusions have no validity.

"So creativeness is not to be striven after. It is not to be learnt, practised, or brought about through any action, through any form of compulsion. I see the truth of that. If I may, I shall think aloud and slowly work this out with you. My mind, which has been ashamed of its mediocrity, is now aware of the significance of condemnation. This condemnatory attitude is brought about by the desire to change; but this very desire to change is the outcome of pettiness, so the mind is still what it was and there has been no change at all. So far I have understood."

What is the state of the mind when it is not attempting to change itself, to become something?

"It accepts what it is."

Acceptance implies that there is an entity who accepts, does it not? And is not this acceptance also a form of effort in order to gain, to experience further? So a conflict of duality is set going, which is again the same problem, for it is conflict that breeds mediocrity of mind and heart. Freedom from mediocrity is that state which comes into being when all conflict has ceased; but acceptance is merely resignation. Or has that word 'acceptance' a different meaning to you?

"I can see the implications of acceptance, since you have given me an insight into its significance. But what is the state of the mind which no longer accepts or condemns?"

Why do you ask, sir? It is a thing to be discovered, not merely to be explained.

"I am not seeking an explanation or being speculative, but is it possible for the mind to be still, without any movement, and yet be unaware of its own stillness?"

To be aware of it breeds the conflict of duality, does it not?

THE PATH WAS rough and dusty, and it led down to a small town below. A few trees remained scattered on the hillside, but most of them had been cut down for firewood, and one had to climb to a good height to find rich shade. Up there the trees were no longer scrubby and mauled by man; they grew to full height, with thick branches and normal foliage. The people would cut down a branch to allow their goats to eat the leaves, and when it was bare they would reduce it to firewood. There was a scarcity of wood at the lower levels, and now they were going higher, climbing and destroying. Rains were not as plentiful as they used to be; the population was increasing, and the people had to live. There was hunger, and one lived as indifferently as one died. There were no wild animals about here, and they must have gone higher up. There were a few birds scratching among the bushes, but even they looked worn out, with some feathers broken. A jay, white and black, was scolding raucously, flying from limb to limb of a solitary tree.

It was getting warm, and it would be very hot by mid-day. There had not been enough rain for many years. The earth was parched and cracked, the few trees were covered with brown dust, and there was not even the morning dew. The sun was relentless, day after day, month in and month out, and the doubtful rainy season was still far away. Some goats went up the hill, with a boy looking after them. He was surprised to see anyone there, but he wouldn't smile, and with a grave look he followed the goats. It was a lonely place, and there was the silence of the coming heat.

Two women came down the path carrying firewood on their heads. One was old and the other quite young, and the burdens they carried looked rather heavy. Each had balanced on her head, protected by a roll of cloth, a long bundle of dried branches tied together with a green vine, and she held it in place with one hand. Their bodies swung freely as they came down the hill with a light, running gait. They had nothing on their feet, though the path was rough. The feet seemed to find their own way, for the women never looked down; they held their heads very straight, their eyes bloodshot and distant. They were very thin, their ribs showing, and the older woman's hair was matted and unwashed. The girl's hair must have been combed and oiled at one time, for there were still some clean, sparkling strands; but she too was exhausted, and there was a weariness about her. Not long ago she must have sung and played with other children, but that was all over. Now, collecting wood among these hills was her life, and would be till she died, with a respite now and then with the coming of a child.

Down the path we all went. The small country town was several miles away, and there they would sell their burden for a pittance, only to begin again tomorrow. They were chatting, with long intervals of silence. Suddenly the younger one told her mother she was hungry, and the mother replied that they were born with hunger, lived with hunger, and died with hunger; that was their lot. It was the statement of a fact; in her voice there was no reproach, no anger, no hope. We continued down that stony path. There was no observer listening, pitying, and walking behind them. He was not part of them out of love and pity; he *was* them; he had ceased and they were. They were not the strangers he had met up the hill, they were of him; his were the hands that held the bundles; and the sweat, the exhaustion, the smell, the hunger, were not theirs, to be shared and sorrowed over. Time and space had ceased. There were no thoughts in our heads, too tired to think; and if we did think, it was to sell the wood, eat, rest, and begin again. The feet on the stony path never hurt, nor the sun overhead. There were only two of us going down that accustomed hill, past that well where we drank as usual, and on across the dry bed of a remembered stream.

"I have read and listened to some of your talks," he said, "and to me, what you say appears very negative; there is in it no directive, no positive way of life. This oriental outlook is most destructive, and look where it has landed the Orient. Your negative attitude, and especially your insistence that there must be freedom from all thought, is very misleading to us westerners, who are active and industrious by temperament and necessity. What you are teaching is altogether contrary to our way of life."

If one may point out, this division of people as of the West or of the East is geographic and arbitrary, is it not? It has no fundamental significance. Whether we live east or west of a certain line, whether we are brown, black, white, or yellow, we are all human beings, suffering and hoping, fearful and believing; joy and pain exist here as they exist there. Thought is not of the West or of the East, but man divides it according to his conditioning. Love is not geographic, held as sacred on one continent and denied on another. The division of human beings is for economic and exploiting purposes. This does not mean that individuals are not different in temperament, and so on; there is similarity, and yet there is difference. All this is fairly obvious and psychologically factual, is it not?

"It may be to you, but our culture, our way of life, is entirely different from that of the East. Our scientific knowledge, slowly developing since the days of ancient Greece, is now immense. East and West are developing along two different lines."

Seeing the difference, we must yet be aware of the similarity. The outward expressions may and do vary, but behind these outward forms and manifestations the urges, compulsions, longings and fears are similar. Do not let us be deceived by words. Both here and there, man wants to have peace and plenty, and to find something more than material happiness. Civilizations may vary according to climate, environment, food, and so on, but culture throughout the world is fundamentally the same: to be compassionate, to shun evil, to be generous, not to be envious, to forgive, and so on. Without this fundamental culture, any civilization, whether here or there, will disintegrate or be destroyed. Knowledge may be acquired by the so-called backward peoples, they can very soon learn the 'know-how' of the West; they too can be war-mongers, generals, lawyers, policemen, tyrants, with concentration camps and all the rest of it. But culture is an entirely different matter. The love of God and the freedom of man are not so easily come by, and without these, material welfare doesn't mean much.

"You are right in that, sir, but I wish you would consider what I said about your teachings being negative. I really would like to understand them, and don't think me rude if I appear somewhat direct in my statements."

What is negative and what is positive? Most of us are used to being told what to do. The giving and following of directions is considered to be positive teaching. To be led appears to be positive, constructive, and to those who are conditioned to follow, the truth that following is evil seems negative, destructive. Truth is the negation of the false, not the opposite of the false. Truth is entirely different from the positive and the negative, and a mind which thinks in terms of the opposites can never be aware of it.

"I am afraid I do not fully understand all this. Would you please explain a little more?"

You see, sir, we are used to authority and guidance. The urge to be guided springs from the desire to be secure, to be protected, and also from the desire to be successful. This is one of our deeper urges, is it not?

"I think it is, but without protection and security, man would . . . "

Please, let us go into the matter and not jump to conclusions. In our urge to be secure, not only as individuals, but as groups, nations and races, have we not built a world in which war, within and outside of a particular society, has become the major concern?

"I know; my son was killed in a war across the seas."

Peace is a state of mind; it is the freedom from all desire to be secure. The mind-heart that seeks security must always be in the shadow of fear. Our desire is not only for material security, but much more for inner, psychological security, and it is this desire to be inwardly secure through virtue, through belief, through a nation, that creates limiting and so conflicting groups and ideas. This desire to be secure, to reach a coveted end, breeds the acceptance of direction, the following of example, the worship of success, the authority of leaders, saviours, Masters, *gurus,* all of which is called positive teaching; but it is really thoughtlessness and imitation.

"I see that; but is it not possible to direct or be directed without making oneself or another into an authority, a saviour?"

We are trying to understand the urge to be directed, are we not? What is this urge? Is it not the outcome of fear? Being insecure, seeing impermanency about one, there is the urge to find something secure, permanent; but this urge is the impulse of fear. Instead of understanding what fear is, we run away from it, and the very running away is fear. One takes flight into the known, the known being beliefs, rituals, patriotism, the comforting formulas of religious teachers, the reassurances of priests, and so on. These in turn bring conflict between man and man, so the problem is kept going from one generation to another. If one would solve the problem, one must explore and understand the root of it. This so-called positive teaching, the what-to-think of religions, including Communism, gives continuity to fear; so positive teaching is destructive.

"I think I am beginning to see what your approach is, and I hope my perception is correct."

It is not a personal, opinionated approach; there is no personal approach to truth, any more than there is to the discovery of scientific facts. The idea that there are separate paths to truth, that truth has different aspects, is unreal; it is the speculative thought of the intolerant trying to be tolerant.

"One has to be very careful, I see, in the use of words. But I would like, if I may, to go back to a point which I raised earlier. Since most of us have been educated to think—or have been taught *what* to think, as you put it—, will it not bring us only more confusion when you keep on saying in different ways that all thought is conditioned and that one. must go beyond all thought?"

To most of us, thinking is extraordinarily important; but is it? It has a certain importance, but thought cannot find that which is not the product of thought. Thought is the result of the known, therefore it cannot fathom the unknown, the unknowable. Is not thought desire, desire for material necessities, or for the highest spiritual goal? We are talking, not about the thought of a scientist at work in the laboratory, or the thought of an absorbed mathematician, and so on, but about thought as it operates in our daily life, in our everyday contacts and responses. To survive, we are forced to think. Thinking is a process of survival, whether of the individual or of a nation. Thinking, which is desire in both its lowest and its highest form, must ever be self-enclosing, conditioning. Whether we think of the universe, of our neighbour, of ourselves, or of God, all our thinking is limited, conditioned, is it not?

"In the sense you are using that word 'thinking', I suppose it is. But does not knowledge help to break down this conditioning?"

Does it? We have accumulated knowledge about so many aspects of life—medicine, war, law, science—and there is at least some knowledge of ourselves, of our own consciousness. With all this vast store of information, are we free from sorrow, war, hate? Will more knowledge free us? One may know that war is inevitable as long as the individual, the group, or the nation is ambitious, seeking power, yet one continues in the ways that lead to war. Can the centre which breeds antagonism, hate, be radically transformed through knowledge? Love is not the opposite of hate; if through knowledge hate is changed to love, then it is not love. This change brought about by thought, by will, is not love, but merely another self-protective convenience.

"I don't follow this at all, if I may say so."

Thought is the response of what has been, the response of memory, is it not? Memory is tradition, experience, and its reaction to any new experience is the outcome of the past; so experience is always strengthening the past. The mind is the result of the past, of time; thought is the product of many yesterdays. When thought seeks to change itself, trying to be or not to be this or that, it merely perpetuates itself under a different name. Being the product of the known, thought can never experience the unknown; being the result of time, it can never understand the timeless, the eternal. Thought must cease for the real to be.

You see, sir, we are so afraid to lose what we think we have, that we never go into these things very deeply. We look at the surface of ourselves and repeat words and phrases that have very little significance; so we remain petty, and breed antagonism as thoughtlessly as we breed children.

"As you said, we are thoughtless in our seeming thoughtfulness. I shall come again, if I may."

HELP

THE STREETS WERE crowded and the shops were full of things. It was the wealthy part of the town, but in the streets were people of every kind, rich and poor, labourers and office workers. There were men and women from all parts of the world, a few in their native costumes, but most of them dressed in western clothes. There were many cars, new and old, and on that spring morning the expensive ones sparkled with chrome and polish, and the people's faces were bright and smiling. The shops too were full of people, and very few seemed to be aware of the blue sky. The shop windows attracted them, the dresses, the shoes, the new cars, and the displays of food. Pigeons were everywhere, moving in and out among the many feet and between the endless cars. There was a bookshop with all the latest books by innumerable authors. The people seemed to have never a care in the world; the war was far away, on another part of the globe. Money, food and work were plentiful, and there was a vast getting and spending. The streets were like canyons between the tall buildings, and there were no trees. It was noisy; there was the strange restlessness of a people who had everything and yet nothing.

A huge church stood amidst fashionable shops, and opposite it was an equally big bank; both were imposing and apparently necessary. In the vast church a priest in surplice and stole was preaching about the One who suffered for the sake of man. The people knelt in prayer; there were candles, idols and incense. The priest intoned and the congregation responded; at last they rose and went out into the sunlit streets and into the shops with

189

their array of things. Now it was silent in the church; only a few remained, lost in their own thoughts. The decorations, the richly coloured windows, the pulpit, the altar and the candles—everything was there to quiet man's mind.

Is God to be found in churches, or in our hearts? The urge to be comforted breeds illusion; it is this urge which creates churches, temples and mosques. We get lost in them, or in the illusion of an omnipotent State, and the real thing goes by. The unimportant becomes all-consuming. Truth, or what you will, cannot be found by the mind; thought cannot go after it; there is no path to it; it cannot be bought through worship, prayer, or sacrifice. If we want comfort, consolation, we shall have it in one way or another; but with it come further pain and misery. The desire for comfort, for security, has the power to create every form of illusion. It is only when the mind is still that there is a possibility of the coming into being of the real.

There were several of us, and B. began by asking whether it is not necessary to have help if we are to understand this whole messy problem of life. Should there not be a guide, an illumined being who can show us the true path?

"Have we not sufficiently gone into all that during these many years?" asked S. "I for one am not seeking a *guru* or a teacher."

"If you are really not seeking help, then why are you here?" insisted B. "Do you mean to say that you have put away all desire for guidance?"

"No, I don't think I have, and I would like to explore this urge to seek guidance or help. I do not now go window-shopping, as it were, running to the various teachers, ancient and modern, as I once did; but I do need help, and I would like to know why. And will there ever be a time when I shall no longer need help?"

"Personally I would not be here if there were no help available from anyone," said M. "I have been helped on previous occasions, and that is why I am here now. Even though you have pointed out the evils of following, sir, I have been helped by you, and I shall continue to come to your talks and discussions as often as I can."

Are we seeking evidence of whether we are being helped or not? A doctor, the smile of a child or of a passer-by, a relationship, a leaf blown by the wind, a change of climate, even a teacher, a *guru*—all these things can help. There is help everywhere for a man who is alert; but many of us are asleep to everything about us except to a particular teacher or book, and that is our problem. You pay attention when I say something, do you not? But when someone else says the same thing, perhaps in different words, you become deaf. You listen to one whom you consider to be the authority, and are not alert when others speak.

"But I have found that what you say generally has significance," replied M., "so I listen to you attentively. When another says something, it is often a mere platitude, a dull response—or perhaps I myself am dull. The point is, it helps me to listen to you, so why shouldn't I? Even if everyone insists that I am merely following you, I shall still come as often as I can manage it."

Why are we open to help from one particular direction, and closed to every other direction? Consciously or unconsciously you may give me your love, your compassion, you may help me to understand my problems; but why do I insist that you are the only source of help, the only saviour? Why do I build you up as my authority? I listen to you, I am attentive to everything you say, but I am indifferent or deaf to the statement of another. Why? Is this not the issue?

"You are not saying that we should not seek help," said L., "but you are asking us why we give importance to the one who helps, making of him our authority. Isn't that it?"

I am also asking why you seek help. When one seeks help, what is the urge behind it? When one consciously, deliberately sets about seeking help, is it help that one wants, or an escape, a consolation? What is it that we are seeking?

"There are many kinds of help," said B. "From the domestic servant to the most eminent surgeon, from the high school teacher to the greatest scientist, they all give some kind of help. In any civilization help is necessary, not only the ordinary kind.

but also the guidance of a spiritual teacher who has attained enlightenment and helps to bring order and peace to man."

Please let us put aside generalities and consider what guidance or help means to each one of us. Does it not mean the resolving of individual difficulties, pains, sorrows? If you are a spiritual teacher, or a doctor, I come to you in order to be shown a happy way of life, or to be cured of some disease. We seek a way of life from the enlightened man, and knowledge or information from the learned. We want to achieve, we want to be successful, we want to be happy, so we look for a pattern of life which will help us to attain what we desire, sacred or profane. After trying many other things, we think of truth as the supreme goal, the ultimate peace and happiness, and we want to attain it; so we are on the lookout to find what we desire. But can desire ever make its way to reality? Does not desire for something, however noble, breed illusion? And as desire acts, does it not set up the structure of authority, imitation and fear? This is the actual psychological process, is it not? And is this help, or self-deception?

"I am having the greatest difficulty not to be persuaded by what you say!" exclaimed B. "I see the reason, the significance of it. But I know you have helped me, and am I to deny that?"

If someone has helped you and you make of him your authority, then are you not preventing all further help, not only from him, but from everything about you? Does not help lie about you everywhere? Why look in only one direction? And when you are so enclosed, so bound, can any help reach you? But when you are open, there is unending help in all things, from the song of a bird to the call of a human being, from the blade of grass to the immensity of the heavens. The poison and corruption begin when you look to one person as your authority, your guide, your saviour. This is so, is it not?

"I think I understand what you are saying," said L., "but my difficulty is this. I have been a follower, a seeker of guidance, for many years. When you point out the deeper significance of following, intellectually I agree with you, but there is a part of me that rebels. Now, how can I integrate this inward contradiction so that I shall no longer follow?"

Two opposing desires or impulses cannot be integrated, and when you introduce a third element, which is the desire for integration, you only complicate the problem, you do not resolve it. But when you see the whole significance of asking help, of following authority, whether it be the authority of another, or of your own self-imposed pattern, then that very perception puts an end to all following.

SILENCE OF THE MIND

BEYOND THE DISTANT haze were the white sands and the cool sea, but here it was insufferably hot, even under the trees and in the house. The sky was no longer blue, and the sun seemed to have absorbed every particle of moisture. The breeze from the sea had stopped, and the mountains behind, clear and close, were reflecting the burning rays of the sun. The restless dog lay panting as though its heart would burst with this intolerable heat. There would·be clear, sunny days, week after week, for many months, and the hills, no longer green and soft with the spring rains, were burnt brown, the earth dry and hard. But there was beauty even now in these hills, shimmering beyond the green oak trees and the golden hay, with the barren rocks of the mountains above them.

The path leading up through the hills to the high mountains was dusty, stony and rough. There were no streams, no sound of running waters. The heat was intense in these hills, but in the shade of some trees along the dry river-bed it was bearable, for here there was a slight breeze coming up the canyon from the valley. From this height the blue of the sea was visible many miles away. It was very quiet, even the birds were still, and a blue jay which had been noisy and quarrelsome was resting now. A brown deer was coming down the path, alert and watchful, making its way to a little pool of water in the otherwise dry bed of the stream; it moved so silently over the rocks, its large ears twitching and its great eyes watching every movement among the bushes. It drank its fill and would have lain down in the shade near the pool, but it must have been aware of the human presence it could not see, for it went uneasily down the path and disappeared. And how difficult it was to watch a coyote, a kind of wild dog, among the hills! It was the same colour as the rocks, and it was doing its best not to be seen. You had to keep your eyes steadily upon it, and even then it disappeared and you could not pick it out again; you looked and looked for any movement, but there was none. Perhaps it might come to the pool. Not too long ago there had been a brutal fire among these hills, and the wild things had gone away; but now some had returned. Across the path a mother quail was leading her new-born chicks, more than a dozen of them; she was softly encouraging, leading them to a thick bush. They were round, yellowish-grey balls of delicate feathers, so new to this dangerous world, but alive and enchanted. There under the bush several had climbed on top of the mother, but most of them were under her comforting wings, resting from the struggles of birth.

What is it that binds us together? It is not our needs. Neither is it commerce and great industries, nor the banks and the churches; these are just ideas and the result of ideas. Ideas do not bind us together. We may come together out of convenience, or through necessity, danger, hate, or worship, but none of these things holds us together. They must all fall away from us, so that we are alone. In this aloneness there is love, and it is love that holds us together.

A preoccupied mind is never a free mind, whether it is preoccupied with the sublime or with the trivial.

He had come from a far-distant land. Though he had had polio, the paralyzing disease, he was now able to walk and drive a car.

"Like so many others, especially those in my condition, I have belonged to different churches and religious organizations," he said, "and none of them has given me any satisfaction; but one never stops seeking. I think I am serious, but one of my difficulties is that I am envious. Most of us are driven by ambition, greed, or envy; they are relentless enemies of man, and yet one cannot seem to be without them. I have tried building various types of resistance against envy, but in spite of all my efforts I get caught up in it again and again; it is like water seeping through the roof, and before I know where I am, I find myself being more intensely envious than ever. You have probably answered this same question dozens of times, but if you have the patience I would like to ask, how is one to extricate oneself from this turmoil of envy?"

You must have found that with the desire not to be envious there comes the conflict of the opposites. The desire or the will not to be *this*, but to be *that*, makes for conflict. We generally consider this conflict to be the natural process of life; but is it? This everlasting struggle between what *is* and what *should* be is considered noble, idealistic; but the desire and the attempt to be non-envious is the same as being envious, is it not? If one really understands this, then there is no battle between the opposites; the conflict of duality ceases. This is not a matter to be thought over when you get home; it is a fact to be seen immediately, and this perception is the important thing, not how to be free from envy. Freedom from envy comes, not through the conflict of its opposite, but with the understanding of what *is;* but this understanding is not possible as long as the mind is concerned with changing what *is*.

"Isn't change necessary?"

Can there be change through an act of will? Is not will concentrated desire? Having bred envy, desire now seeks a state in which there is no envy; both states are the product of desire. Desire cannot bring about fundamental change.

"Then what will?"

Perceiving the truth of what *is*. As long as the mind, or desire, seeks to change itself from *this* to *that*, all change is superficial and trivial. The full significance of this fact must be felt and understood, and only then is it possible for a radical transformation to take place. As long as the mind is comparing, judging, seeking a result, there is no possibility of change, but only a series of unending struggles which it calls living.

"What you say seems so true, but even as I listen to you I find myself caught in the struggle to change, to reach an end, to achieve a result."

The more one struggles against a habit, however deep its roots, the more force one gives to it. To be aware of one habit without choosing and cultivating another, is the ending of habit.

"Then I must remain silently with what *is*, neither accepting nor rejecting it. This is an enormous task, but I see that it is the only way if there is to be freedom.

"Now may I go on to another question? Does not the body affect the mind, and the mind in turn affect the body? I have especially noticed this in my own case. My thoughts are occupied with the memory of what I was—healthy, strong, quick of movement—and with what I hope to be, as compared with what I am now. I seem unable to accept my present state. What am I to do?"

This constant comparison of the present with the past and the future brings about pain and the deterioration of the mind, does it not? It prevents you from considering the fact of your present state. The past can never be again, and the future is unpredictable, so you have only the present. You can adequately deal with the present only when the mind is free from the burden of the past memory and the future hope. When the mind is attentive to the present, without comparison, then there is a possibility of other things happening.

"What do you mean by 'other things'?"

When the mind is preoccupied with its own pains, hopes and fears, there is no space for freedom from them. The self-enclosing process of thought only cripples the mind further, so the vicious circle is set going. Preoccupation makes the mind trivial, petty, shallow. A preoccupied mind is not a free mind, and preoccupation with freedom still breeds pettiness. The mind is petty when it is preoccupied with God, with the State, with virtue, or with its own body. This preoccupation with the body prevents adaptability to the present, the gaining of vitality and movement, however limited. The self, with its preoccupations, brings about its own pains and problems, which affect the body; and concern over bodily ills only further hinders the body. This does not mean that health should be neglected; but preoccupation with health, like preoccupation with truth, with ideas, only entrenches the mind in its own pettiness. There is a vast difference between a preoccupied mind and an active mind. An active mind is silent, aware, choiceless.

"Consciously it is rather difficult to take all this in, but probably the unconscious is absorbing what you are saying; at least I hope so.

"I would like to ask one more question. You see, sir, there are moments when my mind is silent, but these moments are very rare. I have pondered over the problem of meditation, and have read some of the things you have said about it, but for a long time my body was too much for me. Now that I have become more or less inured to my physical state, I feel it is important to cultivate this silence. How is one to set about it?"

Is silence to be cultivated, carefully nurtured and strengthened? And who is the cultivator? Is he different from the totality of your being? Is there silence, a still mind, when one desire dominates all others, or when it sets up resistance against them? Is there silence when the mind is disciplined, shaped, controlled? Does not all this imply a censor, a so-called higher self who controls, judges, chooses? And is there such an entity? If there is, is he not the product of thought? Thought dividing itself as the high and the low, the permanent and the impermanent, is still the outcome of the past, of tradition, of time. In this division lies its own security. Thought or desire now seeks safety in silence, and so it asks for a method or a system which offers what it wants. In place of worldly things it now craves the pleasure of silence, so it breeds conflict between what *is* and what *should* be. There is no silence where there is conflict, repression, resistance.

"Should one not seek silence?"

There can be no silence as long as there is a seeker. There is the silence of a still mind only when there is no seeker, when there is no desire. Without replying, put this question to yourself: Can the whole of your being be silent? Can the totality of the mind, the conscious as well as the unconscious, be still?

CONTENTMENT

THE PLANE WAS crowded. It was flying at twenty-odd thousand feet over the Atlantic and there was a thick carpet of clouds below. The sky above was intensely blue, the sun was behind us, and we were flying due west. The children had been playing, running up and down the aisle, and now tired out, they were sleeping. After the long night everyone else was awake, smoking and drinking. A man in front was telling another about his business, and a woman in the seat behind was describing in a pleased voice the things she had bought and speculating on the amount of duty she would have to pay. At that altitude the flight was smooth, there wasn't a bump, though there were rough winds below us. The wings of the plane were bright in the clear sunlight and the propellers were turning over smoothly, biting into the air at fantastic speed; the wind was behind us and we were doing over three hundred miles an hour.

Two men just across the narrow aisle were talking rather loudly, and it was difficult not to overhear what they were saying. They were big men, and one had a red, weather-beaten face. He was explaining the business of killing whales, how risky it was, what profits there were in it, and how frightfully rough the seas were. Some whales weighed hundreds of tons. The mothers with calves were not supposed to be killed, nor were they permitted to kill more than a certain number of whales within a specified time. Killing these great monsters had apparently been worked out most scientifically, each group having a special job to do for which it was technically trained. The smell of the factory ship was almost unbearable, but one got used to it, as one can to almost anything. But there was lots of money in it if all went well. He began to explain the strange fascination of killing, but at that moment drinks were brought and the subject of conversation changed.

Human beings like to kill, whether it be each other, or a harmless, bright-eyed deer in the deep forest, or a tiger that has preyed upon cattle. A snake is deliberately run over on the road; a trap is set and a wolf or a coyote is caught. Well-dressed, laughing people go out with their precious guns and kill birds that were lately calling to each other. A boy kills a chattering blue jay with his air-gun, and the elders around him say never a word of pity, or scold him; on the contrary, they say what a good shot he is. Killing for so-called sport, for food, for one's country, for peace —there is not much difference in all this. Justification is not the answer. There is only: do not kill. In the West we think that animals exist for the sake of our stomachs, or for the pleasure of killing, or for their fur. In the East it has been taught for centuries and repeated by every parent: do not kill, be pitiful, be compassionate. Here animals have no souls, so they can be killed with impunity; there animals have souls, so consider and let your heart know love. To eat animals, birds, is regarded here as a normal, natural thing, sanctioned by church and advertisements; there it is not, and the thoughtful, the religious, by tradition and culture, never do. But this too is rapidly breaking down. Here we have always killed in the name of God and country, and now it is everywhere. Killing is spreading; almost overnight the ancient cultures are being swept aside, and efficiency, ruthlessness and the means of destruction are being carefully nurtured and strengthened.

Peace is not with the politician or the priest, neither is it with the lawyer or the policeman. Peace is a state of mind when there is love.

He was a man of small business, struggling but able to make ends meet.

"I haven't come to talk about my work," he said. "It gives me what I need, and as my needs are few, I get along. Not being over-ambitious, I am not in the game of dog eat dog. One day, as I was passing by, I saw a crowd under the trees, and I stopped to listen to you. That was a couple of years ago, and what you said set something stirring in me. I am not too well educated, but I now read your talks, and here I am. I used to be content with my life, with my thoughts, and with the few scattered beliefs which lay lightly on my mind. But ever since that Sunday morning when I wandered into this valley in my car and came by chance to hear you, I have been discontented. It is not so much with my work that I am discontented, but discontent has taken hold of my whole being. I used to pity the people who were discontented. They were so miserable, nothing satisfied them—and now I have joined their ranks. I was once satisfied with my life, with my friends, and with the things I was doing, but now I am discontented and unhappy."

If one may ask, what do you mean by that word 'discontent'?

"Before that Sunday morning when I heard you, I was a contented person, and I suppose rather a bore to others; now I see how stupid I was, and I am trying to be intelligent and alert to everything about me. I want to amount to something, get somewhere, and this urge naturally makes for discontent. I used to be asleep, if I may put it that way, but now I am waking up."

Are you waking up, or are you trying to put yourself to sleep again through the desire to become something? You say you were asleep, and that now you are awake; but this awakened state makes you discontented, which displeases you, gives you pain, and to escape from this pain you are attempting to become something, to follow an ideal, and so on. This imitation is putting you back to sleep again, is it not?

"But I don't want to go back to my old state, and I do want to be awake."

Isn't it very strange how the mind deceives itself? The mind doesn't like to be disturbed, it doesn't like to be shaken out of its old patterns, its comfortable habits of thought and action; being disturbed, it seeks ways and means to establish new boundaries and pastures in which it can live safely. It is this zone of safety that most of us are seeking, and it is the desire to be safe, to be secure, that puts us to sleep. Circumstances, a word, a gesture, an experience, may awaken us, disturb us, but we want to be put to sleep again. This is happening to most of us all the time, and it is not an awakened state. What we have to understand are the ways in which the mind puts itself to sleep. This is so, is it not?

"But there must be a great many ways in which the mind puts itself to sleep. Is it possible to know and avoid them all?"

Several could be pointed out; but this would not solve the problem, would it?

"Why not?"

Merely to learn the ways in which the mind puts itself to sleep is again to find a means, perhaps different, of being undisturbed, secure. The important thing is to keep awake, and not ask *how* to keep awake; the pursuit of the 'how' is the urge to be safe.

"Then what is one to do?"

Stay with discontent without desiring to pacify it. It is the desire to be undisturbed that must be understood. This desire, which takes many forms, is the urge to escape from what *is*. When this urge drops away—but not through any form of compulsion, either conscious or unconscious—only then does the pain of discontent cease. Comparison of what *is* with what *should* be brings pain. The cessation of comparison is not a state of contentment; it is a state of wakefulness without the activities of the self.

"All this is rather new to me. It seems to me that you give to words quite a different significance, but communication is possible only when both of us give the same meaning to the same word at the same time."

Communication is relationship, is it not?

"You jump to wider significances than I am now capable of grasping. I must go more deeply into all this, and then perhaps I shall understand."

The Actor

The road curved in and out through the low hills, mile after endless mile. The burning rays of the afternoon sun lay on the golden hills, and there were deep shadows under the scattered trees, which spoke of their solitary existence. For miles around there was no habitation of any kind; here and there were a few lonely cattle, and only occasionally another car would appear on the smooth, well-kept road. The sky was very blue to the north and glary to the west. The country was strangely alive, though barren and isolated, and far away from human joy and pain. There were no birds, and you saw no wild animals apart from the few ground squirrels that scurried across the road. No water was visible except in one or two places where the cattle were. With the rains the hills would turn green, soft and welcoming, but now they were harsh, austere, with the beauty of great stillness.

It was a strange evening, full and intense, but as the road wove in and out among the rolling hills, time had come to an end. The sign said it was eighteen miles to the main road leading north. It would take half an hour or so to get there: time and distance. Yet at that moment, looking at that sign on the roadside, time and distance had ceased. It was not a measurable moment; it had no beginning and no end. The blue sky and the rolling, golden hills were there, vast and everlasting, but they were part of this timelessness. The eyes and the mind were watchful of the road; the dark and lonely trees were vivid and intense, and each separate blade of hay on the curving hills stood out, simple and clear. The light of that late afternoon was very still around the trees and among the hills, and the only moving thing was the car, going so fast. The silence between words was of that measureless stillness. This road would come to an end, joining another, and that too would peter out somewhere; those still, dark trees would fall and their dust would be scattered and lost;

tender green grass would come up with the rains, and it too would wither away.

Life and death are inseparable, and in their separation lies everlasting fear. Separation is the beginning of time; the fear of an end gives birth to the pain of a beginning. In this wheel the mind is caught and spins out the web of time. Thought is the process and the result of time, and thought cannot cultivate love.

He was an actor of some repute who was making a name for himself, but he was still young enough to inquire and suffer.

"Why does one act?" he asked. "To some the stage is merely a means of livelihood, to others it offers a means for the expression of their own vanity, and to still others, playing various rôles is a great stimulation. The stage also offers a marvellous escape from the realities of life. I act for all these reasons, and perhaps also because—I say this with hesitancy—I hope to do some good through the stage."

Does not acting give strength to the self, to the ego? We pose, we put on masks, and gradually the pose, the mask becomes the daily habit, covering the many selves of contradiction, greed, hate, and so on. The ideal is a pose, a mask covering the fact, the actual. Can one do good through the stage?

"Do you mean that one cannot?"

No, it is a question, not a judgment. In writing a play the author has certain ideas and intentions which he wants to put across; the actor is the medium, the mask, and the public is entertained or educated. Is this education doing good? Or is it merely conditioning the mind to a pattern, good or bad, intelligent or stupid, devised by the author?

"Good Lord, I never thought about all this. You see, I can become a fairly successful actor, and before I get lost in it completely, I am asking myself if acting is to be my way of life. It has a curious fascination of its own, sometimes very destructive, and at other times very pleasant. You can take acting seriously, but in itself it is not very serious. As I am inclined to be rather serious, I have wondered if I should make the stage my career.

There is something in me that rebels against the absurd superficiality of it all, and yet I am greatly attracted to it; so I am disturbed, to put it mildly. Through all this runs the thread of seriousness."

Can another decide what should be one's way of life?

"No, but in talking the matter over with another, things sometimes become clear."

If one may point out, any activity that gives emphasis to the self, to the ego, is destructive; it brings sorrow. This is the principal issue, is it not? You said earlier that you wanted to do good; but surely the good is not possible when, consciously or unconsciously, the self is being nourished and sustained through any career or activity.

"Is not all action based on the survival of the self?"

Perhaps not always. Outwardly it may appear that an action is self-protective, but inwardly it may not be at all. What others say or think in this regard is not of great importance, but one should not deceive oneself. And self-deception is very easy in psychological matters.

"It seems to me that if I am really concerned with the abnegation of the self, I shall have to withdraw into a monastery or lead a hermit's life."

Is it necessary to lead a hermit's life in order to abnegate the self? You see, we have a concept of the selfless life, and it is this concept which prevents the understanding of a life in which the self is not. The concept is another form of the self. Without escaping to monasteries and so on, is it not possible to be passively alert to the activities of the self? This awareness may bring about a totally different activity which does not breed sorrow and misery.

"Then there are certain professions that are obviously detrimental to a sane life, and I include mine among them. I am still quite young. I can give up the stage, and after going into all this, I am pretty sure I will; but then what am I to do? I have certain talents which may ripen and be useful."

Talent may become a curse. The self may use and entrench

itself in capacities, and then talent becomes the way and the glory of the self. The gifted man may offer his gifts to God, knowing the danger of them; but he is conscious of his gifts, otherwise he would not offer them, and it is this consciousness of being or having something, that must be understood. The offering up of what one is or has in order to be humble, is vanity.

"I am beginning to get a glimpse of all this, but it is still very complex."

Perhaps; but what is important is choiceless awareness of the obvious and the subtle activities of the self.

THE WAY OF KNOWLEDGE

THE SUN HAD set behind the mountains, and the roseate glow was still on the rocky range to the east. The path led down, wandering in and out through the green valley. It was a calm evening, and there was a slight breeze among the leaves. The evening star was just visible high over the horizon, and presently it would be quite dark, for there was no moon. The trees, which had been open and welcoming, were withdrawing into themselves from the dark night. It was cool and silent among these hills, and now the sky was full of stars and the mountains were clear and sharp against them. That smell peculiar to the night was filling the air, and far away a dog was barking. It was a very still night, and this stillness seemed to penetrate into the rocks, the trees, into all the things about one, and the footsteps on the rough path did not disturb it.

The mind too was utterly still. After all, meditation is not a means to produce a result, to bring about a state which has been or which might be. If meditation is with intention, the desired result may be achieved, but then it is not meditation, it is only the fulfilment of desire. Desire is never satisfied, there is no end to desire. The understanding of desire, without trying to put a stop to it, or sustain it, is the beginning and the end of meditation. But there is something beyond this. It is strange how the meditator persists; he seeks to continue, he becomes the observer, the experiencer, a recollecting mechanism, the one who evaluates, accumulates, rejects. When meditation is of the meditator, it only strengthens the meditator, the experiencer. The stillness of the mind is the absence of the experiencer, of the observer who is aware that he is still. When the mind is still, there is the awakened state. You can be intermittently awake to many things, you can probe, seek, inquire, but these are the activities of desire, of will, of recognition and gain. That which is ever awake is neither desire nor the product of desire. Desire breeds the conflict of duality, and conflict is darkness.

Well-connected and rich, she was now on the hunt for the spiritual. She had sought out the Catholic masters and the Hindu teachers, had studied with the Sufis and dabbled in Buddhism.

"Of course," she added, "I have also looked into the occult, and now I have come to learn from you."

Does wisdom lie in the accumulation of much knowledge? If one may ask, what is it that you are seeking?

"I have gone after different things at different periods of my life, and what I have sought I have generally found. I have gathered much experience, and have had a rich and varied life. I read a great deal on a variety of subjects, and have been to one of the eminent analysts, but I am still seeking."

Why are you doing all this? Why this search, whether superficial or deep?

"What a strange question to ask! If one did not seek, one would vegetate; if one did not constantly learn, life would have no meaning, one might just as well die."

Again, what are you learning? In reading what others have said about the structure and behaviour of human beings, in analysing social and cultural differences, in studying any of the various sciences or schools of philosophy, what is it that you are gathering?

"I feel that if only one had enough knowledge it would save

206

one from strife and misery, so I gather it where I can. Knowledge is essential to understanding."

Does understanding come through knowledge? Or does knowledge prevent creative understanding? We seem to think that by accumulating facts and information, by having encyclopaedic knowledge, we shall be set free from our bondages. This is simply not so. Antagonism, hatred and war have not been stopped, though we all know how destructive and wasteful they are. Knowledge is not necessarily preventive of these things; on the contrary, it may stimulate and encourage them. So is it not important to find out why we are gathering knowledge?

"I have talked to many educators who think that if knowledge can be spread sufficiently widely it will dissipate man's hatred for man and prevent the complete destruction of the world. I think this is what most serious educators are concerned with."

Though we now have so much knowledge in so many fields, it has not stopped man's brutality to man even among those of the same group, nation, or religion. Perhaps knowledge is blinding us to some other factor that is the real solution to all this chaos and misery.

"What is that?"

In what spirit are you asking that question? A verbal answer could be given, but it would only be adding more words to an already overburdened mind. For most people, knowledge is the accumulation of words or the strengthening of their prejudices and beliefs. Words, thoughts, are the framework in which the self-concept exists. This concept contracts or expands through experience and knowledge, but the hard core of the self remains, and mere knowledge or learning can never dissolve it. Revolution is the voluntary dissolution of this core, of this concept, whereas action born of self-perpetuating knowledge can only lead to greater misery and destruction.

"You suggested that there might be a different factor which is the true solution to all our miseries, and I am asking in all seriousness what that factor is. If such a factor exists and one could know and build one's whole life around it, a totally new culture might well be the outcome."

Thought can never find it, the mind can never seek it out. You want to know and build your life around it; but the 'you' with its knowledge, its fears, its hopes, frustrations and illusions, can never discover it; and without discovering it, merely to acquire more knowledge, more learning, will only act as a further barrier to the coming into being of that state.

"If you won't guide me to it, I shall have to seek it out for myself; and yet you imply that all search must cease."

If there were guidance, there would be no discovery. There must be freedom to discover, not guidance. Discovery is not a reward.

"I am afraid I do not understand all this."

You seek guidance in order to find; but if you are guided you are no longer free, you become a slave to the one who knows. He who asserts that he knows is already a slave to his knowledge, and he also must be free to find. Finding is from moment to moment, so knowledge becomes an impediment.

"Would you please explain a little more?"

Knowledge is always of the past. What you know is already in the past, is it not? You do not know the present or the future. The strengthening of the past is the way of knowledge. What may be uncovered may be totally new, and your knowledge, which is the accumulation of the past, cannot fathom the new, the unknown.

"Do you mean that one must get rid of all one's knowledge if one is to find God, love, or whatever it is?"

The self is the past, the power to accumulate things, virtues, ideas. Thought is the outcome of this conditioning of yesterday, and with this instrument you are trying to uncover the unknowable. This is not possible. Knowledge must cease for the other to be.

"Then how is one to empty the mind of knowledge?"

There is no 'how'. The practice of a method only further conditions the mind, for then you have a result, not a mind that is free from knowledge, from the self. There is no way, but only passive awareness of the truth with regard to knowledge.

How BEAUTIFUL IS the earth with its deserts and rich fields, its forests, rivers and mountains, its untold birds and animals and human beings! There are villages, filthy and diseased, where it has not rained enough for many seasons; the wells are all but dry and the cattle are skin and bones; the fields are cracked, and the ground-nut is withering away; the sugar-cane is no longer planted, and the river has not flowed for several years. They beg, they steal, and go hungry; they die waiting for the rains. Then there are the opulent cities with their clean streets and shiny new cars, their washed and well-dressed people, their endless shops filled with things, their libraries, universities and slums. The earth is beautiful and its soil, around the temple and in the arid desert, is sacred.

To imagine is one thing, and to perceive what *is* is another, but both are binding. It is easy to perceive what *is,* but to be free of it is another matter; for perception is clouded with judgment, with comparison, with desire. To perceive without the interference of the censor is arduous. Imagination builds the image of the self, and thought then functions within its shadows. From this self-concept grows the conflict between what *is* and what *should* be, the conflict in duality. Perception of the fact, and idea about the fact, are two entirely different states, and only a mind that is not bound by opinion, by comparative values, is capable of perceiving what is true.

She had come a long distance by train and bus, and the last bit she had had to walk; but as it was a cool day, the climb was not too much.

"I have a rather pressing problem which I would like to talk over," she said. "When two people who love each other are adamant in their diametrically opposed convictions, what is to be done? Must one or the other give in? Can love bridge this separating and destructive gap?"

If there were love, would there be these fixed convictions which separate and bind?

"Perhaps not, but it has now gone beyond the state of love; the convictions have become hard, brutal, unyielding. One may be flexible, but if the other is not, there is bound to be an explosion. Can one do anything to avoid it? One may yield, temporize, but if the other is wholly intransigent, life with that person becomes impossible, there is no relationship with him. This intransigence is leading to dangerous results, but the person concerned doesn't seem to mind inviting martyrdom for his convictions. It all seems rather absurd when one considers the illusory nature of ideas; but ideas take deep root when one has nothing else. Kindliness and consideration vanish in the harsh brilliancy of ideas. The person concerned is completely convinced that his ideas, theories which he has got from reading, are going to save the world by bringing peace and plenty to all, and he considers that killing and destruction, when necessary, are justified as a means to that idealistic end. The end is all-important, and not the means; no one matters as long as that end is achieved."

To such a mind, salvation lies in the destruction of those who are not of the same conviction. Some religions have in the past thought this to be the way to God, and they still have excommunications, threats of eternal hell, and so on. This thing you are talking about is the latest religion. We seek hope in churches, in ideas, in 'flying saucers', in Masters, in *gurus,* all of which only leads to greater misery and destruction. In oneself one has to be free from this intransigent attitude; for ideas, however great, however subtle and persuasive, are illusory, they separate and destroy. When the mind is no longer caught in the net of ideas, opinions, convictions, then there is something wholly different from the projections of the mind. The mind is not our last resort in resolving our problems; on the contrary, it is the maker of problems.

"I know that you do not advise people, sir, but all the same, what is one to do? I have been asking myself this question for many months, and I haven't found the answer. But even now as I put that question I am beginning to see that there is no definite answer, that one must live from moment to moment, taking things as they come and forgetting oneself. Then perhaps it is possible to be gentle, to forgive. But how difficult it is going to be!"

When you say 'how difficult it is going to be', you have already stopped living from moment to moment with love and gentleness. The mind has projected itself into the future, creating a problem—which is the very nature of the self. The past and the future are its sustenance.

"May I ask something else? Is it possible for me to interpret my own dreams? Lately I have been dreaming a great deal and I know that these dreams are trying to tell me something, but I cannot interpret the symbols, the pictures that keep repeating themselves in my dreams. These symbols and pictures are not always the same, they vary, but fundamentally they all have the same content and significance—at least I think so, though of course I may be mistaken."

What does that word 'interpret' mean with regard to dreams?

"As I explained, I have a very grave problem which has been bothering me for many months, and my dreams are all concerned with this problem. They are trying to tell me something, perhaps give me a hint of what I should do, and if I could only interpret them correctly I would know what it is they are trying to convey."

Surely, the dreamer is not separate from his dream; the dreamer is the dream. Don't you think this is important to understand?

"I don't understand what you mean. Would you please explain?"

Our consciousness is a total process, though it may have contradictions within itself. It may divide itself as the conscious and the unconscious, the hidden and the open, in it there may be opposing desires, values, urges, but that consciousness is nevertheless a total, unitary process. The conscious mind may be aware of a dream, but the dream is the outcome of the activity of the whole consciousness. When the upper layer of consciousness tries to interpret a dream which is a projection of the whole consciousness, then its interpretation must be partial, incomplete, twisted. The interpreter inevitably misrepresents the symbol, the dream.

"I am sorry, but this is not clear to me."

The conscious, superficial mind is so occupied with anxiety, with trying to find a solution to its problem, that during the waking period it is never quiet. In so-called sleep, being perhaps somewhat quieter, less disturbed, it gathers an intimation of the activity of the whole consciousness. This intimation is the dream, which the anxious mind upon waking tries to interpret; but its interpretation will be incorrect, for it is concerned with immediate action and its results. The urge to interpret must cease before there can be the understanding of the whole process of consciousness. You are very anxious to find out what is the right thing to do with regard to your problem, are you not? That very anxiety is preventing the understanding of the problem, and so there is a constant change of symbols behind which the content seems to be always the same. So, what now is the problem?

"Not to be afraid of whatever happens."

Can you so easily put away fear? A mere verbal statement does not do away with anxiety. But is that the problem? You may wish to do away with fear, but then the 'how', the method, becomes important, and you have a new problem as well as the old one. So we move from problem to problem and are never free of them. But we are now talking of something wholly different, are we not? We are not concerned with the substitution of one problem for another.

"Then I suppose the real problem is to have a quiet mind."

Surely, that is the only issue: a still mind.

"How can I have a still mind?"

See what you are saying. You want to possess a still mind, as you would possess a dress or a house. Having a new objective, the stillness of the mind, you begin to inquire into the ways and means of getting it, so you have another problem on your hands. Just be aware of the utter necessity and importance of a still mind. Don't struggle after stillness, don't torture yourself with discipline in order to acquire it, don't cultivate or practise it. All these efforts produce a result, and that which is a result is not stillness. What is put together can be undone. Do not seek continuity of stillness. Stillness is to be experienced from moment to moment; it cannot be gathered.

DEATH

THE RIVER WAS very wide here, almost a mile, and very deep; in mid-stream the waters were clear and blue, but towards the banks they were sullied, dirty and sluggish. The sun was setting behind the huge, sprawling city up the river; the smoke and the dust of the town were giving marvellous colours to the setting sun, which were reflected on the wide, dancing waters. It was a lovely evening and every blade of grass, the trees and the chattering birds, were caught in timeless beauty. Nothing was separate, broken up. The noise of a train rattling over the distant bridge was part of this complete stillness. Not far away a fisherman was singing. There were wide, cultivated strips along both banks, and during the day the green, luscious fields were smiling and inviting; but now they were dark, silent and withdrawn. On this side of the river there was a large, uncultivated space where the children of the village flew their kites and romped about in noisy enjoyment, and where the nets of the fishermen were spread out to dry. They had their primitive boats anchored there.

The village was just above, higher up the bank, and generally they had singing, dancing, or some other noisy affair going on up there; but this evening, though they were all out of their huts and sitting about, the villagers were quiet and strangely thoughtful. A group of them were coming down the steep bank, carrying on a bamboo litter a dead body covered with white cloth. They passed by and I followed. Going to the river's edge, they put down the litter almost touching the water. They had brought with them fast-burning wood and heavy logs, and making of these a pyre they laid the body on it, sprinkling it with water from the river and covering it with more wood and hay. A very young man lit the pyre. There were about twenty of us, and we all gathered around. There were no women present, and the men sat on their haunches, wrapped in their white cloth, completely still. The fire was getting intensely hot, and we had to move back. A charred black leg rose out of the fire and was pushed back with a long stick; it wouldn't stay, and a heavy log was thrown on it. The bright yellow flames were reflected on the dark water, and so were the stars. The slight breeze had died down with the setting of the sun. Except for the crackling of the fire, everything was very still. Death was there, burning. Amidst all those motionless people and the living flames there was infinite space, a measureless distance, a vast aloneness. It was not something apart, separate and divided from life. The beginning was there and ever the beginning.

Presently the skull was broken and the villagers began to leave. The last one to go must have been a relative; he folded his hands, saluted, and slowly went up the bank. There was very little left now; the towering flames were quiet, and only glowing embers remained. The few bones that did not burn would be thrown into the river tomorrow morning. The immensity of death, the immediacy of it, and how near! With the burning away of that body, one also died. There was complete aloneness and yet not apartness, aloneness but not isolation. Isolation is of the mind but not of death.

Well advanced in age, with quiet manners and dignity, he had clear eyes and a quick smile. It was cold in the room and he was wrapped in a warm shawl. Speaking in English, for he had been educated abroad, he explained that he had retired from governmental work and had plenty of time on his hands. He had studied various religions and philosophies, he said, but had not come this long way to discuss such matters.

The early morning sun was on the river and the waters were sparkling like thousands of jewels. There was a small golden-green bird on the veranda sunning itself, safe and quiet.

"What I have really come for," he continued, "is to ask about or perhaps to discuss the thing that most disturbs me: death. I have read the *Tibetan Book of the Dead,* and am familiar with what our own books say on the subject. The Christian and Islamic suggestions concerning death are much too superficial. I have talked to various religious teachers here and abroad, but to me at least all their theories appear to be very unsatisfactory. I have thought a great deal about the subject and have often meditated upon it, but I don't seem to get any further. A friend of mine who heard you recently told me something of what you were saying, so I have come. To me the problem is not only the fear of death, the fear of not being, but also what happens after death. This has been a problem for man throughout the ages, and no one appears to have solved it. What do you say?"

Let us first dispose of the urge to escape from the fact of death through some form of belief, such as reincarnation or resurrection, or through easy rationalization. The mind is so eager to find a reasonable explanation of death, or a satisfying answer to this problem, that it easily slips into some kind of illusion. Of this, one has to be extremely watchful.

"But isn't that one of our greatest difficulties? We crave for some kind of assurance, especially from those whom we consider to have knowledge or experience in this matter; and when we can't find such an assurance we bring into being, out of despair and hope, our own comforting beliefs and theories. So belief, the most outrageous or the most reasonable, becomes a necessity."

However gratifying an escape may be, it does not in any way bring understanding of the problem. That very flight is the cause of fear. Fear comes in the movement away from the fact, the what *is.* Belief, however comforting, has in it the seed of fear. One shuts oneself off from the fact of death because one doesn't want to look at it, and beliefs and theories offer an easy way out. So if the mind is to discover the extraordinary significance of death it must discard, easily, without resistance, the craving for some hopeful comfort. This is fairly obvious, don't you think?

"Aren't you asking too much? To understand death we must be in despair; isn't that what you are saying?"

Not at all, sir. Is there despair when there is not that state which we call hope? Why should we always think in opposites? Is hope the opposite of despair? If it is, then that hope holds within it the seed of despair, and such hope is tinged with fear. If there is to be understanding, is it not necessary to be free of the opposites? The state of the mind is of the greatest importance. The activities of despair and hope prevent the understanding or the experiencing of death. The movement of the opposites must cease. The mind must approach the problem of death with a totally new awareness in which the familiar, the recognizing process, is absent.

"I am afraid I don't quite understand that statement. I think I vaguely grasp the significance of the mind's being free from the opposites. Though it is an enormously difficult task, I think I see the necessity of it. But what it means to be free from the recognizing process altogether eludes me."

Recognition is the process of the known, it is the outcome of the past. The mind is frightened of that with which it is not familiar. If you knew death, there would be no fear of it, no need for elaborate explanations. But you cannot know death, it is something totally new, never experienced before. What is experienced becomes the known, the past, and it is from this past, from this known that recognition takes place. As long as there is this movement from the past, the new cannot be.

"Yes, yes, I am beginning to feel that, sir."

What we are talking over together is not something to be thought about later, but to be directly experienced as we go along. This experience cannot be stored up, for if it is, it becomes memory, and memory, the way of recognition, blocks the new, the unknown. Death is the unknown. The problem is not what death is and what happens thereafter, but for the mind to cleanse itself of the past, of the known. Then the living mind can enter the abode of death, it can meet death, the unknown.

"Are you suggesting that one can know death while still alive?"

Accident, disease and old age bring death, but under these circumstances it is not possible to be fully conscious. There is pain, hope or despair, the fear of isolation, and the mind, the self, is consciously or unconsciously battling against death, the inevitable. With fearful resistance against death, we pass away. But is it possible—without resistance, without morbidity, without a sadistic or suicidal urge, and while fully alive, mentally vigorous—to enter the house of death? This is possible only when the mind dies to the known, to the self. So our problem is not death, but for the mind to free itself from the centuries of gathered psychological experience, from ever-mounting memory, the strengthening and refining of the self.

"But how is this to be done? How can the mind free itself from its own bondages? It seems to me that either an outside agency is necessary, or else the higher and nobler part of the mind must intervene to purify the mind of the past."

This is quite a complex issue, is it not? The outside agency may be environmental influence, or it may be something beyond the boundaries of the mind. If the outside agency is environmental influence, it is that very influence, with its traditions, beliefs and cultures, that has held the mind in bondage. If the outside agency is something beyond the mind, then thought in any form cannot touch it. Thought is the outcome of time; thought is anchored to the past, it can never be free from the past. If thought frees itself from the past, it ceases to be thought. To speculate upon what is beyond the mind is utterly vain. For the intervention of that which is beyond thought, thought which is the self must cease. Mind must be without any movement, it must be still with the stillness of no motive. Mind cannot invite it. The mind may and does divide its own field of activities as noble and ignoble, desirable and undesirable, higher and lower, but all such divisions and subdivisions are within the boundaries of the mind itself; so any movement of the mind, in any direction, is the reaction of the past, of the 'me', of time. This truth is the only liberating factor, and he who does not perceive this truth will ever be in bondage, do what he may; his penances, vows, disciplines, sacrifices may have sociological and comforting significance, but they have no value in relation to truth.

EVALUATION

MEDITATION IS A very important action in life; perhaps it is the action that has the greatest and deepest significance. It is a perfume that cannot easily be caught; it is not to be bought through striving and practice. A system can yield only the fruit it offers, and the system, the method, is based on envy and greed.

Not to be able to meditate is not to be able to see the sunlight, the dark shadows, the sparkling waters and the tender leaf. But how few see these things! Meditation has nothing to offer; you may not come begging with folded hands. It doesn't save you from any pain. It makes things abundantly clear and simple; but to perceive this simplicity the mind must free itself, without any cause or motive, from all the things it has gathered through cause and motive. This is the whole issue in meditation. Meditation is the purgation of the known. To pursue the known in different forms is a game of self-deception, and then the meditator is the master, there is not the simple act of meditation. The meditator can act only in the field of the known; he must cease to act for the unknown to be. The unknowable doesn't invite you, and you cannot invite it. It comes and goes as the wind, and you cannot capture it and store it away for your benefit, for your use. It has no utilitarian value, but without it life is measurelessly empty.

The question is not how to meditate, what system to follow, but what is meditation? The 'how' can only produce what the method offers, but the very inquiry into what is meditation will open the door to meditation. The inquiry does not lie outside of the mind, but within the movement of the mind itself. In pursuing that inquiry, what becomes all-important is to understand the seeker himself, and not what he seeks. What he seeks is the projection of his own craving, of his own compulsions, desires. When this fact is seen, all searching ceases, which in itself is enormously significant. Then the mind is no longer grasping at something beyond itself, there is no outward movement with its reaction inwards; but when seeking has entirely stopped, there is a movement of the mind which is neither outward nor inward. Seeking does not come to an end by any act of will, or by a complex process of conclusions. To stop seeking demands great understanding. The ending of search is the beginning of a still mind.

A mind that is capable of concentration is not necessarily able to meditate. Self-interest does bring about concentration, like any other interest, but such concentration implies a motive, a cause, conscious or unconscious; there is always a thing to be gained or set aside, an effort to comprehend, to get to the other shore. Attention with an aim is concerned with accumulation. The attention that comes with this movement towards or away from something is the attraction of pleasure or the repulsion of pain, but meditation is that extraordinary attention in which there is no maker of effort, no end or object to be gained. Effort is part of the acquisitive process, it is the gathering of experience by the experiencer. The experiencer may concentrate, pay attention, be aware; but the craving of the experiencer for experience must wholly cease, for the experiencer is merely an accumulation of the known.

There is great bliss in meditation.

He explained that he had studied philosophy and psychology, and had read what Patanjali had to say. He considered Christian thought rather superficial and given to mere reformation, so he had gone to the East, had practised some kind of yoga, and was fairly familiar with Hindu thought.

"I have read something of what you have been saying and I think I can follow it up to a certain point. I see the importance of not condemning, though I find it extremely difficult not to condemn; but I cannot understand at all when you say, 'Do not evaluate, do not judge'. All thinking, it seems to me, is a process of evaluation. Our life, our whole outlook, is based on choice, on values, on good and bad, and so on. Without values we would just disintegrate, and surely you do not mean that. I have tried to empty my mind of all norm or value, and for me at least it is impossible."

Is there thinking without verbalization, without symbols? Are words necessary to thinking? If there were no symbols, referents, would there be what we call thinking? Is all thinking verbal, or is there thinking without words?

"I do not know, I have never considered the matter. As far as I can perceive, without images and words there would be no thinking."

Shouldn't we find out the truth of this matter now, while we are here talking about it? Is it not possible to find out for oneself whether or not there is thinking without words and symbols?

"But in what way is this related to evaluation?"

The mind is made up of referents, associations, images and words. Evaluation comes from this background. Words like God, love, Socialism, Communism, and so on, play an extraordinarily important part in our lives. Neurologically as well as psychologically words have significance according to the culture in which we are brought up. To a Christian certain words and symbols have enormous significance, and to a Moslem another set of words and symbols has an equally vital significance. Evaluation takes place within this area.

"Can one go beyond this area? And even if one can, why should one?"

Thinking is always conditioned; there is no such thing as freedom of thought. You may think what you like, but your thinking is and will always be limited. Evaluation is a process of thinking, of choice. If the mind is content, as it generally is, to remain within an enclosure, wide or narrow, then it is not bothered with any fundamental issue; it has its own reward. But if it would find out whether there is something beyond thought, then all evaluation must cease; the thinking process must come to an end.

"But the mind itself is part and parcel of this process of thinking, so by what effort or practice can thought be brought to an end?"

Evaluation, condemnation, comparison, is the way of thought, and when you ask through what effort or method can the process of thinking be brought to an end, are you not seeking to gain something? This urge to practise a method or to make further effort is the outcome of evaluation, and is still a process of the mind. Neither by the practice of a method nor by any effort whatsoever can thought be brought to an end. Why do we make an effort?

"For the very simple reason that if we did not make an effort we would stagnate and die. Everything makes an effort, all nature struggles to survive."

Do we struggle just to survive, or do we struggle to survive within a certain psychological or ideological pattern? We want to be something; the urge of ambition, of fulfilment, of fear, shapes our struggle within the pattern of a society which has come about through the collective ambition, fulfilment and fear. We make effort to gain or to avoid. If we were concerned only with survival, then our whole outlook would be fundamentally different. Effort implies choice; choice is comparison, evaluation, condemnation. Thought is made up of these struggles and contradictions; and can such thought free itself from its own self-perpetuating barriers?

"Then there must be an outside agency, call it divine grace or what you will, that steps in and puts an end to the self-enclosing ways of the mind. Is this what you are indicating?"

How eagerly we want to achieve a satisfying state! If one may point out, sir, are you not concerned with arrival, with achievement, with freeing the mind from a particular condition? The mind is caught in the prison of its own making, of its own desires and efforts, and every movement it makes, in any direction, is within the prison; but it is not aware of this, so in its pain and conflict it prays, it seeks an outside agency which will liberate it. It generally finds what it seeks, but what it has found is the outcome of its own movement. The mind is still a prisoner, only in a new prison which is more gratifying and comforting.

"But what in the name of heaven is one to do? If every movement of the mind is an extension of its own prison, then all hope must be abandoned."

Hope is another movement of thought caught in despair. Hope

and despair are words that cripple the mind with their emotional content, with their seemingly opposing and contradictory urges. Is it not possible to stay in the state of despair, or any similar state, without rushing away from it to an opposite idea, or desperately clinging to the state which is called joyous, hopeful, and so on? Conflict comes into being when the mind takes flight from the state called misery, pain, into another called hope, happiness. To understand the state in which one is, is not to accept it. Both acceptance and denial are within the area of evaluation.

"I am afraid I still do not grasp how thought can come to an end without some kind of action in that direction."

All action of will, of desire, of compulsive urge, is born of the mind, the mind that is evaluating, comparing, condemning. If the mind perceives the truth of this, not through argumentation, conviction, or belief, but through being simple and attentive, then thought comes to an end. The ending of thought is not sleep, a weakening of life, a state of negation; it is an entirely different state.

"Our talk together has shown me that I have not thought very deeply about all this. Though I have read a great deal, I have only assimilated what others have said. I feel that for the first time I am experiencing the state of my own thinking and am perhaps able to listen to something more than mere words."

ENVY AND LONELINESS

UNDER THE TREE that evening it was very quiet. A lizard was pushing itself up and down on a rock, still warm. The night would be chilly, and the sun would not be up again for many hours. The cattle were weary and slow coming back from the distant fields where they had laboured with their men. A deep-throated owl was hooting from the hill-top which was its home. Every evening about this time it would begin, and as it got darker the hoots would be less frequent; but occasionally, late in the night, you would hear them again. One owl would be calling to another across the valley, and their deep hooting seemed to give greater silence and beauty to the night. It was a lovely evening, and the new moon was setting behind the dark hill.

Compassion is not hard to come by when the heart is not filled with the cunning things of the mind. It is the mind with its demands and fears, its attachments and denials, its determinations and urges, that destroys love. And how difficult it is to be simple about all this! You don't need philosophies and doctrines to be gentle and kind. The efficient and the powerful of the land will organize to feed and clothe the people, to provide them with shelter and medical care. This is inevitable with the rapid increase of production; it is the function of well-organized government and a balanced society. But organization does not give the generosity of the heart and hand. Generosity comes from quite a different source, a source beyond all measure. Ambition and envy destroy it as surely as fire burns. This source must be touched, but one must come to it empty-handed, without prayer, without sacrifice. Books cannot teach nor can any *guru* lead to this source. It cannot be reached through the cultivation of virtue, though virtue is necessary, nor through capacity and obedience. When the mind is serene, without any movement, it is there. Serenity is without motive, without the urge for the more.

She was a young lady, but rather weary with pain. It was not the physical pain that bothered her so much, but pain of a different sort. The bodily pain she had been able to control through medication, but the agony of jealousy she had never been able to assuage. It had been with her, she explained, from childhood; at that age it was a childish thing, to be tolerated and smiled upon, but now it had become a disease. She was married and had two children, and jealousy was destroying all relationship.

"I seem to be jealous, not only of my husband and children, but of almost anyone who has more than I have, a better garden or a prettier dress. All this may seem rather silly, but I am tortured by it. Some time ago I went to a psycho-analyst, and temporarily I was at peace; but it soon began again."

Doesn't the culture in which we live encourage envy? The advertisements, the competition, the comparison, the worship of success with its many activities—do not all these things sustain envy? The demand for the more is jealousy, is it not?

"But . . ."

Let us consider envy itself for a few moments, and not your particular struggles with it; we shall come back to that later. Is this all right?

"Most certainly."

Envy is encouraged and respected, is it not? The competitive spirit is nourished from childhood. The idea that you must do and be better than another is repeated constantly in different ways; the example of success, the hero and his brave act, are endlessly dinned into the mind. The present culture is based on envy, on acquisitiveness. If you are not acquisitive of worldly things and instead follow some religious teacher, you are promised the right place in the hereafter. We are all brought up on this, and the desire to succeed is deeply embedded in almost everyone. Success is pursued in different ways, success as an artist, as a business man, as a religious aspirant. All this is a form of envy, but it is only when envy becomes distressing, painful, that one attempts to get rid of it. As long as it is compensating and pleasurable, envy is an accepted part of one's nature. We don't see that in this very pleasure there is pain. Attachment does give pleasure, but it also breeds jealousy and pain, and it is not love. In this area of activity one lives, suffers, and dies. It is only when the pain of this self-enclosing action becomes unbearable that one struggles to break through it.

"I think I vaguely grasp all this, but what am I to do?"

Before considering what to do, let us see what the problem is. What is the problem?

"I am tortured by jealousy and I want to be free from it."

You want to be free from the pain of it; but don't you want to hold on to the peculiar pleasure that comes with possession and attachment?

"Of course I do. You don't expect me to renounce all my possessions, do you?"

224

We are not concerned with renunciation, but with the desire to possess. We want to possess people as well as things, we cling to beliefs as well as hopes. Why is there this desire to own things and people, this burning attachment?

"I don't know, I have never thought about it. It seems natural to be envious, but it has become a poison, a violently disturbing factor in my life."

We do need certain things, food, clothing, shelter, and so on, but they are used for psychological satisfaction, which gives rise to many other problems. In the same way, psychological dependence on people breeds anxiety, jealousy and fear.

"I suppose in that sense I do depend on certain people. They are a compulsive necessity to me, and without them I would be totally lost. If I did not have my husband and children I think I would go slowly mad, or I would attach myself to somebody else. But I don't see what is wrong with attachment."

We are not saying it is right or wrong but are considering its cause and effect, are we not? We are not condemning or justifying dependence. But why is one psychologically dependent on another? Isn't that the problem, and not how to be free from the tortures of jealousy? Jealousy is merely the effect, the symptom, and it would be useless to deal only with the symptom. Why is one psychologically dependent on another?

"I know I am dependent, but I haven't really thought about it. I took it for granted that everyone is dependent on another."

Of course we are physically dependent on each other and always will be, which is natural and inevitable. But as long as we do not understand our *psychological* dependence on another, don't you think the pain of jealousy will continue? So, why is there this psychological need of another?

"I need my family because I love them. If I didn't love them I wouldn't care."

Are you saying that love and jealousy go together?

"So it seems. If I didn't love them, I certainly wouldn't be jealous."

In that case, if you are free from jealousy you have also got rid of love, haven't you? Then why do you want to be free from jealousy? You want to keep the pleasure of attachment and let the pain of it go. Is this possible?

"Why not?"

Attachment implies fear, does it not? You are afraid of what you are, or of what you will be if the other leaves you or dies, and you are attached because of this fear. As long as you are occupied with the pleasure of attachment, fear is hidden, locked away, but unfortunately it is always there; and till you are free from this fear, the tortures of jealousy will go on.

"What am I afraid of?"

The question is not what you are afraid of, but are you aware that you are afraid?

"Now that you are pointedly asking that question, I suppose I am. All right, I am afraid."

Of what?

"Of being lost, insecure; of not being loved, cared for; of being lonely, alone. I think that is it: I am afraid of being lonely, of not being able to face life by myself, so I depend on my husband and children, I desperately hold on to them. There is always in me the fear of something happening to them. Sometimes my desperation takes the form of jealousy, of uncontainable fury, and so on. I am fearful lest my husband should turn to another. I am eaten up with anxiety. I assure you, I have spent many an hour in tears. All this contradiction and turmoil is what we call love, and you are asking me if it *is* love. Is it love when there is attachment? I see it is not. It is ugly, completely selfish; I am thinking about myself all the time. But what am I to do?"

Condemning, calling yourself hateful, ugly, selfish, in no way diminishes the problem; on the contrary, it increases it. It is important to understand this. Condemnation or justification prevents you from looking at what lies behind fear, it is an active distraction from facing the fact of what is actually happening. When you say, "I am ugly, selfish", these words are loaded with condemnation, and you are strengthening the condemnatory characteristic which is part of the self.

"I am not sure I understand this."

By condemning or justifying an action of your child, do you understand him? You haven't the time or the inclination to explain, so to get an immediate result you say 'do' or 'don't'; but you haven't understood the complexities of the child. Similarly, condemnation, justification, or comparison prevents the understanding of yourself. You have to understand the complex entity which is you.

"Yes, yes, I grasp that."

Then go into the matter slowly, without condemning or justifying. You will find it quite arduous not to condemn or justify, because for centuries denial and assertion have been habitual. Watch your own reactions as we are talking together.

The problem, then, is not jealousy and how to be free of it, but fear. What is fear? How does it come into being?

"It is there all right, but what it is I do not know."

Fear cannot exist in isolation, it exists only in relation to something, doesn't it? There is a state which you call loneliness, and when you are conscious of that state, fear arises. So fear doesn't exist by itself. What are you actually afraid of?

"I suppose of my loneliness, as you say."

Why do you suppose? Aren't you sure?

"I hesitate to be sure about anything, but loneliness is one of my deepest problems. It has always been there in the background, but it is only now, in this talk, that I am forced to look at it directly, to see that it is there. It is an enormous void, frightening and inescapable."

Is it possible to look at that void without giving it a name, without any form of description? Merely labelling a state does not mean that we understand it; on the contrary, it is a hindrance to understanding.

"I see what you mean, but I cannot help labelling it; it is practically an instantaneous reaction."

Feeling and naming are almost simultaneous, are they not? Can they be separated? Can there be a gap between a feeling and the naming of it? If this gap is really experienced, it will be found that the thinker ceases as an entity separate and distinct

227

from thought. The verbalizing process is part of the self, the 'me', the entity who is jealous and who attempts to get over his jealousy. If you really understand the truth of this, then fear ceases. Naming has a physiological as well as a psychological effect. When there is no naming, only then is it possible to be fully aware of that which is called the void of loneliness. Then the mind does not separate itself from that which *is*.

"I find it extremely difficult to follow all this, but I feel I have understood at least some of it, and I shall allow that understanding to unfold."

THE STORM IN THE MIND

ALL DAY THE fog had lasted, and as it cleared towards evening a wind sprang up from the east—a dry, harsh wind, blowing down the dead leaves and drying up the land. It was a tempestuous and menacing night; the wind had increased, the house creaked, and branches were being torn from the trees. The next morning the air was so clear you could almost touch the mountains. The heat had returned with the wind; but as the wind died in the late afternoon, the fog rolled in again from the sea.

How extraordinarily beautiful and rich the earth is! There is no tiring of it. The dry river-beds are full of living things: gorse, poppies, tall yellow sunflowers. On the boulders there are lizards; a brown-and-white-ringed king snake is sunning itself, its black tongue shooting in and out, and across the ravine a dog is barking, pursuing a gopher or a rabbit.

Contentment is never the outcome of fulfilment, of achievement, or of the possession of things; it is not born of action or inaction. It comes with the fullness of what *is*, not in the alteration of it. That which is full does not need alteration, change. It is the incomplete which is trying to become complete that knows the turmoil of discontent and change. The what *is* is the incomplete, it is not the complete. The complete is unreal, and the pursuit of the unreal is the pain of discontent which can never be healed. The very attempt to heal that pain is the search for the unreal, from which arises discontent. There is no way out of discontent. To be aware of discontent is to be aware of what *is,* and in the fullness of it there is a state which may be called contentment. It has no opposite.

The house overlooked the valley, and the highest peak of the distant mountains was aglow with the setting sun. Its rocky mass seemed hung from the sky and alight from within, and in the darkening room the beauty of that light was beyond all measure.

He was a youngish man, eager and searching.

"I have read several books on religion and religious practices, on meditation and the various methods advocated for attaining the highest. I was at one time drawn to Communism, but soon found that it was a retrogressive movement in spite of the many intellectuals who belonged to it. I was also attracted to Catholicism. Some of its doctrines pleased me, and for a time I thought of becoming a Catholic; but one day, while talking to a very learned priest, I suddenly perceived how similar Catholicism was to the prison of Communism. During my wanderings as a sailor on a tramp-ship I went to India and spent nearly a year there, and I thought of becoming a monk; but that was too withdrawn from life and too idealistically unreal. I tried living alone in order to meditate, but that too came to an end. After all these years I still seem to be utterly incapable of controlling my thoughts, and this is what I want to talk about. Of course I have other problems, sex and so on, but if I were completely the master of my thoughts I could then manage to curb my burning desires and urges."

Will the controlling of thought lead to the calming of desire, or merely to its suppression, which will in turn bring other and deeper problems?

"You are of course not advocating giving way to desire. Desire is the way of thought, and in my attempts to control thought I had hoped to subjugate my desires. Desires have either to be subjugated or sublimated, but even to sublimate them they must first be held in check. Most of the teachers insist that desires must be transcended, and they prescribe various methods to bring this about."

Apart from what others have said, what do you think? Will mere control of desire resolve the many problems of desire? Will suppression or sublimation of desire bring about the understanding of it, or free you from it? Through some occupation, religious or otherwise, the mind can be disciplined every hour of the day. But an occupied mind is not a free mind, and surely it is only the free mind that can be aware of timeless creativity.

"Is there no freedom in transcending desire?"

What do you mean by transcending desire?

"For the realization of one's own happiness, and also of the highest, it is necessary not to be driven by desire, not to be caught in its turmoil and confusion. To have desire under control, some form of subjugation is essential. Instead of pursuing the trivial things of life, that very same desire can search out the sublime."

You may change the object of desire from a house to knowledge, from the low to the very highest, but it is still the activity of desire, is it not? One may not want worldly recognition, but the urge to attain heaven is still the pursuit of gain. Desire is ever seeking fulfilment, attainment, and it is this movement of desire which must be understood and not driven away or under. Without understanding the ways of desire, mere control of thought has little significance.

"But I must come back to the point from which I started. Even to understand desire, concentration is necessary, and that is my whole difficulty. I can't seem to control my thoughts. They wander all over the place, tumbling over each other. There is not a single thought that is dominant and continuous among all the irrelevant thoughts."

The mind is like a machine that is working night and day, chattering, everlastingly busy whether asleep or awake. It is speedy and as restless as the sea. Another part of this intricate and complex mechanism tries to control the whole movement, and so begins the conflict between opposing desires, urges. One may be called the higher self and the other the lower self, but both are within the area of the mind. The action and reaction of the mind, of thought, are almost simultaneous and almost automatic. This whole conscious and unconscious process of accepting and denying, conforming and striving to be free, is extremely rapid. So the question is not how to control this complex mechanism, for control brings friction and only dissipates energy, but can this very swift mind slow down?

"But how?"

If it may be pointed out, sir, the issue is not the 'how'. The 'how' merely produces a result, an end without much significance; and after it is gained, another search for another desirable end will begin, with its misery and conflict.

"Then what is one to do?"

You are not asking the right question, are you? You are not discovering for yourself the truth or falseness of the slowing down of the mind, but you are concerned with getting a result. Getting a result is comparatively easy, isn't it? Is it possible for the mind to slow down without putting on brakes?"

"What do you mean by slowing down?"

When you are going very fast in a car, the nearby landscape is a blur; it is only at a walking speed that you can observe in detail the trees, the birds and the flowers. Self-knowledge comes with the slowing down of the mind, but that doesn't mean forcing the mind to be slow. Compulsion only makes for resistance, and there must be no dissipation of energy in the slowing down of the mind. This is so, isn't it?

"I think I am beginning to see that the effort one makes to control thought is wasteful, but I don't understand what else is to be done."

We haven't yet come to the question of action, have we? We are trying to see that it is important for the mind to slow down, we are not considering how to slow it down. Can the mind slow down? And when does this happen?

"I don't know, I have never thought of it before."

Have you not noticed, sir, that while you are watching something the mind slows down? When you watch that car moving along the road down there, or look intently at any physical object, is not your mind functioning more slowly? Watching, observing, does slow down the mind. Looking at a picture, an image, an object, helps to quiet the mind, as does the repetition of a phrase; but then the object or the phrase becomes very important, and not the slowing down of the mind and what is discovered thereby.

"I am watching what you are explaining, and there is an awareness of the stillness of the mind."

Do we ever really watch anything, or do we interpose between the observer and the observed a screen of various prejudices, values, judgments, comparisons, condemnations?

"It is almost impossible not to have this screen. I don't think I am capable of observing in an inviolate manner."

If it may be suggested, don't block yourself by words or by a conclusion, positive or negative. Can there be observation without this screen? To put it differently, is there attention when the mind is occupied? It is only the unoccupied mind that can attend. The mind is slow, alert, when there is watchfulness, which is the attention of an unoccupied mind.

"I am beginning to experience what you are saying, sir."

Let us examine it a little further. If there is no evaluation, no screen between the observer and the observed, is there then a separation, a division between them? Is not the observer the observed?

"I am afraid I don't follow."

The diamond cannot be separated from its qualities, can it? The feeling of envy cannot be separated from the experiencer of that feeling, though an illusory division does exist which breeds conflict, and in this conflict the mind is caught. When this false separation disappears, there is a possibility of freedom, and only then is the mind still. It is only when the experiencer ceases that there is the creative movement of the real.

AT ANY SPEED there was always dust, fine and penetrating, and it poured into the car. Though it was early in the morning and the sun wouldn't be up for an hour or two, there was already a dry, crisp heat which was not too unpleasant. Even at that hour there were bullock-carts on the road. The drivers were asleep, but the oxen, keeping to the road, were going slowly back to their village. Sometimes there would be two or three carts, sometimes ten, and once there were twenty-five, a long line of them with all the drivers asleep and a single kerosene lamp on the leading cart. The car had to go off the road to pass them, raising mountains of dust, and the oxen, their bells ringing rhythmically, never swerved.

It was still rather dark after an hour of steady driving. The trees were dark, mysterious and withdrawn. The road was now paved but narrow, and every cart meant more dust, more tinkling of bells, and still more carts ahead. We were going due east, and soon there was the beginning of dawn, opaque, soft and shadowless. It was not a clear dawn, bright with sparkling dew, but one of those mornings which are rather heavy with the coming heat. Yet how beautiful it was! Far away were the mountains; they could not yet be seen, but one felt they were there, immense, cool and time-free.

The road passed through every kind of village, some clean, orderly and well-kept, others filthy and rotting with hopeless poverty and degradation. Men were going off to the fields, women to the well, and the children were shouting and laughing in the streets. There were miles of government farms, with tractors, fish-ponds, and experimental agricultural schools. A powerful new car passed by, laden with wealthy, well-fed people. The mountains were still far away, and the earth was rich. In several places the road went through a dry river-bed where it was no longer a road, but the buses and carts had made a way

233

across. The parrots, green and red, called to each other in their crazy flight; there were also smaller birds, gold and green, and the white rice-birds.

Now the road was leaving the plains and beginning to ascend. The thick vegetation in the foothills was being cleared away with bulldozers, and miles of fruit-trees were being planted. The car continued to climb as the hills became mountains covered with chestnut and pine trees, the pines slender and straight, and the chestnuts heavy with bloom. The view was opening now, measureless valleys stretching away below, and ahead were the snowy peaks.

At last we rounded a bend at the summit of the climb, and there stood the mountains, clear and dazzling. They were sixty miles away, with a vast blue valley between them and us. Stretching for over two hundred miles, they filled the horizon from end to end, and with a turn of the head we could see from one end to the other. It was a marvellous sight. The intervening sixty miles seemed to disappear, and there was only that strength and solitude. Those peaks, some of them rising over 25,000 feet, had divine names, for the gods lived there, and men came to them from great distances on pilgrimages, to worship and to die.

He had been educated abroad, he said, and had held a good position with the government; but over twenty years ago he had made the decision to give up this position and the ways of the world in order to spend the remaining days of his life in meditation.

"I practised various methods of meditation," he went on, "till I had complete control of my thoughts, and this has brought with it certain powers and domination over myself. However, a friend took me to one of your talks in which you answered a question on meditation, saying that as generally practised meditation was a form of self-hypnosis, a cultivation of self-projected desires, however refined. This struck me as being so true that I sought out this conversation with you; and considering that I have given my life to meditation, I hope we can go into the matter rather deeply.

"I would like to begin by explaining somewhat the course of my development. I realized from everything I had read that it was necessary to be completely the master of one's thoughts. This was extremely difficult for me. Concentration on official work was something wholly different from steadying the mind and harnessing the whole process of thought. According to the books, one had to have all the reins of controlled thought in one's hand. Thought could not be sharpened to penetrate into the many illusions unless it was controlled and directed; so that was my first task."

If one may ask without breaking into your narration, is control of thought the first task?

"I heard what you said in your talk about concentration, but if I may I would like as far as possible to describe my whole experience and then take up certain vital issues connected with it."

Just as you like, sir.

"From the very beginning I was dissatisfied with my occupation, and it was a comparatively easy matter to drop a promising career. I had read a great many books on meditation and contemplation, including the writings of the various mystics, both here and in the West, and it seemed obvious to me that control of thought was the most important thing. This demanded considerable effort, sustained and purposive. As I progressed in meditation I had many experiences, visions of Krishna, of Christ, and of some of the Hindu saints. I became clairvoyant and began to read people's thoughts, and acquired certain other *sidhis* or powers. I went from experience to experience, from one vision, with its symbolic significance, to another, from despair to the highest form of bliss. I had the pride of a conqueror, of one who was the master of himself. Asceticism, the mastery of oneself, does give a sense of power, and it breeds vanity, strength, and self-confidence. I was in the rich fullness of all that. Though I had heard of you for many years, the pride in my achievement had always prevented me from coming to listen to you; but my friend, another *sannyasi,* insisted that I should come, and what I heard has disturbed me. I had previously thought that I was beyond all disturbance! This briefly has been my history in meditation.

"You said in your talk that the mind must go beyond all experience, otherwise it is imprisoned in its own projections, in its own desires and pursuits, and I was deeply surprised to find that my mind was caught up in these very things. Being conscious of this fact, how is the mind to break down the walls of the prison it has built around itself? Have these twenty years and more been wasted? Has it all been a mere wandering in illusion?"

What action should take place can presently be talked over, but let us consider, if you will, the control of thought. Is this control necessary? Is it beneficial or harmful? Various religious teachers have advocated the control of thought as the primary step, but are they right? Who is this controller? Is he not part of that very thought which he is trying to control? He may think of himself as being separate, different from thought, but is he not the outcome of thought? Surely, control implies the coercive action of will to subjugate, to suppress, to dominate, to build up resistance against what is not desired. In this whole process there is vast and miserable conflict, is there not? Can any good come out of conflict?

Concentration in meditation is a form of self-centred improvement, it emphasizes action within the boundaries of the self, the ego, the 'me'. Concentration is a process of narrowing down thought. A child is absorbed in its toy. The toy, the image, the symbol, the word, arrests the restless wanderings of the mind, and such absorption is called concentration. The mind is taken over by the image, by the object, external or inward. The image or the object is then all-important, and not the understanding of the mind itself. Concentration on something is comparatively easy. The toy does absorb the mind, but it does not free the mind to explore, to discover what is, if there is anything, beyond its own frontiers.

"What you say is so different from what one has read or been taught, yet it appears to be true and I am beginning to understand the implications of control. But how can the mind be free without discipline?"

Suppression and conformity are not the steps that lead to freedom. The first step towards freedom is the understanding of bondage. Discipline does shape behaviour and mould thought to the desired pattern, but without understanding desire, mere control or discipline perverts thought; whereas, when there is an awareness of the ways of desire, that awareness brings clarity and order. After all, sir, concentration is the way of desire. A man of business is concentrated because he wants to amass wealth or power, and when another concentrates in meditation, he also is after achievement, reward. Both are pursuing success, which yields self-confidence and the feeling of being secure. This is so, is it not?

"I follow what you are explaining, sir."

Verbal comprehension alone, which is an intellectual grasp of what is heard, has little value, don't you think? The liberating factor is never a mere verbal comprehension, but the perception of the truth or the falseness of the matter. If we can understand the implications of concentration and see the false as the false, then there is freedom from the desire to achieve, to experience, to become. From this comes attention, which is wholly different from concentration. Concentration implies a dual process, a choice, an effort, does it not? There is the maker of effort and the end towards which effort is made. So concentration strengthens the 'I', the self, the ego as the maker of effort, the conqueror, the virtuous one. But in attention this dual activity is not present; there is an absence of the experiencer, the one who gathers, stores and repeats. In this state of attention the conflict of achievement and the fear of failure have ceased.

"But unfortunately not all of us are blessed with that power of attention."

It is not a gift, it is not a reward, a thing to be purchased through discipline, practice, and so on. It comes into being with the understanding of desire, which is self-knowledge. This state of attention is the good, the absence of the self.

"Is all my effort and discipline of many years utterly wasted and of no value at all? Even as I ask this question I am beginning to see the truth of the matter. I see now that for over twenty years I have pursued a way that has inevitably led to a self-created prison in which I have lived, experienced and suffered. To weep over the past is self-indulgence, and one must begin again with a different spirit. But what about all the visions and experiences? Are they also false, worthless?"

Is not the mind, sir, a vast storehouse of all the experiences, visions and thoughts of man? The mind is the result of many thousands of years of tradition and experience. It is capable of fantastic inventions, from the simplest to the most complex. It is capable of extraordinary delusions and of vast perceptions. The experiences and hopes, the anxieties, joys and accumulated knowledge of both the collective and the individual are all there, stored away in the deeper layers of consciousness, and one can relive the inherited or acquired experiences, visions, and so on. We are told of certain drugs that can bring clarity, a vision of the depths and the heights, that can free the mind from its turmoils, giving it great energy and insight. But must the mind travel through all these dark and hidden passages to come to the light? And when through any of these means it does come to the light, is that the light of the eternal? Or is it the light of the known, the recognized, a thing born of search, struggle, hope? Must one go through this weary process to find that which is not measurable? Can we by-pass all this and come upon that which may be called love? Since you have had visions, powers, experiences, what do you say, sir?

"While they lasted I naturally thought they were important and had significance; they gave me a satisfying sense of power, a certain happiness in gratifying achievement. When the various powers come they give one great confidence in oneself, a feeling of self-mastery in which there is an overwhelming pride. Now, after talking all this over, I am not at all sure that these visions, and so on, have such great meaning for me as they once had. They seem to have receded in the light of my own understanding."

Must one go through all these experiences? Are they necessary to open the door of the eternal? Can they not be by-passed? After all, what is essential is self-knowledge, which brings about a still mind. A still mind is not the product of will, of discipline, of the various practices to subjugate desire. All these practices and disciplines only strengthen the self, and virtue is then another rock on which the self can build a house of importance and respectability. The mind must be empty of the known for the unknowable to be. Without understanding the ways of the self, virtue begins to clothe itself in importance. The movement of the self, with its will and desire, its searching and accumulation, must wholly cease. Then only the timeless can come into being. It cannot be invited. The mind that seeks to invite the real through various practices, disciplines, through prayers and attitudes, can only receive its own gratifying projections, but they are not the real.

"I perceive now, after these many years of asceticism, discipline and self-mortification, that my mind is held in the prison of its own making, and that the walls of this prison must be broken down. How is one to set about it?"

The very awareness that they must go is enough. Any action to break them down sets in motion the desire to achieve, to gain, and so brings into being the conflict of the opposites, the experiencer and the experience, the seeker and the sought. To see the false as the false is in itself enough, for that very perception frees the mind from the false.

Is There Profound Thinking?

FAR BEYOND THE palms was the sea, restless and cruel; it was never calm, but always rough with waves and strong currents. In the silence of the night its roar could be heard some distance inland, and in that deep voice there was a warning, a threat. But here among the palms there were deep shadows and stillness. It was full moon and almost like daylight, without the heat and the glare, and the light on those waving palms was soft and beautiful. The beauty was not only of the moonlight on the palms, but also of the shadows, of the rounded trunks, of the

239

sparkling waters and the rich earth. The earth, the sky, the man walking by, the croaking frogs, and the distant whistle of a train—it was all one living thing not measurable by the mind.

The mind is an astonishing instrument; there is no man-made machinery that is so complex, subtle, with such infinite possibilities. We are only aware of the superficial levels of the mind, if we are aware at all, and are satisfied to live and have our being on its outer surface. We accept thinking as the activity of the mind: the thinking of the general who plans wholesale murder, of the cunning politician, of the learned professor, of the carpenter. And is there profound thinking? Is not all thinking a surface activity of the mind? In thought, is the mind deep? Can the mind, which is put together, the result of time, of memory, of experience, be aware of something which is not of itself? The mind is always groping, seeking something beyond its own self-enclosing activities, but the centre from which it seeks remains ever the same.

The mind is not merely the surface activity, but also the hidden movements of many centuries. These movements modify or control the outer activity, so the mind develops its own dualistic conflict. There is not a whole, total mind, it·is broken up into many parts, one in opposition to another. The mind that seeks to integrate, co-ordinate itself, cannot bring peace among its many broken parts. The mind that is made whole by thought, by knowledge, by experience, is still the result of time and sorrow; being put together, it is still a thing of circumstances.

We are approaching this problem of integration wrongly. The part can never become the whole. Through the part the whole cannot be realized, but we do not see this. What we do see is the particular enlarging itself to contain the many parts; but the bringing together of many parts does not make for integration, nor is it of great significance when there is harmony between the various parts. It is not harmony or integration that is of importance, for this can be brought about with care and attention, with right education; but what is of the highest importance is to let the unknown come into being. The known can never receive the unknown. The mind is ceaselessly seeking to live happily in the puddle of self-created integration, but this will not bring about the creativity of the unknown.

Essentially, self-improvement is but mediocrity. Self-improvement through virtue, through identification with capacity, through any form of positive or negative security, is a self-enclosing process, however wide. Ambition breeds mediocrity, for ambition is the fulfilment of the self through action, through the group, through idea. The self is the centre of all that is known, it is the past moving through the present to the future, and all activity in the field of the known makes for shallowness of mind. The mind can never be great, for what is great is immeasurable. The known is comparable, and all the activities of the known can only bring sorrow.

IMMENSITY

THE VALLEY LAY far below and was filled with the activity of most valleys. The sun was just setting behind the distant mountains, and the shadows were dark and long. It was a quiet evening, with a breeze coming off the sea. The orange trees, row upon row, were almost black, and on the long straight road that ran through the valley there were occasional glints as moving cars caught the light of the setting sun. It was an evening of enchantment and peace.

The mind seemed to cover the vast space and the unending distance; or rather, the mind seemed to expand without an end, and behind and beyond the mind there was something that held all things in it. The mind vaguely struggled to recognize and remember that which was not of itself, and so it stopped its usual activity; but it could not grasp what was not of its own nature, and presently all things, including the mind, were enfolded in that immensity. The evening darkened, and the distant barking of dogs in no way disturbed that which is beyond all consciousness. It cannot be thought about and so experienced by the mind.

But what is it, then, that has perceived and is aware of something totally different from the projections of the mind? Who is it that experiences it? Obviously it is not the mind of everyday memories, responses and urges. Is there another mind, or is there a part of the mind which is dormant, to be awakened only by that which is above and beyond all mind? If this is so, then within the mind there is always that which is beyond all thought and time. And yet this cannot be, for it is only speculative thought and therefore another of the many inventions of the mind.

Since that immensity is not born of the process of the mind, then what is it that is aware of it? Is the mind as the experiencer aware of it, or is that immensity aware of itself because there is no experiencer at all? There was no experiencer when this happened coming down the mountain, and yet the awareness of the mind was wholly different, in kind as well as in degree, from that which is not measurable. The mind was not functioning; it was alert and passive, and though cognizant of the breeze playing among the leaves, there was no movement of any kind within itself. There was no observer who measured the observed. There was only *that,* and *that* was aware of itself without measure. It had no beginning and no word.

The mind is aware that it cannot capture by experience and word that which ever abides, timeless and immeasurable.

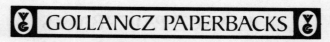

GOLLANCZ PAPERBACKS

GOD OF A HUNDRED NAMES
Prayers and meditations from many faiths and cultures
Collected and arranged by Barbara Greene and Victor Gollancz

Reaching across the barriers of time and place, the prayers in this moving and often surprising collection range in author from Elizabeth I to an Arab chieftain, from Socrates to Edith Sitwell. Together they express the deepest needs of the human spirit.

"A book to cling on to when the world seems falling to bits"—Sir John Betjeman

ISBN 0 575 03645 1

ORGANON OF MEDICINE
Samuel Hahnemann

The classic work on homoeopathy, written by its founding father and translated from the definitive sixth edition.

ISBN 0 575 03880 2

EVERYBODY'S GUIDE TO HOMEOPATHIC MEDICINES
Stephen Cummings and Dana Ullman

An easy-to-follow and reliable handbook for treating yourself and your family at home. Includes all common ailments and first-aid situations and clearly states when to seek outside medical help.

ISBN 0 575 03897 7

GOLLANCZ PAPERBACKS

THE USE OF THE SELF
F. M. Alexander
Introduced by Wilfred Barlow

First published in 1932, this is the classic exposition of the Alexander Technique—the revolutionary theory of movement and body function.

ISBN 0 575 03720 2

WORLD ARMAMENT AND WORLD HUNGER
A Call for Action
Willy Brandt

A powerful personal manifesto and an up-to-the-minute assessment of the dangerously disparate positions of the rich North and underdeveloped South. By the former West German Chancellor and Chairman of the influential 'North–South' commission.

"A tract of rare sense which should be common but isn't"—*Sunday Times*

ISBN 0 575 03827 6

ETHIOPIA
The Challenge of Hunger
Graham Hancock

Formerly the *Economist*'s East Africa correspondent, Graham Hancock provides a clear, unbiased explanation of Ethiopia's famine disaster, analyses the international implications and offers long term solutions.

"Excellent"—*New Society*

ISBN 0 575 03681 8